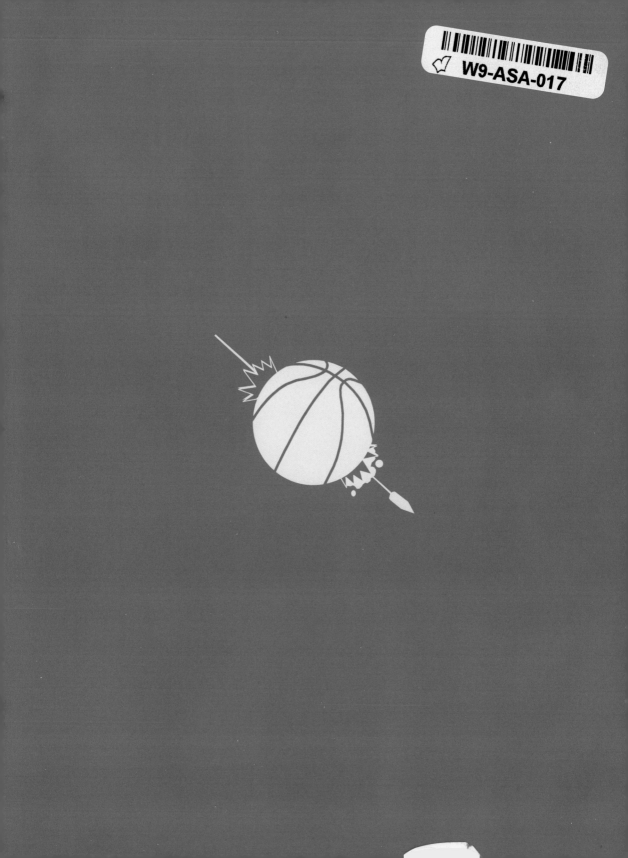

THE
MACROPHENOMENAL
PRO BASKETBALL ALMANAC

FreeDarko presents

THE MACROPHENOMENAL
PRO BASKETBALL ALMANAC

Styles, Stats, and Stars in Today's Game

B L O O M S B U R Y

Published by Bloomsbury USA, New York

All papers used by Bloomsbury USA are natural,
recyclable products made from wood grown
in well-managed forests. The manufacturing
processes conform to the environmental
regulations of the country of origin.

LIBRARY OF CONGRESS CATALOGING-IN-PUBLICATION DATA
HAS BEEN APPLIED FOR.

ISBN-10: 1-59691-561-7

ISBN-13: 978-1-59691-561-9

First U.S. Edition 2008

10 9 8 7 6 5 4 3 2 1

Printed in China by RR Donnelley, South China Printing Co. Ltd.

CONTENTS

Foreword 7
The FreeDarko Manifesto 11
Periodic Table of Style 14

Chapter I
Master Builders
KOBE BRYANT 18
TIM DUNCAN 26
KEVIN GARNETT 34
Jerseys for Every Occasion 42

Chapter II
Uncanny Peacocks
GILBERT ARENAS 50
GERALD WALLACE & JOSH SMITH 58
LEANDRO BARBOSA 70
Euro for Beginners 76

Chapter III
Lost Souls
LAMAR ODOM 82
TRACY McGRADY 92
JOE JOHNSON 100
Where They Are Now 108

Chapter IV
Phenomenal Tumors
RON ARTEST 116
VINCE CARTER 124
STEPHON MARBURY 130
The 2000 NBA Draft 136

Chapter V
People's Champs
CARMELO ANTHONY 144
YAO MING 152
RASHEED WALLACE 160
When They Were Mayors 168

Chapter VI
Destiny's Kids
LeBRON JAMES 178
CHRIS PAUL 186
AMARE STOUDEMIRE 194
Myth of the Next 202

Glossary 209
Bios 218
Thank-yous 219

FOREWORD

by Gilbert Arenas

I became a real NBA fan when I first saw Anfernee Hardaway on TV on draft night back in 1993. They were showing his highlights, and after seeing the way he played the game, I gravitated towards it. It was such a smooth style. He played with a West Coast flavor to his game, even though he was from Memphis. He was quiet on the court, never really got emotional; he just played with a smooth swagger. That's when *Blue Chips* came out, too, and I watched him in that and he had this whole little persona.

At the time, I was into basketball, but I wasn't *really* into it. After I saw him, it made me fall in love with the game. I was eleven years old, and all I could think was, "I want to be like him, that's who I want to be."

When he started to make a name for himself in the league, it made basketball fun. The same guy I picked to be a fan of started showing up everywhere. There was the Penny nickname and the commercials with the Lil' Penny doll—those made me laugh—and the attitude line in his hair. Plus there was the signature shoe and the armband with the little 1¢ symbol—it all made me fall in love with his style of basketball.

Now that I'm in the NBA, I realize that fans are following every little thing we do as players. The summer after Detroit played in the finals, I went to the park, and I saw a kid doing the little free-throw routine that Rip Hamilton does where he lines up his right hand with the rim and then bends down and takes a hard dribble to his right before shooting it. I went over to the kid and straight-up asked him:

Me: "Uhh, why do you shoot free throws like that?"

Kid: "Because of Rip Hamilton."

I'm thinking, "Oh, man, I didn't know kids actually paid attention to stuff like that." So that day, I came up with a routine of my own where I circle the ball around my waist before I shoot free throws so kids can do that at the park, too. And they have.

A basketball player's style is defined in a lot of ways—what they wear, how they play, what they do. We all know Dennis Rodman had style coming out of his ears. My dad was a Bulls fan and loved Rodman, because he knew how to get under everybody's skin. When Rodman went up against Karl Malone in the finals, my dad would watch the Rodman-Malone matchup the whole game. In the first quarter, he'd be like, "Watch, watch, watch! He's about to irritate him!"

Second quarter: "He's about to grab his booty!"

Third quarter: "Yeah, yeah, he's about to trip him!"

Fourth quarter: "He's about to grab his shirt!"

I was like, "Dad, that's dirty." And he told me, "It's entertainment. That's all it is. Look how much fun he's having, look at him high-stepping!" You'd have to just smile seeing Dennis bounce down the court, clapping his hands, doing the high step with those shorts riding up his thighs.

Matter of fact, I got the whole thing about throwing my jersey to the fans from Dennis Rodman. He would throw it into the stands in frustration, after getting kicked out of a game, but everybody was screaming for that jersey. Home crowd, away crowd, it didn't matter. They would push down their grandmother to get to that number 91. I told myself, "If I ever make it to the NBA, that's going to be my trademark—giving out stuff." I stayed true to it, and I give out my jersey every game, every year.

There have been trendsetters who came from the NBA and impacted the whole world, whether you were a sports fan or not. AI was a trendsetter for the black community. He was the first person to wear braids and have a whole bunch of tattoos. That wasn't in the NBA before him; people hadn't seen anything like that before.

His image only grew because of what he did on the basketball floor. He had his crossover that everybody copied but nobody could stop. Then there was the way he played the game as a little man saying, "You're not gonna stop me."

I've never really shaped my image with what I wear, other than the number zero, of course. I keep it simple, right down to the low-top sneakers. (I tried the headband at one point because everybody was wearing headbands, but it didn't look right on me.) Some people wear their wristband on their forearm because that's where Michael Jordan wore it. I mean, it's called a *wrist*band! But you want to be like Mike. Some people wear their practice shorts under their game shorts to be like Jordan, too. When you're a little kid, you pick up these habits, and when you become older those habits are all you know. When LeBron James wears number 23, he's not telling everybody it's because of Michael Jordan, even though it is. It becomes his own style. Now LeBron fans think *he's* number 23.

There are armbands and arm sleeves and tights and knee braces and long socks—everybody has something. Kerry Kittles wore one high sock in college and one low. Ed O'Bannon wore a T-shirt under his jersey. Ain't nobody bringing back the goggles again, though—I think they retired along with Horace Grant.

In the basketball realm, you pick up on these things. They are a part of what every player pays attention to, but to the average fan it doesn't even have to be that intricate. Truthfully, when fans go to a game all they want is entertainment. They want to see somebody playing their heart out, and for the guy who's playing his heart out to have fun doing it. All it takes is for him to throw a smile, raise the roof, do *something*. That's all they're waiting for. You pay all this money to sit up close, believe it or not, you want to get hit with a ball and get your drink knocked over. You want to leave with something to talk about. You want Shaq to fall on you and get drenched in his sweaty-sweat-sweat. That's all part of the game. It's just a big show.

Showboating is part of entertainment, of expression. And if you take away expression, you take away from the game. The fans feed off that energy. You expect to see Jordan with the tongue wagging like you expect Urkel to say "Did I do that?" You expect Dikembe Mutombo to do the finger wave like you expect Martin to say "Dammmn, Gina." It's like a punch line. I guarantee if Dikembe blocks a shot and then he doesn't bring out the finger like that, people in the stands would be like, "What the hell is going on?"

Basketball is up and down, quick baskets, constant little victories. You can do more things to celebrate. In the NFL, you score one touchdown and that's it. You get your one chance to do a little spike or whatever with the play dead and the clock stopped. But in the NBA, I can dunk on somebody and run down the court doing my little antics and keep it fluid, keep it flowing.

That's what they are: they're antics. They're a little extra. People may think it's something silly that has just come into the game now, but you've been seeing antics since the NBA started. Isiah Thomas with the kiss on Magic's cheek, Magic wearing the Celtics T-shirt under his warm-ups when he played Bird, Jordan with the shoulder shrug against Portland . . . they're all part of the antics.

And the antics are what this book is all about.

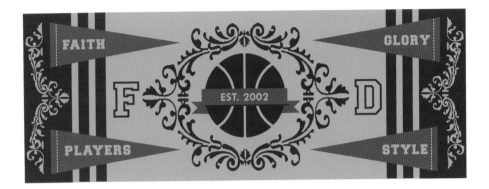

THE FREEDARKO
MANIFESTO

THE SIGNATORIES HERETO CONSECRATE THE
PRINCIPLES SET FORTH IN THIS DOCUMENT:

THE **DISSOLUTION** OF THE OLD LEAGUE;

THE **RENEWAL** OF **FAITH** IN INDIVIDUAL **PLAYERS**;

THE **CELEBRATION** OF THE **NEW LEAGUE** IN ITS FULL **GLORY**.

WHEREAS:

WE REJECT THE OLD NBA

LARGE CONTRACTS, inappropriate behavior, Meaningless Games, and craven misman-
agement have tarnished this great League in the eyes of the land. The Citizens who support it affirm their right to be entertained and diverted by the League, no matter what
the month. We further acknowledge that its nervous center, its Governing Body, has
lost grip of its wits; specifically, we cite an awkward Playoff format and various confusing marketing campaigns as signs that the League's primacy has been abrogated.

WE DISCOUNT MERE WINS AND LOSSES

THE OLD WISDOM HOLDS that Winning is the essential function of an NBA team. But we ask: Is there no such thing as a beautiful Loss? A noble Failure? A compelling Train Wreck? The collapse of the 2000 Portland Trail Blazers in the fourth quarter of Game 7 was tragicomic and memorable; it confirms that Victory need not be the most prized outcome. We assert our right to be amused by non-Champions. Some of the most masterful moves to the basket yield not points and die a replayless death, excluded forever from the Kingdom of Highlight Posterity. These we reclaim in the name of the People.

WE FIND ROOTING FOR THE HOME TEAM
SPIRITUALLY AND EMOTIONALLY LIMITING

IN AN AGE LESS ADVANCED, man's allegiance was determined by proximity alone. Tribalism and peer pressure conspired to make the fan see only "us" and "them," no matter what genius wore the color of the enemy. We believe that these are the ways of provincials and fascists, and in this brave century man must stand on his own and open his fandom to new possibilities.

THEREFORE:

WE EMBRACE THE PRIMACY OF THE INDIVIDUAL

THE FEELINGS OF LIBERATED FANDOM begin with Respect for the individual player. The League is strengthened by its most compelling Personalities, including: Players with inscrutable Superstitions; Players with genetically improbable Body Types; Players whose Emotional Baggage is visible during Play; and other Interesting Players: those whose time has yet to come, and those who, through no curse of their own, find themselves stranded on the margins of visibility.

As a consequence thereof,

The appeal of individual Players transcends the boundaries between Teams. Coaches and General Managers respect the Team first, and in so doing compromise our attachments to favorite Players. We assert our right to sustain those attachments. Further, we acknowledge our skepticism of the decision-making powers of General Managers and Coaches. As Liberated Fans, we should favor shifts in personnel, to better expand the variety of basketball experience within our minds.

WE ASPIRE TO FORM A MORE PERFECT BASKETBALL UNION

IN THE NEW BROTHERHOOD of NBA appreciation, players will be viewed for their personal Styles, both during and outside of Play. We embrace their Foibles, even those that prevent them from Winning. We exalt their Particularities and intriguing Backstories, and endorse a League in which these Virtues are fostered. When victory is attained, it shall come as a by-product of a life well lived, not as an all-sacrificing end. Every night is an adventure and a revelation.

THIS IS NOT THE DEATH OF THE GAME,
IT IS THE RIGHTFUL BEGINNING IT NEVER HAD

IN REJECTING THE OLD NBA, we seek not to spite our forebears but to silence those who proclaim the League's decrepitude. Our Mission is to shed this heavy mantle. The League persists; may its legend grow. May we grow stronger through it, involved and inspired as it cycles through artificial periods of drought and return.

We have come to take up this banner, and hold it aloft as a beacon to all Mankind.

SIGNED, THE FREEDARKO COLLECTIVE:

BETHLEHEM SHOALS

BIG BABY BELAFONTE

BROWN RECLUSE, ESQ.

DR. LAWYER INDIANCHIEF

SILVERBIRD5000

PERIODIC TABLE OF STYLE

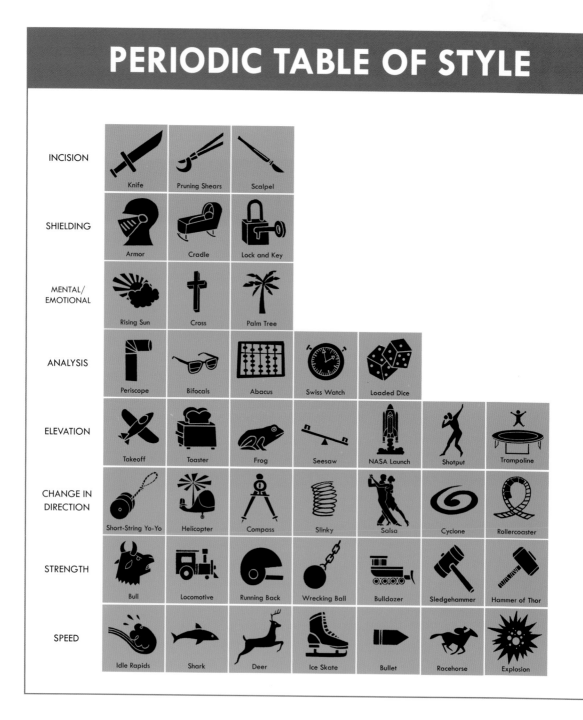

INCISION	Knife	Pruning Shears	Scalpel			
SHIELDING	Armor	Cradle	Lock and Key			
MENTAL/ EMOTIONAL	Rising Sun	Cross	Palm Tree			
ANALYSIS	Periscope	Bifocals	Abacus	Swiss Watch	Loaded Dice	
ELEVATION	Takeoff	Toaster	Frog	Seesaw	NASA Launch	Shotput	Trampoline
CHANGE IN DIRECTION	Short-String Yo-Yo	Helicopter	Compass	Slinky	Salsa	Cyclone	Rollercoaster
STRENGTH	Bull	Locomotive	Running Back	Wrecking Ball	Bulldozer	Sledgehammer	Hammer of Thor
SPEED	Idle Rapids	Shark	Deer	Ice Skate	Bullet	Racehorse	Explosion

THE STYLE GUIDE

Every basketball player approaches the game uniquely. By means of signs and symbols, we have broken down various players' games on a second-by-second basis. The icons indicate exactly what occurs in a instant, revealing style as a mix of the physical, the emotional, and the spiritual.

FIG. A: Factual View
(Player leaping over other player)

FIG. B: Stylistic View
(Player as "Rising Sun")

Snowflake	This Is Not a Pipe	Witchcraft	Extra Gear	Sand Dollar	Spring Showers	Triple Layer Chocolate Cake	MYSTERIES
Bullhorn	Showman	Rag Doll	Duck	Custer's Last Stand	Parachute	Freeze Frame	SUPERFICIAL
Cockroach	Baseball Bat	Wheeled Ottoman	Knight	Paddle Ball	Headless Chicken	Baby Steps	CHANGE IN DIRECTION (Cont.)
Mortar and Pestle	Loading Ramp	Doorstop	Crab	Hard Hat	Screw	Crane	STRENGTH (Cont.)
Mercury	Missile Launcher	Sling	Motocross	Bear Trap	Harpoon	Falcon	SPEED (Cont.)

Chapter I

Master Builders

For Whom Dominance Has Become a Truism

The NBA is a monument to man's persuasive capacity for self-invention—if that monument were made of shiny goo in a constant state of flux. Men scramble about its innards, leaving imprints, dents, and paths that subtly shift the structure. And then, hovering above this gloppy construction site, are the men wielding the hammers. They're the Master Builders, the forces who make and destroy the very parameters of the league. In each of them, we find not only a tremendous talent, but also a key facet of the way the game is today played. Few players can claim membership in this select genus—while excellence is one thing, influence and stature are that next level. They don't just play basketball; for all intents and purposes, they *are* this era of basketball.

We know them as performers and commodities; the game lionizes them as experts. Yet in certain revealing moments, we get a glimpse at the human being beneath all this. And then, all the on-court brilliance and off-court fronting is shot through with a new perspective.

KOBE BRYANT

Chasing Perfection

Check the résumé—it's absolutely impeccable. A 6'6" shooting guard with limitless physical tools, a hell-bent perfectionist, Kobe Bryant works tirelessly to condition his body and enhance his game. He's fearless in the clutch, voraciously competitive, and serious to the point of bleakness.

Drafted out of high school in 1996, and an All-Star starter by his second season, World Champion from 2000 to 2002, perennial presence on the All-NBA and All-Defensive teams. Weathered three seasons of uncertain rebuilding, during which he still managed to make the playoffs twice in the rough-and-tumble Western Conference. That, and on January 22, 2006, 81 points against Toronto—the second-highest total in NBA history. Come 2007–08, he was at the height of his powers and once again surrounded with top talent. Hence that season's MVP, only his first.

You couldn't script a more stellar career or offer up a stronger candidate for the league's all-around finest. And yet no superstar has cut a stormier path through his era than Kobe Bean Bryant. Kobe may be the Great American Shooting Guard, and indeed, he has spent his whole life aspiring to this kind of abstract dignity. But just as *Moby-Dick* defines our national literature despite its rollicking imperfections, Kobe's drives and desires have made him equal parts pristine legend and unwieldy mess of humanity.

In the NBA, the greatest players are always, to some degree, alone at the top. But this isolation is always buffered by other

WHAT HE GIVES US:
The game's most proficient, and polarizing, figure.

WHAT HE STANDS FOR:
Landslides, great and crippling.

WHY WE CARE:
Where others see only their own love or hate for Kobe, we see a complex mess of man's best and worst qualities.

aspects of their professional or private lives. Michael Jordan's obsessive need to be the best was counterbalanced by his respect for Dean Smith and the UNC tradition.

Allen Iverson, who entered the league one year after Kobe, was routinely criticized for his independence on and off the court. But his rebellious egoism spoke for many, just as Tupac's or Brando's had.

Kobe, however, is no such jazzy outsider. Few players better fit the bill of athletic aristocracy or defy the blacktop-and-bulletholes come-up more. Bryant was born with an NBA-colored spoon 'tween his gums: his father, Joe "Jelly Bean" Bryant, was a former 76er; he played high school ball in the Philly suburbs; and he took R&B starlet Brandy to his senior prom, just because he could. And yet, throughout his life, Bryant has dealt with various forms of dislocation, displacement, and distance.

He spent his early years in Italy as Papa Joe pursued the overseas option. Bryant learned the language, developed an affinity for soccer, and idolized Mike D'Antoni, the zippy expat who would one day turn the Phoenix Suns into a basketball think tank. When he returned to the States, Bryant's game hit the stratosphere, but the kid himself now had to cultivate the swagger of an American jock. Never was this more evident—or awkward—than when he wore sunglasses indoors during the press conference announcing his decision to go pro.

Bryant was drafted by Charlotte, but his agent engineered a trade to the Lakers, whose GM, Jerry West, coveted the scrawny teen. During his rookie season, Kobe was the subject of a *New York Times* profile; while he put on a brave face, it was hard not to feel sorry for the millionaire kid who spent every night alone in his hotel room, as his older teammates begrudged his inability to contribute immediately. These experiences made him uniquely vulnerable to the lonely-at-the-top predicament of the marquee athlete, while denying him the means to see beyond it. It also made his drive to win, to constantly improve, into something private and puritanical—quite distinct from Jordan's megalomania or Iverson's righteous indignation.

Paired with Shaquille O'Neal, Kobe was supposed to bring on a new Lakers golden age—and he did, once Hall of Fame coach Phil Jackson stepped into the scene. However, Kobe and Shaq could not have been more different, and eventually they clashed because of it. Shaq was a boundless extrovert, a popular, lovable guy who fed off of outside affirmation. He cruised like a hungry whale shark through the tide of media superlatives and took those three titles as a sign of infallibility. He looked upon Kobe as a sidekick, an understudy in his school of self-fulfilling greatness. Kobe, by contrast, was aloof, restless, and more interested in improving himself than in garnering the admiration of others. The world saw the three-peat, but inside the Lakers, tensions simmered, especially when Shaq's conditioning and work ethic flagged. Many read this as Kobe's ego crying out, dying to take control of the team. But it was just as likely his deep-seated sense of justice.

Shaq thought that the team could coast along like a never-ending championship parade; Kobe didn't mistake nostalgia for fuel, or camaraderie for chemistry. In 2004, the Lakers added future Hall of Famers Karl

Malone and Gary Payton in a clumsy attempt to regain the throne. They were upset in the finals by a far more organic, hungry Pistons team; Jackson exited; and the dynasty was officially deceased. When Bryant marched into the Lakers' front office and forced them to choose between their two superstars, it was as much a matter of anxiety as of arrogance. Kobe might have begrudged Shaq's dominance a little, but more importantly, he recognized that their era was over, and this was no time to make decisions based on the past. Shaq went to the Heat, won them a ring, and in the short term made a fool of Kobe. However, O'Neal then declined quickly and considerably, his contract becoming an albatross. Kobe had recognized the importance of looking toward the uncertain future; you could even say he'd been there all along.

Kobe sees the world with a healthy skepticism; perhaps because of this, he's often seen this way by others. No one ever really believed the wholesome, anodyne mask he wore through those first few years of endorsements; when he was accused in 2004 of raping a Colorado coed, his detractors thought they'd located his dark side. Once considered merely paranoid or phony, Bryant was now the Grand Deceiver. But as the details came out and the charges were eventually dropped, felon Kobe gave way to man torn between overbearing self-control and ghoulish indiscretion.

This duality has always been present in his game: Kobe is both the league's smartest player and one of its most impulsive.

He plays with unquenchable fire, skirting the fine line between craft and artistry. Once, Bryant was a propulsive slasher with an uncommon mid-range game. Now, when he's

NAME: Kobe Bean Bryant
BORN: August 23, 1978
HEIGHT: 6 ft 6 in (1.98 m)
WEIGHT: 205 lb (93 kg)
HOMETOWN: Lower Merion, PA/Italy

SPIRIT ANIMAL: He calls himself "Black Mamba."

PLAYER COMPARISON: A smarter, more neurotic Michael Jordan.

NOTABLE REMARK: "These young guys are playing checkers. I'm out there playing chess."

HOPES AND DREAMS: In 2006, Kobe started a foundation that sends minority college students to Italy. Unclear whether it's for their benefit or it's his own backward version of Birthright.

DISTINGUISHING MARKS: During his legal troubles, Bryant got his first tattoos: a few family-centric doodles and a Bible verse with angel wings.

MUSICAL CAREER: In 2000, dropped two singles: the tawdry Tyra Banks collabo "K.O.B.E.," and the thoroughly unconvincing "Thug Poet." His *Visions* full-length never saw the light of day. Eventually redeemed himself by recording with dirty Philly don Beanie Sigel.

met by a defender, the curtain rises on an interaction of frightening detail and determination. Only Tim Duncan is as adept at milking every single square inch of space in a precise, Terminator-like assessment of complex obstacles. But for Duncan, the action's near the basket, and the shots—aided by his height—tend to resolve into something fairly routine. Kobe, operating all over the floor, doesn't take the simple shot, throw up prayers, or gamble on his pride. He figures out how to make the impossible shot viable, going out of his way to demonstrate his superiority. It's frustrating enough to see someone excel with no apparent effort; Kobe infuriates by working hard in an effortless manner.

During the Lakers' lean years, Bryant struggled with his own inability to make an inferior team into a winner. It was hardly his fault, though; even after Phil returned to the fold, the front office steadfastly refused to trade for available All-Stars like Jason Kidd and Baron Davis. They continued to wait on big man Andrew Bynum, drafted in 2005 straight out of high school and still unformed. In May 2007, after being ousted in the first round of the playoffs yet again, Bryant exploded, telling any and all media outlets that he wanted out of L.A. Rumors abounded, and several important-sounding meetings took place. But that fall Kobe was still a Laker. He was chummier than ever with his teammates and had made a point of reaching out to Bynum, who suddenly became a force to be reckoned with. The Lakers then swung a one-sided deal for Memphis big man Pau Gasol, who alongside Bynum and Lamar Odom made for the West's most imposing frontcourt.

What exactly had happened between spring and fall? Had Kobe lost control, let out his frustration, and then thought the better of it? Was it all a Machiavellian public relations coup on the part of Bryant, who ended up getting the help he wanted? Had he set foot in camp and instantly realized that Bynum was ready to contribute? Did he actually feel betrayed by the organization, emotionally wounded? Or was he just irritated that they'd impeded his still-vital career?

We don't know for sure. But most likely, there's a grain of truth to all of it. And that's why Kobe Bryant would fascinate us even if he weren't the world's best basketball player. For in addition to his mastery of the game—the kind of catchall supremacy that led him to pick up Duncan's bank shot on a whim—Bryant's also shown what happens when the full thrust of greatness flies off the rails. He's at once the mastermind and the victim of his own powers.

To his detractors, Kobe Bryant is Dracula: a spooky, inhuman being that gets shit done. Starstruck fans regard him as the epitome of glitz, glam, and accomplishment. In truth, he's that most stormy, and mortal, kind of great man. If Shaquille O'Neal always represented Superman, then Kobe's the Dark Knight: vulnerable, but all the stronger for it.

While it's hard to argue with the outcomes in his life, the process behind Bryant's perfection—the "how" of his imposing "what"—hides a humanity even more craggy and flawed than our own. He alarms us by appearing both above and beneath us, inspiring exultation and revulsion alike. And for all his brazen confidence, there's no question that the ever-isolated Kobe sustains himself through a similarly combustible dynamic.

Kobe Bryant: A Life of Ambivalence

What's most fascinating about Kobe Bryant's reputation isn't how wildly it's split—it's that, without fail, the same things that bring him praise from some corners bring hellfire from the others. Depending on who you ask, Bryant can truly do nothing wrong, or nothing right. But we suspect he likes it this way: the polarized reception, providing equal parts love and scornful motivation.

KOBE LOVER:

Scores 81 Points:
Virtuosic display of skill

Colorado Rape Trial:
Naive about NBA
road life

Shaq Partnership:
Kobe was necessary
for Shaq's dominance

**Butterfly-Crown
Tattoo:**
Butterflies reveal
his sensitive side.

**Dressed up as
Lord Voldemort
for Halloween:**
Kobe's kids love
Harry Potter, and
Kobe loves his kids

**Switches Jersey
Number to 24:**
Represents his 24-7
focus on basketball

Youth in Italy:
Showed him
the world

Bought a Helicopter:
The most efficient way
to deal with L.A.'s
rush hour traffic

KOBE HATER:

Scores 81 Points:
Statistical glutton

Colorado Rape Trial:
The monster
revealed

Shaq Partnership:
Kobe was nothing
without the big guy

**Butterfly-Crown
Tattoo:**
Crown reveals his
arrogance

**Dressed up as
Lord Voldemort
for Halloween:**
Is a competitive prick,
even when it comes
to parenting

**Switches Jersey
Number to 24:**
Just had to be one
more than Jordan

Youth in Italy:
Embittered by
separation

Bought a Helicopter:
Really self-indulgent,
and just terrible for
the environment

STYLE GUIDE

1 Kobe tests the defender with a series of jab steps at the three-point line.

 STYLE: Abacus
Technical computations, study tool

2 Catches his defender off balance and bursts forward.

 STYLE: Explosion
Combustible, propulsive

3 Beats his man and picks up his dribble as he turns into the lane.

 STYLE: Lock and Key
Protection, lots of complex rotating mechanisms.

4 Leaps upward as the other defenders collapse into the lane.

 STYLE: Knife
Slices through things

5 Draws contact, then contracts and spins in midair so that his back is to the basket.

STYLE: (Open to interpretation)

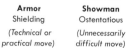

Witchcraft	Armor	Showman
Irrational, magical	Shielding	Ostentatious
(Improvisatory or spontaneous move)	*(Technical or practical move)*	*(Unnecessarily difficult move)*

6 Throws it up at the last minute for the basket and the foul.

 STYLE: Loaded Dice
A calculated gamble

How 81 Trumps 100

More than fifty years later, Wilt Chamberlain's 100-point game against the New York Knicks, on March 2, 1962, remains the greatest single display of scoring virility the NBA has ever known. But in many ways, Kobe's 81-point game against the Raptors was equally impressive, if not more so. Many have pointed to the natural advantage a towering post player enjoys over a guard like Kobe. However, what is usually ignored is just how uncompetitive Wilt's game was, with the Warriors leading the Knicks by an average of 17.5 points at the end of each quarter. In comparison, Kobe's Lakers were down for over two thirds of the game, which one could argue made his baskets that much more vital to a real competitive effort. Bryant may have been shooting like crazy, but it was with a higher goal in mind.

Point Differential at Time of Basket

-20   -15   -10   0   +10   +15   +20

Though no play-by-play data for Wilt's game exists, according to firsthand reports the Warriors had established a 19–3 lead over the Knicks "within minutes," with Wilt scoring 16 points. Thus we can assume that only Wilt's very first baskets of the game were of competitive importance.

The Warriors led by 16 at the end of the first quarter, but by halftime the Knicks had narrowed the score to 79–68—the closest recorded point of the game. Incidentally, Wilt scored the smallest number of points (only 15) during the closest quarter of the game, the second.

By the end of the third the Warriors led by 21 and the game had clearly turned into a blowout. Entering the fourth, Wilt realized he had a shot at breaking his previous record of 78 points, and the match quickly deteriorated into a one-man game, with the Warriors feeding Wilt the ball on every possession to help him reach 100 and the Knicks frantically fouling in an attempt to keep the ball out of Wilt's hands. Speaking later about the game, Wilt said, "I'm embarrassed by it . . . I pushed for a hundred and it destroyed the game, because I took shots that I normally never would have."

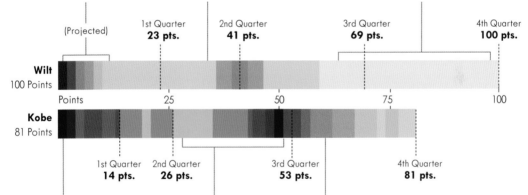

| | (Projected) | 1st Quarter **23 pts.** | 2nd Quarter **41 pts.** | 3rd Quarter **69 pts.** | 4th Quarter **100 pts.** |

Wilt
100 Points

Points   25   50   75   100

Kobe
81 Points

| | 1st Quarter **14 pts.** | 2nd Quarter **26 pts.** | 3rd Quarter **53 pts.** | 4th Quarter **81 pts.** |

Although the first quarter of Kobe's game was fairly close, Toronto established a lead within the first two minutes and was able to maintain it throughout the quarter.

With 9:55 left in the third quarter, the Lakers fell behind 18 points, their largest deficit of the game. Kobe responded by going 6 for 7 on field goals, 4 for 4 on threes, and hitting one free throw, for a total of 25 points in just 9 minutes. With 1 minute left in the third the Lakers finally took an 87–85 lead, their first in 32 minutes.

Even during much of the fourth quarter, the game was still tight. Only five of Kobe's shots were taken with the Lakers up by more than 15 points. Though Chamberlain's feat remains the stuff of Precambrian lore, a look at the available details reveals a tawdry fluke that not even its author felt wholly comfortable with. Kobe's 81-point performance may have also been against an inferior team, but it certainly wins out in the credibility department.

MY NAME IS DUNCAN
KING OF KINGS:
LOOK ON MY WORKS,
YE MIGHTY, AND DESPAIR!

TIM DUNCAN

Mechanical Gothic

Tim Duncan proves that absence of style can be style in and of itself, a paradox that defines his daily actions and decisions. Duncan is a figure seemingly birthed from Mount Rushmore's granite façade, yet his movement is fluid. He faces up to his opponents with the saucer-like eyes of a German shepherd, yet with his empty stare he intimidates all who face him. Duncan hails from the Virgin Islands, a location that should evoke images of relaxation and respite, yet Duncan's citizenship status instead elicits a bothersome uncertainty, as no one actually knows what the Virgin Islands are. Duncan's off-court obsession with video gaming, his apparent introversion, and his Wayne Brady–as-Milhouse vocal tone convey an overall tenor of erudite boredom. Nonetheless, all who have faced him hold unbounded respect for him, because so many have met their fate by his hand.

Throughout his career, Duncan has maintained his role as the NBA's gatekeeper, yet his term is unlike that of others who held the position before him. Michael Jordan halted the likes

WHAT HE GIVES US:
The methodical plumbing that allows the NBA universe to function.

WHAT HE STANDS FOR:
The magnificence of the mundane.

WHY WE CARE:
Redefines style to encompass elements completely devoid of stylishness.

of Ewing, Malone, Stockton, and Barkley, denying them championships with a hand in their faces and a dagger in their hearts. Shaquille O'Neal, as Jordan's successor, towered over the most competent Kings and Nets teams during his reign. Duncan, by contrast, provides no abrupt reaction to an opponent's push. As Duncan denies scores of aspirants an opportunity at the title, they simply collapse at his feet.

Duncan entered the NBA after four years of college at Wake Forest. The circumstances were suspicious: An already championship-ready San Antonio Spurs team implodes for one single season—just long enough to attain the first overall pick in the draft and net the stoic young power forward. Because winning came so immediately for Duncan—in his first year he led the Spurs to one of the biggest single-season turnarounds in NBA history—aesthetics became an afterthought to success. This suited the dull and routine mastery that would soon become Duncan's calling card.

Duncan has always kept his uniform shorts at an appropriate length. Off the court, he rarely dons a suit and is more likely to be seen in the blandest of Banana Republics or the grayest of sweat suits, giving press conferences unpolluted by slang or foul speech. At his most striking, he resembles an oversized and popular Carnegie Mellon engineering student or a recently bankrupt and divorced stock trader. More often, however, Duncan looks like the most glorious human being ever produced in a factory, pristine and plain faced. He is a monument to bottom lines, permanent but not necessarily memorable.

With a game founded on a geometrically accurate bank shot and simple three-step

NAME: Timothy Theodore Duncan

BORN: April 25, 1976

HEIGHT: 6 ft 11 in (2.11 m)

WEIGHT: 260 lb (118 kg)

HOMETOWN: Christiansted, VI

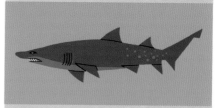

SPIRIT ANIMAL: Nurse shark

CREATION MYTH: As a youth, Tim Duncan was an avid swimmer. He only took up basketball in his teens, when his local pool was destroyed in a hurricane; Duncan's fear of sharks was so pronounced that he couldn't bear to step foot into the ocean, and thus had to find a new hobby. As a basketball player, Duncan came to embrace what he initially feared. He learned to circle his opponents and attack instinctually at the scent of blood. This remorseless method of terror has both brought Duncan overwhelming success and allowed him to exorcise the demons of his youth.

NOTABLE REMARK: "The time when there is no one to feel sorry for you or to cheer for you is when a player is made."

DISTINGUISHING MARKS: Duncan has two tattoos. One is a skeletal jester and the other is the legendary wizard Merlin, but since these are on his chest and back, respectively, they are almost always hidden from view.

footwork in the post, he has become the modest Carhartt coat that blankets a league full of precious metals. In making a defensive stop, Duncan is not feverish or quick footed; he is a concrete wall of disregard for a player's intention to score. In completing a powerful dunk, Duncan uses an efficiency of motion, rarely jumping higher than necessary, and in speech never emits any proclamation of greatness or dominance. Duncan is known for his dissatisfaction with foul calls, but he generally expresses such angst in a silent widening of his nostrils and eyelids. He is incapable of histrionics. A scholar of psychology and Chinese literature while in college, he confronts the unbridled emotion of his opponents with circumspect reason.

While other players wind-sprint through the season, Duncan marathons, going deep into the playoffs year after year. While his foes throw their hearts and minds into the thick of competition, Duncan stands at a remove, his every action rich with intent. His brain operates with the dull precision of the TI-83 calculator. Can Duncan feel pain? He has faced his share of knee and foot injuries over the years, yet they have slowed him only as an oil leak slows a robot. Does Duncan love? His wife, Amy, a former Wake Forest cheerleader, conveys a forced plastic smile in public appearances, suggesting that not even she knows. Do the concepts of free will or consciousness mean anything to him? If so, he does not experience these capacities as you and I do. Referee Joey Crawford once issued a technical foul to Duncan simply for laughing while on the bench; Crawford more than anything was probably startled at Timmy's capacity to display human feeling. In his eter-

nal drudgery, Duncan moves forward with a single purpose, as though preprogrammed to achieve the sole end of winning. Cognition, emotion, intention—all are merely incidental to the goal at hand.

A world champion multiple times over, Tim Duncan is a human trophy, not a flighty canvas of mood and invention: not a winner, just someone who wins games. His first two championships with the Spurs were more attributable to the aging torpedo David Robinson, Duncan's frontcourt-mate and mentor, than they were to Duncan himself. Although Robinson's skills were declining at this point, it was his spirit and leadership that carried Duncan and the Spurs unto victory. Duncan's third championship, which occurred after Robinson's retirement, lacked any authoritative moment of self-definition—the clutch shooting of Robert Horry and the unstoppable penetration of Tony Parker were as important as Duncan's geologic whir. The Spurs' unwatchable 2007 championship was aided by circumstance: questionable refereeing, the Warriors' first-round upset of the Mavericks (the Spurs' chief competition), and unwarranted suspensions of players on the Spurs' Western Conference Finals foes, the Phoenix Suns. However, the Spurs' eventual victory was not the product of luck or white-hot destiny. These things came to be because of who Tim Duncan is: an automaton of success.

Duncan has little need to probe his own being or to carol his findings to the world. He is style by default—all that is left when time ends and only judgment remains. He is the holiest of all ghosts, occupying a dimension that is not captured by Newtonian laws or Quantum theory, but only by spiritual discourse.

Duncan is a vessel through which a beam of magnificence passes. He is the NBA's designated holder of pure athletic dignity, the kind that danced around the ring with Joe Louis and that ran with Joe DiMaggio around the base paths. Duncan emanates such honor and humility that many members of the media have idealized him, fashioning him as some sort of puritanical savior to the league. And although this status is somewhat overblown, without Duncan, one wonders if the Association would ring hollow to the public, who might view it as merely a noisy shell of celebrity and finesse. Duncan keeps us honest. His righteous and calming presence provides balance—and enables the NBA to unashamedly pursue its primary function as a flabbergasting playground for all to enjoy.

Despite all of Duncan's glory, a restlessness envelops him. We watch a player with infinite talent, with MVP, All-Star, and All-Defensive Team honors, with a loving fan base, and we wonder why he expresses no joy. We rarely cheer for him, because at some point all of us have watched him destroy a player or team we love. And even this distaste for him makes us uncomfortable, because he is not villainous. We watch perhaps the greatest power forward in the history of the NBA go relatively unnoticed among his flashier colleagues and wonder why he does not express frustration. Duncan's mind is just as likely to hold the perversions of a serial killer as it is the rote mechanism of success. It is this vacancy—the potential that Duncan's soul may be composed of *any substance at all*, even the substance of turmoil—that keeps us compelled as he plods through his life on-court.

The Boring Quiz

Match the numbered items with the quotes about them below.

---

1. Tim Duncan

2. Al Gore

3. Wynton Marsalis

4. *The Bridges of Madison County*

5. Lewis & Clark's winter at Fort Clatsop

6. Potatoes

A. "Dull, monotonous, boring, and scientifically productive."

B. "Crazy-talented but largely a boring romantic."

C. "In those days, he was so stiff and robotic he could have played a supporting role in *March of the Penguins*."

D. "Technically brilliant, sterilely detached and downright boring . . . there's no anger, no frustration, no anything."

E. "Arguably the world's longest greeting card."

F. "I know of nothing more completely tasteless."

ANSWERS:

1. D *The Denver Post* 2. C *The St. Petersburg Times*
3. B PopMatters.com 4. E *The New York Times*
5. A *The Trails of Lewis & Clark* 6. F *The Physiology of Taste*

Filling the Void

The elegant simplicity of the Fibonacci sequence has delighted mathematicians and stoned college students for centuries. This sequence (a series of numbers, starting with one, in which each new number is derived by adding the previous two, ad infinitum) is not technically found in nature, but there is startling similarity between the Fibonacci sequence and the growth patterns of pinecones, sunflowers, and seashells—exactly the sort of deceptively innocuous creatures that, if left to their own devices, one suspects would eventually take over the universe, much as Tim Duncan has the NBA. Thus, it is no surprise that Duncan's statistics reflect these proportions, as if he were king of the pinecones or the chief architect of the seashell.

The Fibonacci Sequence vs. Tim Duncan's Career Averages

1	1	2	3	5	8	13	21
0.508	0.8	2.4	3.1	5	8.3	11.8	21.6
FG%	Steals	Blocks	Assists	FTs Made	FGs Made	Rebounds	Points

It's almost uncanny how closely Tim Duncan's stats hew to the first eight numbers of the Fibonacci sequence. While he falls just shy of perfection, the correlation reads like a statement of purpose. And compared to his contemporaries—represented here by a sample of expert power forwards and centers—he's undoubtedly the Fibonacci-est of the bunch, with only 3.39 units of deviation.

Perfect Fibonacci Player: 0.00 (Deviation)

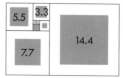

Tim Duncan: 3.39

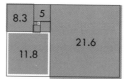

Dirk Nowitzki: 8.53

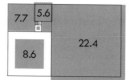

Jermaine O'Neal: 18.54

Kevin Garnett: 6.01

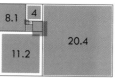

Shawn Marion: 11.82

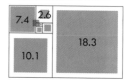

Marcus Camby: 22.53

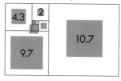

All career averages through 2007-2008 season

The Gothic Dimensions of Tim Duncan

AMERICAN GOTHIC

Presents to the world a demure aesthetic, reinforced by core American values of hard work, moral uprightness, and honesty.

GOTH SUBCULTURE

Conveys a quiet bookishness to cloak a deeply violent essence. Harbors a penchant for Dungeons & Dragons, knives, and the movie *The Crow*.

VISIGOTH BARBARIANS

Prone to exerting brute strength over opponents; allied with teammates of varying ethnicities.

GOTHIC ARCHITECTURE

Relies for its beauty on angles and arches, the ornate character of which is overshadowed by their repetition. Gargoyle-like when angry.

SIMPLE MECHANICS

Although Duncan's nickname is "the Big Fundamental," his game actually consists of *several* fundamental mechanical concepts.

THE INCLINED PLANE
(SHOULDERS)

A plane set at an angle to the horizontal, used to raise or lower a load by rolling or sliding.

THE WEDGE
(BUTT)

A double inclined plane, used to split an object through force or brace an object through friction.

THE SCREW
(TORSO)

A helical inclined plane, used to convert a rotational force to a linear force and vice versa.

THE PULLEY
(KNEES & ELBOWS)

A series of wheels and cables, used to change the direction of the pull and thereby lift a load.

THE WHEEL & AXLE
(BODY & LEGS)

A lever that rotates in a circle around a center point or fulcrum.

THE LEVER
(FEET)

A rigid object with a fixed pivot point, used to raise weight on one end by pushing down on the opposite end.

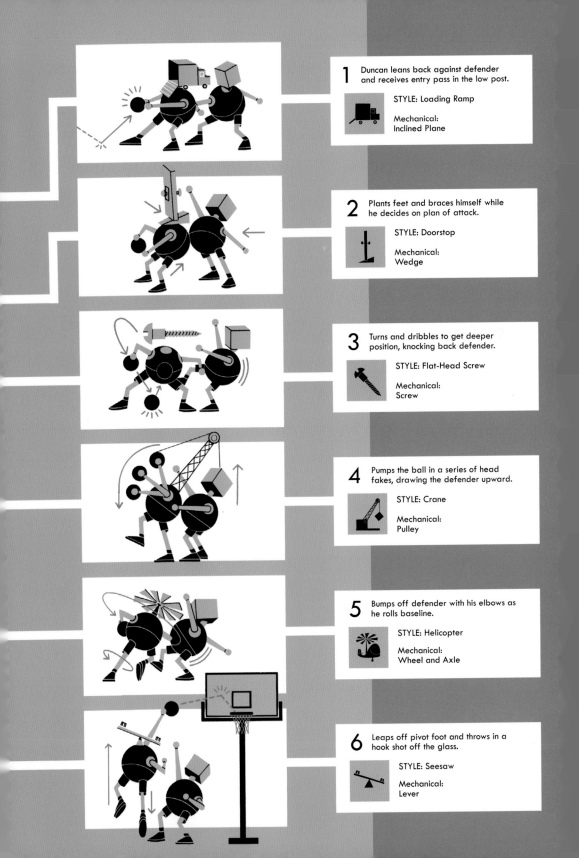

1 Duncan leans back against defender and receives entry pass in the low post.

STYLE: Loading Ramp

Mechanical: Inclined Plane

2 Plants feet and braces himself while he decides on plan of attack.

STYLE: Doorstop

Mechanical: Wedge

3 Turns and dribbles to get deeper position, knocking back defender.

STYLE: Flat-Head Screw

Mechanical: Screw

4 Pumps the ball in a series of head fakes, drawing the defender upward.

STYLE: Crane

Mechanical: Pulley

5 Bumps off defender with his elbows as he rolls baseline.

STYLE: Helicopter

Mechanical: Wheel and Axle

6 Leaps off pivot foot and throws in a hook shot off the glass.

STYLE: Seesaw

Mechanical: Lever

KEVIN GARNETT

The Schism that Bridges

Midlife turmoil. The unbridled self-doubt of an honest and well-traveled salesman. The purchase of luxuries to compensate for an unfulfilling life. Gently careening over the hill. Kevin Garnett, whose NBA existence has hurried him directly from adolescence into elderhood, has experienced none of these.

Garnett's childhood reads like a Great Migration novel. As a teen, racial injustice drove him from his hometown of Mauldin, South Carolina. He moved up north, becoming a teenage Gargantua on the basketball court at the predominantly Mexican Farragut Academy in Chicago. After an explosive senior year there, Garnett made a then-unprecedented decision to enter the NBA draft.

Although Moses Malone, Bill Willoughby, and Darryl Dawkins had entered the anarchic ABA straight out of high school, Garnett's leap was viewed incredulously, like a baby constructing a refrigerator. Basketball had not experienced such a delicate moment of uncertainty and confusion since the Russians stole the gold medal from the U.S. in the 1972 Olympics. How to treat this prodigious man-child? Isiah Thomas, then the executive vice president of the Toronto Raptors, declared that if he drafted Garnett he would "only let him play home games. Have him play forty-one home games, enroll him in college here [in Toronto] and not really allow him to travel on the road, with the exceptions of maybe two or three places." Shawn Respert, an eventual college-to-NBA disappointment, noted, "If he has the right mentors and the right peers to guide him the right way

WHAT HE GIVES US:
A man continually faced with the discomforting excitement of growth.

WHAT HE STANDS FOR:
The point of near-explosion.

WHY WE CARE:
Garnett embodies the ideal that a man can become bigger than the battles he fights.

he'll be very successful . . . But if he doesn't, I mean, there have been a lot of players that have been busts."

Just prior to the 1995 NBA draft, Garnett appeared on the cover of *Sports Illustrated* on what appeared to be the set of Michael Jordan's Playground. The cover read, "Ready Or Not . . . Three Weeks Ago Kevin Garnett Went to His High School Prom. Next Week He'll Be a Top Pick in the NBA Draft." Garnett's appearance was a novelty: Eddie Gaedel and *Close Encounters of the Third Kind* all in one.

Throughout the circus of it all, the one thing that stood out was how truly young Garnett looked. For the sweet life of him, he could not and would not control his exuberance. Whether it was his giddiness on draft night or his emphatic on-court bellowing, Garnett epitomized the defiance of adolescence. Knowing his own naïveté, he looked up to teammates Terry Porter and Sam Mitchell as spiritual figures and took their lessons to heart.

How Garnett then managed to age so fast is a matter of some debate. Some suggest it happened in the whirlwind of his second season, when Garnett became a starter and an All-Star, and the Timberwolves made the playoffs for the first time in franchise history. Others point to Garnett's first playoff series victory, in 2004, when the Timberwolves triumphed over both Denver and Sacramento. Close observers of Garnett's legacy, however, will note a far more critical period.

From 1998 to 2000, Garnett was faced with disloyalty, death, and deceit. It was the end of innocence, a slamming, shuddering express train from youth to elderhood. On the court, he was transformed from an unbridled, slam-dunking up-and-comer to a more calculating veteran.

The change was touched off, appropriately, by an issue of money, that ignominious marker of adulthood. When Garnett signed a record-setting $125 million contract, Stephon Marbury, a childhood confidant who had risen to NBA stardom alongside him on the Timberwolves, began to grumble. Marbury eventually forced a trade from Minnesota, leaving KG and the rest of the Minnesota organization stupefied. This was Garnett's first lesson: There are no friends in this life.

As a result of Garnett's enormous contract, the Timberwolves were thrown into salary cap hell. To maneuver around the league's restrictions and Garnett's mammoth paycheck, the Wolves completed an under-the-table deal with power forward Joe Smith. The Wolves promised Smith, a favorite of Garnett, that if he signed with the team for below market value, they would grant him a future multimillion dollar deal. When Commissioner Stern and his goons found out about this negotiation, they punished the Timberwolves severely, initially taking away five future first-round draft picks. The lack of picks would ultimately cripple Minnesota's personnel flexibility far more than the salary cap restrictions. Garnett learned his second lesson: Subterfuge will never lead to prosperity.

The final lesson came in 2000, when Garnett's teammate Malik Sealy's SUV was hit by a drunk driver's pickup truck. Sealy, Garnett's closest friend on the team, had been returning home from Garnett's twenty-fourth birthday. This would be Garnett's final indoctrination into elderhood. With Sealy's memory forever weighing on him, there would be no "settling down" period in Garnett's life. This third lesson: All is impermanent.

Garnett had not merely learned some valuable life lessons; rather, it was as though he became educated with the wisdom of one million Vedas. He adopted a greater leadership role on the Timberwolves. With that big contract heavy around his neck, Garnett began to take responsibility for Minnesota's continual playoff failures and occasional late-game collapses. Even in winning seasons, each loss ate away at him. Garnett's style of play became more sinewy and less powerful. He relied ever more on his patented turnaround baseline jumper than on back-to-the-basket post-moves and thunderous dunks. He also began averaging more assists, deferring to teammates and distributing the ball like an egalitarian quarterback. Many Timberwolves followers found this maddening, as they longed for the less cerebral Garnett of old who would jaunt to the hoop without deliberation, without hesitation in his trajectory.

In 2004, Garnett captured the MVP award with statistics indicative of his expanding wisdom. There was the 2.2 blocks per game, reflecting Garnett's calm certainty in knowing when to explore risk. His 24.2 points per game told of his sheer will to find and make shots despite the consistent pressure from opponents' double-teams. His five assists a game demonstrated his capacity for integrating his new teammates Sam Cassell and Latrell Sprewell into the flow of the game. With the veterans Cassell and Spree, Garnett found kinship in elderhood, and the Timberwolves ground their way to the Western Conference Finals that year. But after falling to the Lakers just shy of the promised land, KG and the

NAME: Kevin Maurice Garnett
BORN: May 19, 1976
HEIGHT: 6 ft 11 in (2.11 m)
WEIGHT: 220 lb (100 kg)
HOMETOWN: Mauldin, SC

SPIRIT ANIMAL: Snakehead

PLAYER COMPARISON: Like one of those cool-as-hell 1970s Walt Frazier/Moses Malone type players, but without all of the getting laid.

NOTABLE REMARK: "It's not about me . . . It's about us" [hands clasped].

ACTING ROLES: Played himself on *The Jamie Foxx Show*. Also portrayed Wilt Chamberlain in the made-for-TV movie *Rebound: The Legend of Earl "The Goat" Manigault*.

DISTINGUISHING MARKS: Has heart-encircled tribute to deceased teammate Malik Sealy on his wrist. KG also has his motto, "Blood, Sweat, and Tears," inscribed on his arm. Additionally, Garnett wears rubber bands on his wrists, a tradition he began in high school, substituting the bands for jewelry to create a style that was all his own.

BEST NBA FRIENDS: Tyronn Lue, Chauncey Billups, Dean Garrett.

Timberwolves began a three-year period of steep decline. Cassell and Sprewell left the team and Garnett found himself surrounded with younger and younger players, such as Rashad McCants, Craig Smith, and Bracey Wright. Now actually the elder, Garnett became more obtuse in his wisdom, spouting off aphorisms such as "We have to do the impossible, but it is possible." He also became more crotchety, allowing the young guys in the league to disrupt his game and his mental stability. Every other night, it seemed, Tyson Chandler, Matt Bonner, Al Jefferson, or Joel Przybilla was getting under Garnett's skin. Garnett wasted his breath on these youngsters, calling them "fake thugs," and occasionally collected an embarrassing flagrant foul for shoving one of them. For the first time, Garnett showed signs of breaking down physically, developing tendinitis and other knee problems throughout the 2005 and 2006 seasons. The end of KG's term as a Timberwolf was in sight.

Just before the 2007–08 season, as though this modern-day Paul Bunyan never really stomped through Minnesota's expansive plains, our great midwestern folk hero departed to Boston. And it is in Boston where he is certain to live out his golden years. He is again paired with a duo of wily and capable veterans in Paul Pierce and Ray Allen. He belongs to a franchise watched over by the most sacred ghosts of basketball history, from Red Auerbach to Dennis Johnson. And yet, we must ask ourselves whether we forced him to age so artificially or whether Garnett brought it on himself. Either way, here he stands, wise, worn, and almighty. And with all of his experience, it is a wonder he does not collapse right before our eyes.

ATLAS BONE (first cervical vertebra): Permanently bent from years of carrying subpar Timberwolves teammates. When asked if he puts the burden of his team losing on his shoulders, Garnett responded, "I've got no choice. It's killing me."

THORACIC CURVE: Identical to the land route of Cherokee removal on the Trail of Tears. Garnett is familiar with both crying— "These are tears of pain, tears of pride," he told Coach John Thompson in a legendarily weepy/tearful interview—and with displacement. As a youngster, he was forced to transfer to Farragut Academy in Chicago from his hometown high school in Mauldin, SC, due to his involvement in a racially charged scuffle.

Charleston
Nashville
Hopkinsville
Cape Girardeau
Springfield
Tahlequah

SACRAL CURVE: Slight horizontal character of lower vertebral column reveals definitive evidence of skeletal resemblance to *R. Tarandus*; as Garnett put it, "I'm like Rudolph the Red-Nosed Reindeer. If I'm not ready, the sled isn't going to go."

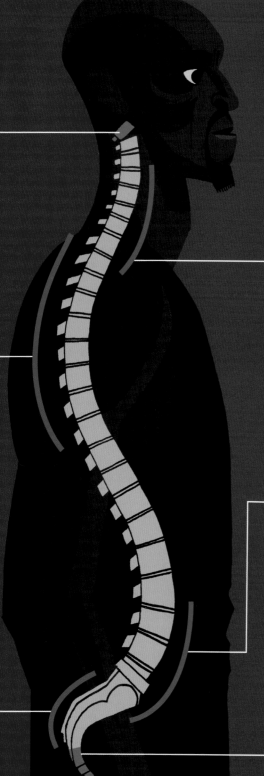

Backbone of a True Soul

For years, Kevin Garnett has been the backbone of the NBA, demonstrating loyalty to those who have supported him, toughness in playing through injuries, and sophistication in accepting responsibility for the shortcomings of his teammates. As it provides character to the league, Garnett's backbone also provides insight into his very soul.

CERVICAL CURVE: Forms the shape of the thirty-round magazine of an M16, the gun that Garnett once referenced in discussing preparation for a playoff battle with the Sacramento Kings: "It's Game 7, man. That's it. It's for all the marbles . . . sitting in the house, I'm loadin' up the pump, I'm loadin' up the Uzi. I got a couple M16s, a couple 9s . . . I'm just loading clips. I'm ready for war."

LUMBAR CURVE: Similar to the value function below zero on the y-axis in graphic demonstrations of Kahneman and Tversky's prospect theory (1979). This theory posits that the psychological impact of losses is greater than the psychological impact of gains, reflective of KG's own aversion to loss. As he once stated, "I'm losing, I'm losing, I'm losing, I'm losing . . . I hate to lose."

VALUE

LOSSES GAINS

COCCYX: The "tailbone" is necessary for performing the dance specified by "The Bump," the Commodores' disco classic containing the lyric "I want your back / If you bump my side, I'll bump you right back." During the 2006 All-Star Game introductions, amid the smoke and pyrotechnics, KG uttered, "I feel like the Commodores . . . I feel like the Commodores."

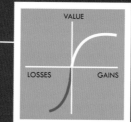

STYLE GUIDE

1 Garnett receives entry pass while fighting off defender.

STYLE: **Crab**
Low to the ground, strong forearms

2 Straightens himself out, sets his feet, and checks for cutters.

STYLE: **Periscope**
Scouting from protected position

3 Dribbles to his left, creating contact with defender.

STYLE: **Mortar and Pestle**
Grinding through repeated motion

Center of Production

Comparing Garnett's on-court production with every other player who played for the Timberwolves during Garnett's twelve seasons on the team.

SEASONS WITH TIMBERWOLVES

1 season or less
2–3 seasons
4–5 seasons
6–7 seasons
12 seasons

Production $= \text{FGs} + 1/2 \times \text{FTs} + \text{AST} + \text{REB} + \text{STL} + \text{BLK}$

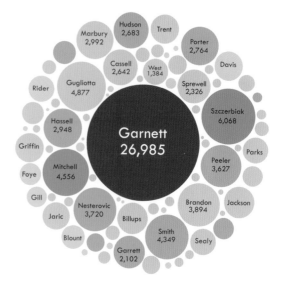

Hudson 2,683
Trent
Marbury 2,992
Porter 2,764
Cassell 2,642
West 1,384
Davis
Rider
Gugliotta 4,877
Sprewell 2,326
Szczerbiak 6,068
Hassell 2,948
Garnett 26,985
Griffin
Parks
Foye
Mitchell 4,556
Peeler 3,627
Gill
Brandon 3,894
Jackson
Jaric
Nesterovic 3,720
Billups
Blount
Smith 4,349
Sealy
Garrett 2,102

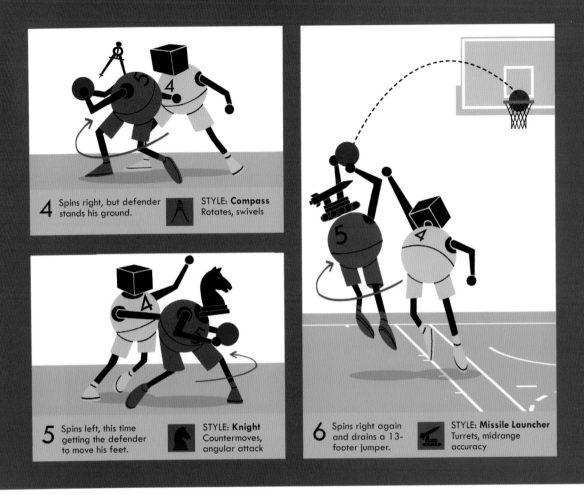

4 Spins right, but defender stands his ground.

STYLE: **Compass**
Rotates, swivels

5 Spins left, this time getting the defender to move his feet.

STYLE: **Knight**
Countermoves, angular attack

6 Spins right again and drains a 13-footer jumper.

STYLE: **Missile Launcher**
Turrets, midrange accuracy

CUTTING THE PIE FIVE WAYS

Percentage of production among the five players who played the most minutes on each of four teams.

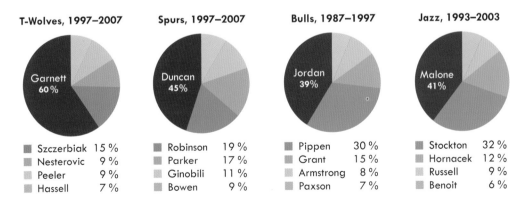

T-Wolves, 1997–2007

Garnett
60%

■ Szczerbiak	15%
■ Nesterovic	9%
■ Peeler	9%
■ Hassell	7%

Spurs, 1997–2007

Duncan
45%

■ Robinson	19%
■ Parker	17%
■ Ginobili	11%
■ Bowen	9%

Bulls, 1987–1997

Jordan
39%

■ Pippen	30%
■ Grant	15%
■ Armstrong	8%
■ Paxson	7%

Jazz, 1993–2003

Malone
41%

■ Stockton	32%
■ Hornacek	12%
■ Russell	9%
■ Benoit	6%

JERSEYS
FOR EVERY OCCASION

Once, fankind donned jerseys only to show loyalty to a team: to claim a partisan place in the tale of armies that has swept along men of sport since time immemorial. However, in the Age of Liberated Fandom, these garments have taken on a more expansive role. They are purchased as much for the individual as for the team—and to express affinity, rather than mere support. Rocking a Kobe Bryant jersey doesn't mean simply that one likes the Lakers or hopes Kobe will help them win; instead, it speaks to one's admiration for Bryant himself, as both a man and an idea. In this age, wearing a jersey tells others more about *you* than about the player you admire.

At the same time, only the most simplistic of fans would own merely one. Jerseys allow us to tap into the richness of our personality, by refracting it through the fun-house mirrors of the NBA sideshow. Who am I today? Am I the upright Bird? The implacable LeBron? Or the bruising Artest, leveling all in my path?

Part of existing as a socialized creature is adapting oneself to the situation at hand. This is altogether consistent with the principles of the NBA, in which every possession is at once a fresh opportunity, a chance to assert one's identity, and a script to interpret. The Master Builders of basketball have not only defined the game; they have become part of our culture's fabric, symbolic figures whose meaning resonates even in the non-basketball world. A Bill Russell jersey tells those around you how you view the matter at hand; a Dominique Wilkins jersey bespeaks something entirely different. How better, then, to show one's gamesmanship in life than by sporting the proper jersey for every occasion?

FUNERAL:

Michael Jordan, Chicago Bulls: The murder of Jordan's father drove him to early retirement in 1994; upon his 1995 comeback, he donned number 45 instead of his signature 23, which had itself been retired. From now till infinity, the Jordan 4-5 links death with rebirth and adjustment.

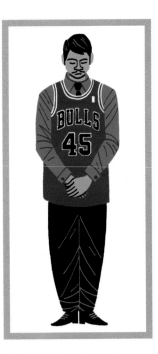

ALTERNATE **Len Bias,** Boston Celtics: The Celtics took Len Bias with the first overall pick in the 1986 draft, after which he promptly died of a cocaine overdose. This tragedy derailed a dynasty; wearing this jersey says to the family "I know you'll never be happy again, and that's okay."

ALTERNATE **Kareem Abdul-Jabbar,** Los Angeles Lakers: Kareem is a very serious man. In his early pro days, he seemed morose and off-putting. But by the time he got to Los Angeles, he'd aged gracefully and transmuted it into gravitas, making him the perfect source of strength in a time of need.

BAR MITZVAH:

Moses Malone, Utah Stars: In 1974, Malone joined the league out of high school; within minutes, he had shown himself as a pillar of strength, courage, and hard work. A worthy template for any young Jew invested in the power of this occasion.

ALTERNATE **Rick Barry,** San Francisco Warriors: Barry scored points at every level and in every league, and went on to spawn a bunch of little ball-playing Barrys. However, he's remembered mostly for his silly-looking underhand foul shots. This day may be the gateway into adulthood, but it will also yield the most awkward photos of your natural-born life.

ALTERNATE **Dolph Schayes,** Syracuse Nationals: The ranks of great coaches overflow with Semitic glory, as do certain chapters of the sport's prehistory. But since the dawn of the NBA, only Schayes has pulled off the unlikely combination of Hebrew heritage and sustained on-court relevance.

WEDDING:

BEST MAN
Charles Barkley, Houston Rockets:
A ferocious defender, Charles Bark-ley liked to party while he was at the height of his powers, and as he eyed retirement that urge can only have gotten stronger. The best man's there for moral support and all, but his main job is picking out the stripper.

GROOM
Oscar Robertson, Cincinnati Royals:
In 1970, the superhuman Robertson was traded to Milwaukee when Cincy coach Bob Cousy got jealous of his aptitude. Let that be a lesson for ev-ery groom on his wedding day.

FATHER OF THE BRIDE
Elgin Baylor, Los Angeles Lakers:
Before Julius Erving, Earl Monroe, or Jordan, Baylor birthed the improvi-sational beauty that gives this game life. Likewise, behind every lovely, fertile lady is a handsome, if wizened and faded, dad.

BRIDESMAID
Chris Webber, Sacramento Kings:
Like the bridesmaid, Webber's Kings were perennially so close, yet so far away. Like Webber, people eventu-ally started to ask if it was fate.

BRIDE
Walt Frazier, New York Knicks:
Hands-down the most flamboyant dresser the NBA has ever known, Frazier knew to play it up in the NYC spotlight. A wedding dress should be extravagant and the bride confident in it, or else the occasion is ruined.

RING BEARER
Allen Iverson, Philadelphia 76ers:
When Iverson entered the league, he brought a brash, hip-hop-inflected style crashing through the gates. He also wore more ice than any athlete before or since, thus establishing him-self as the reigning authority on dia-monds—and keeping that shit safe.

JOB INTERVIEW

Jerry Lucas, Cincinnati Royals: Lucas was never the most athletic player on the court, but he won at every level through hard work and savvy. Blessed with a legendary memory, he has the ability to retain key facts about the company and the names of people he meets during interviews.

Willis Reed, New York Knicks: An inspirational leader who puts his job first, Reed can excel in any work environment. A great team player, a hard-nosed defender, and a tenacious rebounder, he is probably best suited for middle management.

James Worthy, Los Angeles Lakers: First impressions mean everything, and with an athletic 6'9" frame and scholarly spectacles, Worthy passes any looks test one could imagine. When you consider his impeccable collegiate pedigree and penchant for stepping up when it matters most, you can see why he'd be at the top of any headhunter's wish list.

COOKING AT A FIVE-STAR RESTAURANT

HEAD CHEF **Karl Malone,** Utah Jazz: The tyrant of the kitchen should seek to capture Malone's spirit as a take-charge individual known to kick ass (literally). Additionally, Malone contributed his famous "hot crab salad" to a book of NBA players' favorite recipes, suggesting he can bring the heat with a broiler, too.

SOUS-CHEF **Ricky Davis,** Cleveland Cavaliers: Never the focal point of any offense, Davis has added additional spice to every team he's played on. Also, Davis presumably spent some time in the kitchen himself after his personal chef was stabbed outside of his apartment by one of Davis's friends.

PASTRY CHEF **Stanley Roberts,** Minnesota Timberwolves: The king of sweets and all things unhealthy. While a member of the Timberwolves, Roberts once paid a ball boy to locate a bag of popcorn before a game. Kevin McHale, upon finding out about this, confiscated the bag.

FIRST DATE

THE GUY **Scottie Pippen,** Portland Trailblazers: Pippen is the classic underdog, a late bloomer from middle-of-nowhere Arkansas. He eventually earned the trust of his teammates and became a smooth, confident performer, although plagued by moments of insecurity.

THE GIRL **Kwame Brown,** Washington Wizards: Kwame was a hot commodity in 2001, a tall, fit nineteen-year-old who caught the eye of Michael Jordan and many others. He was shy and soft-spoken, but there were indications that intelligence lurked behind that smooth-faced exterior.

THE GIRL'S DAD **Charles Oakley,** New York Knicks: Oakley is one of the league's all-time tough guys, playing the enforcer for Michael Jordan early in his career and Vince Carter toward the end. If he stood up for his teammates that way, just imagine what he'd do to you if you tried to dog out his daughter.

JURY DUTY

Adonal Foyle, Golden State Warriors: He started the student organization Democracy Matters, demonstrating a deep commitment to doing his civic duty. Since he rarely sees the court, he has a good attitude when he actually gets there.

Isiah Thomas, Detroit Pistons: Stubborn and fond of bossing people around, Thomas is ideally suited to the job of jury foreman. He's a sure bet to piss off the judge and attorneys on both sides.

Len Elmore, Indiana Pacers: Elmore began his career with the Pacers in the lawless ABA; thirteen years later, he graduated from Harvard Law School. By far the most informed juror to ever don a pro basketball jersey.

CIVIL WAR REENACTMENT

UNION SOLDIERS **Phil Jackson,** New York Knicks: This jersey connotes victory: The Zen master does not lose. As a player, Phil Jackson fought for the north; as a coach, he has embraced egalitarian values. Plus, in those old 1970s Knicks days, he bore a striking resemblance to General Ambrose Burnside.

CONFEDERATE SOLDIERS **Jason Williams,** Memphis Grizzlies: An outfit for the proud but confused. Williams is from West Virginia, which technically housed both Confederate and Union soldiers, yet nothing says south-of-the-Mason-Dixon-line backcountry like White Chocolate.

MID-VICTORIAN FEMALE CIVILIANS **Glenn Robinson,** San Antonio Spurs: The decoration of subordination. During the Spurs' 2005 championship run, Robinson was deemed unfit for battle, spending most of his time looking on from the sidelines. Although pundits believed he contributed something to the Spurs' victory, it is unclear what exactly.

1998 SMOKING GROOVES CONCERT

Wayman Tisdale, Sacramento Kings: A professional lite-jazz bassist with six albums to his credit, Tisdale was neo-soul before green tea and headwraps hit the mainstream. The silky-smooth Tisdale wouldn't likely get down with Cypress Hill's death-kill raps, but one imagines he could vibe out to Spearhead or some early Black Eyed Peas with the best of them.

Jason Kapono, Toronto Raptors: This jersey, like Kapono himself, exemplifies the demeanor of the Caucasian backpacker who won't shut up about the latest Rawkus compilation. Kapono would give you a ride to the show, let you indulge in whatever you needed to indulge in, and drive you home afterward.

Brian Grant, Miami Heat: The jersey of the true fanboy. Grant purchased a private beach in Jamaica and had it detailed with sand sculptures of Ziggy Marley. This type of devotion to one of music's most nonprovocative figures is both inspiring and incredibly depressing.

Chapter 11

Uncanny Peacocks

Cutting Through the League with Idiosyncratic Flair

Few of us can imagine the life of a peacock: an animal dressed in finery who, beneath it all, desires simply to hunt and fuck like any other hardy organism. In the courts of ancient Persia, they roamed the lawns as decoration. Much later, at a predominantly Jewish school in Dallas, these birds were employed to stand guard against intruders. They sparkle in the light, but that light drives them to kill, just as their beauty lends itself to luxuriance. But this species is not Nature's ruse, or a vehicle for her crassest whimsy. Instead, it is death and beauty rolled up into one, a mending of the very division that so delighted Eve and Adam.

Where eccentricity is fuel for might, the song of the peacock rises up into the skies. These are men who could be lost to their own perplexing qualities; instead, they come roaring into known basketball with authority, demanding respect while enforcing their singularity. While all NBA players make the sport their own, few do so with as much defiant energy as these men. And few players draw us as absolutely into their corner. That peacock's cry you hear isn't a tune or a language. It's the piercing tone poem of a creature that can't help but show itself to the world.

GILBERT ARENAS
The Court Is a Carnival

Gilbert Arenas is the NBA's court jester, a font of outrageous utterances and unfathomable behavior. But even if he weren't an inveterate ham, he'd still be one of the NBA's most peculiar creatures. The Washington Wizards guard has earned a reputation for outlandish pranks, Byzantine rituals, and a good-natured form of grandstanding that borders on parody. But above all, it's Arenas's approach to the actual game of basketball that defies logic and twists convention.

Arenas entered the NBA draft in 2001, an underclassman too short to be a shooting guard, too impulsive to man the point. This was true to form: In every phase of his young career, he had been doubted, scorned, and left to fend for himself. As a freshman at Arizona, he had taken the jersey number zero because it was "the number of minutes people predicted I would play." When Arenas was finally scooped up by Golden State in the second round, it seemed that his only hope was to reinvent himself as a real PG—or at least alter his outlook to jibe with the position's solemnity.

But Gilbert being Gilbert, this was not to happen. Given an opportunity at the point, he promptly established himself as a one-man scoring onslaught. Somewhere along the way, the Warriors and the Wizards—who signed him to a lucrative long-term contract—both decided to sit back and enjoy the ride. He became Washington's new franchise player: a man who had not only beaten the odds, but actually made the odds longer than they had to be and then beat them anyway. It was the only way he knew how to motivate himself—or perhaps defying the impossible was all he was after in the first place.

WHAT HE GIVES US:
A breathlessly effective, slightly kooky take on the underdog come-up.

WHAT HE STANDS FOR:
The stream of consciousness as power's will, not a form of weakness.

WHY WE CARE:
He's proof that the modern athlete can succeed in making a circus out of a profession too often cast as warfare.

In spite of his All-Star appearances and playoff heroics, Arenas somehow remains the eternal underdog; he's one of the league's most visible young stars, yet hailed mostly as a cult figure. While Arenas exudes humor and glee, his triumphs are pure acid, revenge against a basketball establishment that has continually done him wrong. At this point, his goofball reputation seems like an elaborate, high-concept taunt. The world sees him as a fool, but this fool fucks up his opponents like he was the baddest man on the planet. Gilbert Arenas knows that people underestimate him; he'll take advantage of this on the court and in the media, using slights as table settings at what amounts to an endless coming-out party. There are streamers on the walls and cake, but about half his guests end up watching from a stretcher.

What marks Gilbert Arenas as a true enig-ma, though, is the way he sees the game unfold before him. It's inaccurate to label him a ball hog, or sloppy, or rash, though he dabbles in all these vices. He's a roundball savant, doing what he feels as guilelessly and wholeheartedly as possible. It's the difference between blinding arrogance and just really, really believing in yourself. Arenas's discipline comes in his cultivation of this belief. He is a notorious gym rat, logging hours upon hours practicing from a single spot on the floor. Most players concentrate on learning the game as a rich assortment of sequences and probabilities. By contrast, Arenas has atomized it, exhaustively breaking it down to blips that he then strings together in fits of untoward zeal.

After Arenas dropped 60 points on Kobe in early 2006, the Laker accused him of "having no conscience" and not taking "quality shots." To paraphrase religious thinkers of various

The Unconscionable Acts of Arenas, Explained

Arenas is frequently criticized for his poor shot selection. However, this criticism assumes that what's bad for the rest of the world is also bad for Gilbert Arenas, which couldn't be further from the truth. Take, for instance, the three-pointer, that most self-indulgent of shots. As illustrated below, Arenas actually shoots a higher percentage on his three-pointers from the hinterlands than he does from up close.

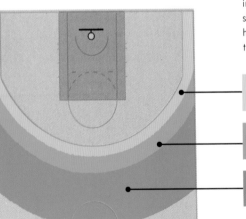

| ZONE 1 | FG%: **0.323** | SOME |
| 23–24 FT | FGS: 42/99 | CONSCIENCE |

| ZONE 2 | FG%: **0.381** | MINIMAL |
| 25–27 FT | FGS: 121/318 | CONSCIENCE |

| ZONE 3 | FG%: **0.435** | NO |
| 28–38 FT | FGS: 20/46 | CONSCIENCE |

persuasions, Kobe was asking the wrong question. Arenas's decision making isn't lacking in rhyme or reason; instead, he makes up the rules as he goes along. In a sport defined by spur-of-the-moment creativity, Arenas is neither contrived nor defiantly free-flowing. He's the NBA's answer to Thelonious Monk, devising his own fractured language system on the fly.

Few moments in his career captured this quality as perfectly as Game 6 of the Wizards' 2006 playoff tangle with the Cleveland Cavaliers. With the Wizards down by three points, facing elimination, and staring at ten seconds left to rescue their season, Arenas nonchalantly dribbled down the court and launched a three from at least five feet behind the line. It was not a quality shot, it left time on the clock, and almost nothing about it made sense. But it sent the game into overtime—where Arenas, normally an effortless free throw shooter, bricked two key ones that handed the ballgame to the Cavs. For any other baller, this would be an agonizing medley of grace and shame. For Gilbert Arenas, it was just something that happened.

Game in and game out, this stance rewards Agent Zero and his followers. And it's likely that being Arenas demands a similar form of haywire faith. What's more, the sheer strangeness of his character—and his ability to continually play the outsider—is also sustained mainly through perverse determination. Many athletes can boast of a single-minded insistence on improving their play. Arenas sustains himself not through a desire to be someone or something, but through the denial of all the things he should be.

Arenas is now recognized as one of the

NAME: Gilbert Jay Arenas
BORN: January 6, 1982
HEIGHT: 6 ft 4 in (1.93 m)
WEIGHT: 215 lb (95 kg)
HOMETOWN: Los Angeles

SPIRIT ANIMAL: Tasmanian devil

PLAYER COMPARISON: Either a beefier Allen Iverson or a more compact, less cerebral Kobe Bryant.

NOTABLE REMARK: "My swag was phenomenal." After shooting a long game-winning three-pointer against the Bucks on January 3, 2007, and then turning around, arms raised triumphantly in the air, before the ball even hit the net.

HOPES & DREAMS: Arenas has publicly stated his desire to invest in floating real estate: "I want to buy an island in Tahiti. Because Diana Ross has an island. Marlon Brando had an island."

DISTINGUISHING MARKS: Arenas has a giant tattoo of a tiger's face that stretches across his entire chest and torso. When his father saw the tattoo for the first time, he scornfully remarked, "Dwyane Wade would never have done that."

league's most feared scorers. He's also gone from local eccentric to large-scale weirdo, dubbing himself "The Black President," launching a signature shoe with twenty autobiographical variations, and setting the gold standard for athlete blogs. Arenas found novel (if somewhat tacky) ways to make his money talk: trying to save Barry Bonds's record-breaking ball from defamation, or taking his rivalry with college teammate Richard Jefferson into the realm of seven-figure alma mater donations. And his collection of autographed memorabilia became an obsession; as Arenas later revealed, "All the jerseys I've collected, these are my memories right here. Truthfully, that's all you have as an athlete when you leave and you go into real society again, it's all you have to keep you going." Which, of course, is why he had to include Beyoncé.

Yet as a player, Arenas has decided to meet the future as if he's still at the bottom staring up. At the beginning of an injury-marred 2007–08, he gave a now-infamous *Sports Illustrated* interview, in which he compared himself favorably to Kobe Bryant, LeBron James, and Dwyane Wade. Arenas later claimed he'd just wanted his due as one of the game's five finest guards. But the way in which he did so—excessively verbal, rationalized, and based on a selective system of his own design—came across as peculiar. What's more, his exaggerated confidence ended up sounding like critiques of his peers; when Arenas asserted that he alone had coexisted with two other 20-point-per-game scorers, it implied that Kobe and the rest were selfish. The backlash was swift.

But realistically, why would Gilbert Arenas suddenly sober up? Wouldn't his elevated status simply raise the stakes—and make them that much more contentious? Arenas will never be content to call himself a great player but not the greatest, or accept that the world loves and respects him. For better or worse, Arenas can't stop, won't stop.

The closer Arenas gets to undisputed superstardom, the more inflamed his underdog complex becomes. Before his takeover, he was entertaining, amusing, curious, and mischievous, a dybbuk inflicted upon the public consciousness. Now, Arenas really, truly has the potential to cause havoc, on the court and in the game's mind. He's gone from perplexing to, in his own screwy way, downright threatening. No longer the underground hero, or the first Internet superstar, Gilbert Arenas now has to prove to every player, fan, and media hack the inherent worth of going a little crazy. A tall order, and yet still preferable to backing down, settling, and saying that his uncompromising ways came only with hunger.

Gilbert Arenas could be a more orthodox decision maker, a less unpredictable teammate, and a full-fledged superstar. But if that happened, he might lose the edge that's allowed for his most jaw-dropping accomplishments. For Arenas, the improbable holds the key to the impossible. And so improbable is Gilbert Arenas that, with every season he spends in the league, he wants nothing more than to take down as much impossible as he can. This is not the way basketball is supposed to be played, and it's certainly a roundabout way to arrive at one's hopes and dreams. But when you've started below nothing and found your way through self-assurance, you might as well always go for broke.

1 Arenas brings the ball across half-court
and sees a possible opening to the basket.

STYLE: Falcon
Analysis in motion, descends
from great heights quickly

STYLE GUIDE

2 He pulls back for a split second to draw the
defender forward (A) then continues in original
direction, throwing the defender off balance (B).

STYLE: Short-String Yo-Yo
Like a normal yo-yo,
but with a short string

3 He then shoots forward directly
toward the basket.

STYLE: Bottle Rocket
Straight-line speed, disregard
for temporary chaos

4 Collides with two defenders in the lane, but
uses upper-body strength to stay on course.

STYLE: Bull
Power, horns

5 Dunks the ball.

STYLE: Sand Dollar
Irrelevant, though
not unpleasant

The Alchemy of Arenas

Maybe you've been told that alchemy, a medieval precursor to modern chemistry, was just an attempt to make some gold out of lead. But this crude science was about more than getting paid and blowing shit up in the process. Really, it was about a journey of the mind, in which a "philosophy of chaos" was refined into the "craft of philosophy." The methods of Gilbert Arenas may seem unpredictable and unaccountable, but once you become familiar with the theoretical framework of this sacred tradition (outlined in a reproduction of a rare ancient diagram on the right), you'll see that Arenas is nothing if not a modern-day alchemist, a beacon unto scores of men and women who currently carry out this lifestyle in secret.

7 ALCHEMICAL STAGES	7 KOOKY ARENAS STORIES
CALCINATION: On the summit of the Black Mountain, the archetypal elements are cooked in an athanor (alchemical furnace).	To improve his stamina and endurance, Gilbert Arenas has altered the oxygen levels in his home to simulate high-altitude conditions.
DISSOLUTION: The athanor then releases the "Retort of Transformation," which melts away the pretenses of the former self.	At the 2001 predraft camp in Chicago, Arenas stunned a roomful of scouts by revealing that "international pimp" was his fallback career choice.
SEPARATION: During Separation, symbolized by a bird taking flight, the sacrificed self rises from a baptism of Fire and Water.	When criticized by his coach Eddie Jordan for shooting too much, Arenas responded by going an entire game without a single field goal attempt.
CONJUNCTION: During Conjunction, the King and Queen, who symbolize the Sun and Moon, work together to lift the Child of the Philosophers into the higher stages of transformation.	In 2003, Arenas hit the free agent market as its most scorching commodity. He narrowed his decision down to the Clippers and the Wizards, and then let a single flip of a coin choose for him.
DISTILLATION: After Conjunction the refined essence leaves the vessel of transformation and is sublimated into an entirely new level of being or state of consciousness.	Arenas once responded to a poor first half by taking a halftime shower in his uniform, then didn't bother to change out of it afterward. Sopping and energized, he led a Wizards comeback.
FERMENTATION: The ensuing Fermentation is symbolized by the sudden emergence of a peacock, who possesses a tail of colorful blooming flowers.	For his twenty-fifth birthday, Arenas threw a multimillion-dollar bash, complete with celebrity guests, a stage full of hip-hop heavyweights, and a life-size ice sculpture of himself.
COAGULATION: This final step is symbolized by the Crown of Coagulation, which partakes of both the material forces Below and the spiritual forces Above.	In the summer of 2007, Arenas was recovering after knee surgery. As part of his rehab, he endeavored to make 100,000 shots in the course of 73 days.

GERALD WALLACE & JOSH SMITH

Holy Warriors of Potential

I n the ten years from 1995—that fateful summer Kevin Garnett entered the draft—until the league set the minimum age at nineteen, NBA scouting fell to the speculators. This was the Age of Potential, when teams hunted for eighteen-year-old prodigies and untested international prospects who might, in theory, make beautiful basketball music one day. Gone was the age of proven student-athletes, hand-groomed by the NCAA to compete at the next level. A scrawny, bouncy, untutored youth from backwoods Arkansas, or a gangly Balkan lad who grew up dodging heavy artillery—these were the draft picks du jour.

Draft hysteria became a cottage industry and a ritualistic cult, with media outlets like ESPN stoking the flames of enthusiasm. "Ceiling" and "upside" became the industry buzzwords. Young players were always moving toward some highly desirable archetype, but at any moment might rewrite the script by attaining something as yet unknown.

"Ceiling" meant that fans got used to hearing late first-rounders compared to current All-Stars; each year's crop of incoming players included one Shawn Marion–like forward, a poor man's Baron Davis, and one of many Baby Shaqs. "Upside," on the other hand, was an altogether more profound, and profoundly disturbing, tonic. Front offices wanted to be right, to accurately predict the diamond's final form by looking at the unformed lump of coal. Yet secretly, shamefully, they dreamed of being confounded and amazed, or having the very contours

WHAT THEY GIVE US:
An unrivaled display of fireworks and revelation.

WHAT THEY STAND FOR:
The ultimate in strength through uncertainty.

WHY WE CARE:
Basketball is inherently improvisational; these two take that mandate to dizzying and ungodly extremes.

of their expectations warped into new molds. It takes a sharp man to pick out the best sofa in the room, but discovering that it also flies and talks is how men get religion. To understand why LeBron James came into this league bearing nicknames like "the Chosen One" and "King James," you must accept into your heart the power that draft picks once held in the hearts and minds of NBA executives and media types.

There also existed a dark effect to this era, one that allowed players to languish—or, some would say, consigned them to eternal infancy. One day, the league told itself, Eddy Curry (or Kwame Brown, or Darius Miles) will have that breakthrough, and a star will be born. That hopefulness allowed these players to keep their market value up, and thus stay paid. But it also burdened them with someone else's heavy dreams, grandiose plans for a lame team's future that brought unwonted attention and succeeded only in inflicting further trauma.

To the cynic, Josh Smith and Gerald Wallace are trapped within the amber of eternal potential. Since entering the league, both have remained only vaguely defined, bundles of ability whose output is both fantastic and confounding. Wallace and Smith are holy warriors of Potential, making radiant possibility into a hard-edged statement of purpose.

The persistent notion that "anything can happen" in basketball provides much of the excitement of the game—and, when something does inevitably happen, gives us the chance to rhapsodize over the theater of sports. But Wallace and Smith so amplify this strain of uncertainty—and make it such

a personal calling—that it becomes at once liberating and deeply unsettling. They find their identities in the unpredictability of the game, and in that assertion there is ecstasy and chaos. They have no signature or consistency, other than the promise of indecency, activity, and flashes of brilliance.

Both Wallace and Smith began their careers under the sign of Potential, in that cradle of lore and omens that is the American South. Wallace, who hails from the Alabama hamlet of Childersburg (population 4,927) burst onto the national scene in 2000 and fast became the nation's top recruit. Amazingly, Wallace spent a year on the campus of his state's great university, despite solid invitations to become an instant millionaire. But, stuck playing power forward off the bench, Wallace stagnated and decided to enter the 2001 draft. As he later said, "I think if I didn't go to the NBA, that I probably wouldn't have gone back to college."

On potential alone, the Sacramento Kings picked him up late in the first, which meant he rode the bench for a perennial contender. Whenever injury or other circumstances pushed him onstage, Wallace would put on a show, have Kings diehards speaking in tongues, and then disappear again into the mists. Says Kings blogger Tom Ziller, "The fans craved Gerald more than any other King, owing to some mix of his visceral explosiveness and the innocent fervor he exhibited on the floor. Any time the Kings got up by 10 in the second half, the chants would start. No matter the team's success, garbage time itself was a reason to be at the arena." In 2004, the Charlotte Bobcats nabbed Wallace in the expansion draft. The Kings let him go; on the hunt for a championship, they were looking for cohesive pieces rather than a head-scratching wild card.

Smith came up in suburban Atlanta, where he played on the same AAU team as Dwight Howard. Picked by the Hawks just outside of the 2004 lottery, Smith was derided by ESPN expert Jay Bilas as the pick "most likely to be a bust." In his first months in the league, it became apparent that Smith could conjure up highlight dunks and blocks with the best of them, even if the rest of his time on the floor was slippery and disjointed. In 2005, he lit up the Slam Dunk Contest, where his long arms, fast-twitch pounce, and sheer strength gave him a runaway victory.

By the end of the next season, both Wallace and Smith had begun putting together the kind of grotesque stat lines that screamed "misprint." On many nights, Smith looked totally incompetent and self-absorbed, and Wallace could be found listlessly floating around until someone threw him a lob. On the other hand, every few nights Wallace would end up with a 30/12 line from the small forward spot, throwing his body around with abandon and hustling way more than jump-out-the-gym specimens usually do. And Smith might mess around and start getting some assists to go with his five or six blocks—as a small forward.

It wouldn't even make sense to call them "versatile" like James, Kevin Garnett, or Lamar Odom, because those players presumably have access to all their skills, all the time. Wallace and Smith are wormholes of ability, random mutations of action that reveal themselves in sporadic fashion.

This effect was made all the more striking

NAME: Gerald Jermaine Wallace
BORN: July 23, 1982
HEIGHT: 6 ft 7 in (2.01 m)
WEIGHT: 220 lb (99.8 kg)
HOMETOWN: Childersburg, AL

SPIRIT ANIMAL: Appalachian puma

CULINARY LIFE: Wallace may be the only NBA player who ever cooks for himself. During Wallace's second year in Sacramento, his mother, who had come along to look after him, moved back home to Alabama, leaving Gerald to master the art of steak, mashed potatoes, corn, and cabbage.

NAME: Joshua Smith
BORN: December 5, 1985
HEIGHT: 6 ft 9 in (2.06 m)
WEIGHT: 235 lb (106.6 kg)
HOMETOWN: College Park, GA

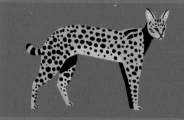

SPIRIT ANIMAL: Serval

CULINARY LIFE: Favorite meal is fried tilapia and yellow rice. Enjoys meaningful lunch meetings with Hawks coaching staff.

by the obscurity of their teams. The Hawks and Bobcats almost never graced national television and were among the league's least noticed franchises. Watching either of these teams play was like experiencing an alternate reality, an unknown land where basketball as we know it did not exist. History had not yet been written, and the old languages, rules, and conventions didn't apply. There were no reference points, and these strange, intermittent blasts of playmaking demanded to light the way—even as their syntax and rhythm registered as mildly insane.

Talented as Wallace and Smith were, you could never have built a team around them, since their production on the court so depended on that day's, week's, or month's latest development. It's fashionable to say that a Garnett or James can bring on a "positional revolution," since they allow for an organic redistribution of labor on the court. Wallace and Smith are either the lunatic fringe of this logic or the anarchists whose desire to change the existing order borders on nihilism.

Stats guru John Hollinger is enamored of Wallace, especially the Wallace of 2005–06, when he became only the third NBA player to average 2 steals and 2 blocks per game—the others being David Robinson and Hakeem Olajuwon. Smith has a shot at setting the all-time swats record; in 2007, he became the youngest man to reach the 500-block plateau. Yet this kind of hard data doesn't make Wallace and Smith any easier to comprehend. Instead, it just shows how they wreak havoc on the norms that govern the rest of the game. They're scary, deviant; they send us hiding under the table in fear of what's next.

It's worth noting that, for all their oddity,

Wallace and Smith remain professionals—and thus commodities within a market. Both present problems for any team looking to invest in them. Smith is still regarded as immature, which may make teams hesitant to anoint him their franchise player; some have suggested that he might be best deployed as a high-energy role player. Wallace has a long-term deal with the Bobcats, but he sustained a serious concussion in 2008. This was the fourth such head injury of his career, which is practically unheard of in the NBA; for a football player, this would likely spell automatic retirement. Wallace returned to the court, but he's become a walking paradox. His style is dependent on sowing the seeds of chaos, disruption, and recklessness—in principle, it prevents him from learning how to break his fall. But with another concussion now all the more likely, Wallace has become his own worst enemy.

If Wallace and Smith could harness all of their powers at once, they'd instantly be among the game's ten best. That's part of what makes them such intriguing figures for general managers, who see in them both a wide array of skills and a blank slate of functionality.

Josh Smith and Gerald Wallace are sometimes world-class virtuosos, sometimes vessels for something greater than themselves. Some eagerly await the day that they mature or find their inner equalibrium. But the real fate of these two comes down to the question of free will. Are Gerald Wallace and Josh Smith erratic, or deliberately evasive? Or have they reached new heights of creativity and flexibility? To ask the question another way: Does inspiration come from within? Or is it a free and elusive quantity that occasionally deigns to use us as its host?

Without Warning or Reason

Josh Smith and Gerald Wallace's Short-Form Explosions

S ome players excel at taking away possessions, while others specialize in giving them back. In comparison, Gerald Wallace and Josh Smith are distinguished by their unique mastery of both. More so than any other players in the league, Wallace and Smith have a remarkable propensity to either block, steal, or turn the ball over at any particular moment of a game—a kind of manic ambivalence toward the very principle of the possession.

More remarkable still is Wallace and Smith's ability to commit these three acts in rapid succession. The charts on the following two pages diagram every possible combination of these three stats up to a factor of five, making 243 different combinations of blocks, steals, and turnovers. The charts then note how many of these different combinations have been recorded by either player from the beginning of the 2004–05 season, the year Josh Smith first entered the league, through the end of the 2006–07 season.

Top Ten Chaos Collectors

Gerald Wallace and Josh Smith have recorded the most unique combinations of blocks, steals, and turnovers in the NBA. Of the 243 possible combinations diagrammed on the next page, Smith has completed 82 of them, while Wallace has completed 75, ranking them first and second in the league respectively.

Looking at the other players in the top ten brings into stark contrast just how sui generis Smith and Wallace really are. While Kirilenko, a fellow statistical schizo, is clearly a kindred soul and only slightly behind Wallace and Smith with 73 sequences completed, the other players include perennial All-Stars Wade, Howard, Webber, James, and Duncan, as well as All-Defensive Team stalwarts Marcus Camby and Ben Wallace. These are either superstars who handle the ball for long periods of time or big men renowned for their defensive prowess—both categories of player that one would expect to have a high frequency of blocks, steals, and turnovers. The fact that Smith and Wallace, neither of whom dominate the ball or are big men, can lead the league in unique block, steal, and turnover combinations is evidence of their disproportionate and somewhat terrifying ability to disrupt the game of basketball—and speaks to their almost perverse fascination with constantly inventing new and creative ways to do so.

	NUMBER OF DIFFERENT SEQUENCES COMPLETED FROM 243 POSSIBLITIES	% OF 243 COMPLETED
1. **Josh Smith**	**82/243**	**0.34**
2. **Gerald Wallace**	**75/243**	**0.31**
3. Andrei Kirilenko	73/243	0.30
4. Marcus Camby	67/243	0.28
5. Dwyane Wade	63/243	0.26
6. Dwight Howard	60/243	0.25
7. Ben Wallace	54/243	0.22
8. Chris Webber	54/243	0.22
9. LeBron James	52/243	0.21
10. Tim Duncan	53/243	0.21

HOW TO READ THIS CHART

Colored circles represent either blocks, steals, or turnovers. The number following a string of circles indicates the number of times the player has executed that particular sequence.

In 2 minutes or less, Wallace has recorded 2 turnovers and 1 steal (in that order) 6 times.

In 3 minutes or less, he has recorded 2 turnovers, 1 steal, and 1 block once.

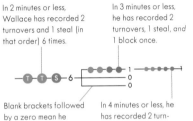

Blank brackets followed by a zero mean he has not recorded that particular combination.

In 4 minutes or less, he has recorded 2 turnovers, 1 steal, 1 block, and 1 turnover once.

Sequence Masters

Of the 243 possible combinations of blocks, steals, and turnovers listed here, Wallace and Smith rank or are tied for first in the following categories—they have executed these sequences more than any other player in the league:

GERALD WALLACE	
BLK STL STL	BLK BLK BLK TO
STL BLK STL	BLK BLK STL STL
STL BLK TO	BLK BLK TO STL
STL STL BLK	BLK BLK TO TO
STL STL TO	BLK STL BLK STL
BLK BLK TO STL	BLK STL BLK TO
BLK STL STL BLK	BLK STL TO TO
BLK TO BLK STL	BLK TO STL TO
BLK TO STL STL	BLK TO TO STL
BLK TO TO STL	STL BLK BLK TO
STL BLK STL BLK	STL BLK STL BLK
STL BLK STL STL	STL BLK STL TO
STL STL BLK TO	TO BLK BLK BLK
TO BLK STL STL	TO STL BLK BLK
TO STL BLK BLK	TO STL STL BLK
TO STL STL BLK	BLK BLK BLK BLK STL
BLK TO BLK STL TO	BLK BLK TO STL BLK
BLK TO STL STL BLK	BLK BLK TO TO STL
STL BLK STL STL BLK	BLK STL BLK STL TO
STL TO STL STL STL	BLK TO STL BLK SL
TO STL STL BLK TO	BLK TO TO STL BLK
TO STL TO TO STL	STL BLK BLK TO STL
TO TO STL BLK STL	STL BLK STL BK TO
	STL BLK STL TO TO
JOSH SMITH	TO BLK BLK BLK BLK
BLK STL BLK	TO BLK STL TO TO
STL BLK BLK	TO STL TO BLK STL
STL BLK STL	TO TO BLK STL STL
TO STL BLK	TO TO TO BLK STL

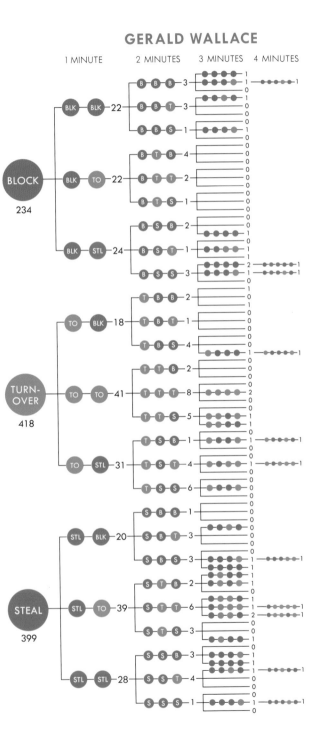

GERALD WALLACE

JOSH SMITH

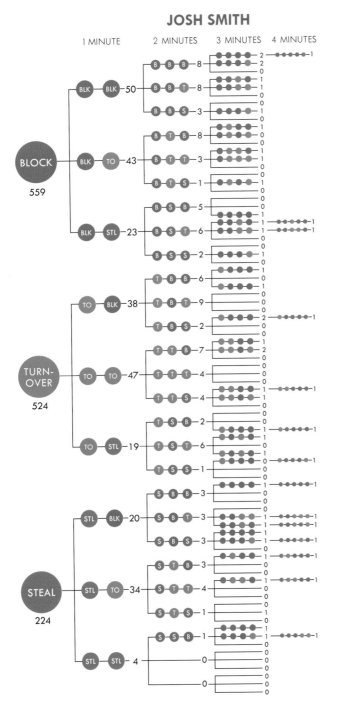

Great Moments in Wallace/Smith Block/Steal/Turnover History

January 22, 2007
Atlanta Hawks vs. Boston Celtics

During the second quarter of a game against the Boston Celtics, Josh Smith executes this literally off-the-charts (not pictured on the left) *six* stat combination in just one and a half minutes of play: Block-Steal-Turnover-Block-Block-Steal.

21:08   Al Jefferson's layup blocked by Smith
21:17   Allan Ray's pass stolen by Smith
21:22   Smith's pass stolen by Sebastian Telfair
21:53   Al Jefferson's layup blocked by Smith
21:58   Al Jefferson's layup blocked by Smith
22:35   Al Jefferson's pass stolen by Smith

January 11, 2005
Atlanta Hawks vs. Milwaukee Bucks

One of the two Block-Block-Block-Block combinations recorded in Josh Smith's career; note Smith's exceptional quickness (eighty seconds) and his incredible focus (Zaza Pachulia).

15:50   Zaza Pachulia's layup blocked by Smith
15:53   Zaza Pachulia's layup blocked by Smith
16:00   Zaza Pachulia's layup blocked by Smith
17:03   Zaza Pachulia's jumper blocked by Smith

March 20, 2007
Charlotte Bobcats vs. Cleveland Cavaliers

Gerald Wallace comes up with a phenomenal Block-Block-Block-Turnover-Block combination during the final four minutes of play against the Cavaliers—his second block on LeBron James sending the game into overtime.

43:34   Eric Snow's layup blocked by Wallace
45:45   LeBron James's layup blocked by Wallace
46:26   Eric Snow's layup blocked by Wallace
46:31   Wallace's pass stolen by Larry Hughes
47:51   LeBron James's layup blocked by Wallace

STYLE GUIDE

WALLACE: DUNK

From a dead stop, he heaves himself upward and right into the basket like it was a put-back.

STYLE: Shotput
Force and loft, blunt flight

WALLACE: STEAL

As an opponent receives the pass, Wallace sprints by and wrenches the ball out of the guy's hands.

STYLE: Harpoon
Speed and force, some accuracy

WALLACE: BLOCK

Rises majestically and then violently swipes the ball away with a wild swing.

STYLE: Cyclone
Spinning, swirling, diruptive, chaotic

SMITH: DUNK

Jumps really high, leans back really far, and throws it down really, really hard.

STYLE: Bear Trap
Coiled tension, vicious release

SMITH: STEAL

Uses great length to move in and disrupt dribbling even while backing off his man.

STYLE: Pruning Shears
Extended reach, trimming

SMITH: BLOCK

Rises straight up, seemingly too late, and smothers the ball.

STYLE: Spring Showers
Comes out of nowhere, hovering, obstructive

Hawks vs. Bobcats

As far as civilizations go, the Aztecs were one of the best. When they weren't busy drinking chocolate, ripping the still-beating hearts out of their sacrificial victims, or playing a sacred sport involving a rubber ball, a hoop, and a stone court (bearing an uncanny resemblance to modern basketball), they were busy expanding on the already sizable cultural and architectural achievements of their predecessors, the Mayans.

But perhaps most impressive of the Aztecs' many accomplishments was their complex calendar system, which by some accounts was even more accurate than our own Gregorian calendar. The Aztecs' intricate system actually consisted of several circular, interlocking calendars, which they used to simultaneously chart religious, agricultural, and astronomical events. But when these calendars happened to coincide—when multiple calendars ended on the same day—it was viewed as a possibly apocalyptic event. On these "Nameless Days," the Aztecs believed, anything could happen, as the boundaries between their world and the underworld dissolved, allowing gods and evil spirits to wreak havoc among them and potentially even destroy the earth.

The NBA too has its gods and monsters, and an equally intricate calendar system.

While the best teams in the league follow the traditional seasonal calendar, stretching from the preseason to the playoffs, those lowly teams at the bottom of the standings set their stars by an additional calendar—the holy calendar of "Rebuilding," a mystical long-term plan that promises an eventual resurrection of the NBA's worst teams. And over the last four seasons, the league's worst records have belonged to the Atlanta Hawks and Charlotte Bobcats, who together have won fewer games than any other two teams during this period.

As the following pages show, four times each season the Hawks and Bobcats' seasonal calendars coincide, and these woeful gods do battle among themselves. Untethered from history, a commitment to defense, or any sort of national media coverage, the collision of these two teams threatens to destroy all forms of basketball logic as we know it.

But more terrifying still are those games that also coincide with a "Black Day" on the Calendar of Rebuilding. On these truly cursed occasions, the Hawks' and Bobcats' high priests, Gerald Wallace and Josh Smith, threaten to unleash a statistical apocalypse from the heavens, and natural disasters wrack the globe as the very fate of the universe hangs in the balance.

November 27, 2004, at Charlotte
Bobcats (3-9)   **107**
Hawks (2-11)   92

The first historic meeting between Charlotte and Atlanta. Both teams shoot over .500 from the field, and the Hawks lose their sixth-straight game. Josh Smith makes only one field goal, and Gerald Wallace, going after a loose ball near midcourt, violently crashes into NASCAR star Jeff Gordon, who is sitting in the front row. On the same day there is a 3.1-magnitude earthquake at Mount St. Helens.

April 11, 2005, at Atlanta
Bobcats (16-61) **110** (OT)
Hawks (12-65)   105

The Bobcats snap an eight-game losing streak and beat the Hawks in overtime in a matchup of Southeast Division rivals with the two worst records in the league. Uncontested jump shots and breakaway dunks are common as the two teams—each allowing more than 100 points per game—display a similar disinterest in defense. In the postgame media session, Charlotte coach Bernie Bickerstaff says the Bobcats and Hawks are "kindred spirits." That afternoon, the World Health Organization announces 206 people have died in Angola from the Marburg virus.

March 28, 2006, at Charlotte
Bobcats (20-52) **125**
Hawks (21-48)   117

In a truly epic game, both teams shoot at least .520 from the floor and score an average of at least 30 points each quarter. Wallace has 41 points, 8 rebounds, 4 assists, 3 steals, and 2 blocks for the victorious Bobcats. Smith has 20 points, 14 rebounds, 8 assists, 2 steals, and 5 blocks for the defeated Hawks. "It's ridiculous. Our commitment to defense is awful," Atlanta coach Mike Woodson says. "We're not even trying to defend." Bobcats coach Bernie Bickerstaff concurs, saying, "Neither team seemed to have any kinship to defense." Later that night, a rare solar eclipse plunges the opposite side of the globe into total darkness.

Nov. 27, 2004
Bobcats 107
Hawks 92

Jan. 15, 2005
Hawks 103
Bobcats 95

Apr. 11, 2005
Bobcats 110 (OT)
Hawks 105

Apr. 13, 2005
Bobcats 105
Hawks 84

Dec. 27, 2005
Bobcats 93
Hawks 90

Feb. 1, 2006
Hawks 92
Bobcats

Mar. 28, 2006
Bobcats 125
Hawks 117

Apr. 14, 2006
Bobcats 116
Hawks 110

Start of Calendar — Hawks vs. Bobcats Game Calendar (outer ring)

Seasonal Dividers —

"Dark Days" — Calendar of Rebuilding (inner ring)

Mar. 7, 2008
Bobcats 108
Hawks 93

Feb. 13, 2008,
Bobcats 100 (OT)
Hawks 98

Dec. 15, 2007
Hawks 93
Bobcats 84

Nov. 14, 2007
Hawks 117
Bobcats 109

Mar. 28 2007
Bobcats 101
Hawks 87

Jan. 20, 2007
Bobcats 105
Hawks 85

Jan. 19, 2007
Bobcats 96
Hawks 75

Nov. 29, 2006
Hawks 99
Bobcats 90

December 15, 2007, at Atlanta
Hawks (11-12) **93**
Bobcats (8-14) 84

By winning, the Hawks guarantee they won't lose a season series to the Bobcats for the first time in the illustrious rivalry. Smith has 19 points, 10 rebounds, 6 assists, 3 steals, and 2 blocks. Wallace has 24 points, 7 rebounds, and 2 assists. Just hours before the game, Hawks backup forward Shelden Williams is carjacked at gunpoint; brutal snowstorms continue to blanket North America, paralyzing transportation and leading to 25 storm-related deaths that day alone.

March 28, 2007, at Charlotte
Bobcats (27-45) **101**
Hawks (27-46) 87

With this game at the end of the season, the two teams once again do battle for the distinction of "least worst team in the NBA." Wallace has 31 points, 9 rebounds, 3 assists, 4 steals, and 4 blocks. Smith has 25 points, 15 rebounds, 4 assists, and 6 blocks. Cyclone Becky continues to tear through the South Pacific.

November 29, 2006, at Atlanta
Hawks (6-7) **99**
Bobcats (4-11) 90

The Bobcats miss their first 13 field goal attempts, the longest initial scoring drought by any team that season. Before this game, the Bobcats and Hawks shared that unfortunate distinction, having both started games 0–9. Wallace is 0–3 from the floor, gets one rebound, and—uncharacteristically—fails to record a single block, steal, or turnover. Smith has 10 points, 13 rebounds, 5 assists, 4 blocks, and 3 turnovers. Tropical Storm Epsilon forms east of Bermuda, and a 6.1-magnitude earthquake rocks Indonesia.

LEANDRO BARBOSA
Fast, Nice, and Good at Basketball

The Suns brought fast back to the NBA. In 2004, the league had ground to an agonizing slog; since Michael Jordan's 1998 exit (the one that mattered), all but one of the titles had gone to teams led by imperious big men: Shaquille O'Neal, Hakeem Olajuwon, Tim Duncan. The one exception was the Detroit Pistons of 2003–04, hard-hatted grunts who made you long for Goliath's grandeur.

The breakthrough in Phoenix is usually attributed to free-thinking coach Mike D'Antoni or two-time MVP Steve Nash, the team's on-floor architect. But before D'Antoni was named interim coach or Nash signed with the Suns as a free agent, the seeds of change had been sown. The previous summer, the team had traded for the rights to Brazilian guard Leandro Barbosa. And so, before the revolution reached even its infancy, it found its mascot.

Barbosa entered the NBA draft in 2003. He was a source of intrigue for many teams: very young, very raw, a basketball griffin with the arms of a center and the speed of a laser. At one point, ESPN's Chad Ford projected him as a lottery pick, suggesting he might one day amount to a Brazilian Gary Payton.

Barbosa was a basketball prodigy in a country synonymous with soccer. He had been taught the game in São Paulo by his brother Arturo, a paratrooper and Micheal Ray Richardson fan who had once played against David Robinson. Arturo drilled the young Leandro for hours, at times employing a menacing stick for motivation. As Barbosa recounted through an interpreter during his rookie season: "He would have me hold out my hands and he would hold the stick . . . It was for agility. He'd move the stick, and if the hands didn't move, that stick would hit really hard . . . Sometimes, I almost couldn't play in organized games because my hands were so sore."

Barbosa spoke no English when he reached the NBA, and it was hampering his development. When D'Antoni took the reins, he brought on his older brother Dan—who just happened to speak Portuguese—to take a special interest in Barbosa. It was only fitting that, with this new blissful brand of basketball, Barbosa would become a priority. He was full of the infectious energy that had become the Suns' calling card. His speed

seemed inseparable from his angelic aspect, just as the Suns' exhilarating play stemmed not from arrogance but from a sheer sense of fun. Watching Barbosa bound down the court or languidly maneuver his jumble of limbs near the basket, you understand the thin, thin line between hotshot showboating and life-affirming creativity. Without Barbosa, it is impossible to say if the Suns would have ended up on the right side of that line or found the inspiration to be much more than just another high-scoring offense.

As the Suns became less of a novelty and more of an institution, it was Barbosa—now known by a single name, "Leandrinho," his nation's true mark of celebrity—who never failed to enchant and amaze. In 2005–06, Barbosa's minutes increased and he was

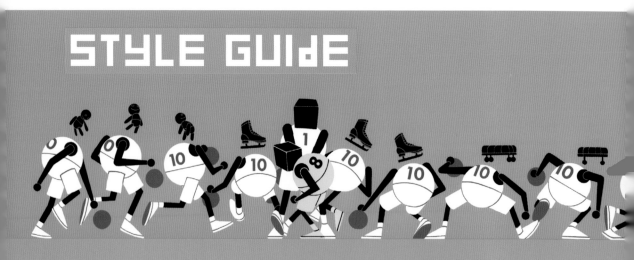

STYLE GUIDE

1 Barbosa idly dribbles the ball up the court.

 STYLE: **Rag Doll**
Gangly, loose-limbed, innocent

2 As a teammate sets a screen, he glides around the first defender.

 STYLE: **Ice Skate**
Quick changes of direction, smooth turns

3 Coming off the screen he swivels and lowers his body.

 STYLE: **Wheeled Ottoman**
Wide feet, low center of gravity, easy rotation

reliably the first player off the bench. The next season, he won the NBA's Sixth Man of the Year award.

When Shaquille O'Neal arrived in Phoenix, there was no shortage of press on the big man's joie de vivre and locker room presence. The irony was that, in Barbosa, they already had a player who could spread love throughout the land without contradicting it with his play. No one will ever giggle with delight as Shaq backs down his man, no matter how many jokes he has. That's work, plain and simple. Barbosa, on the other hand, marked the perfect synergy of one man's style and an entire club's attitude. Fast, nice, and good at basketball, he is the embodiment of an idea whose time may have passed, even as the legacy of Leandro Barbosa continues to unfold.

NAME: Leandro Mateus Barbosa
BORN: November 28, 1982
HEIGHT: 6 ft 3 in (1.91 m)
WEIGHT: 188 lb (85 kg)
HOMETOWN: São Paulo, Brazil

SPIRIT ANIMAL: Barbosa *is* the Phoenix Suns' spirit animal.

4 Accelerates forward, with his body low to the ground.

 STYLE: **Bullet**
Aerodynamic projectile

5 Beats second defender and with one giant stride moves upward.

 STYLE: **Takeoff**
Seamless transition from land to air

6 Uses long arms to evade a third defender and lay the ball in.

 STYLE: **Slinky**
Contracts and expands, springy

How Do You Say "Seven Seconds or Less" in Portuguese?

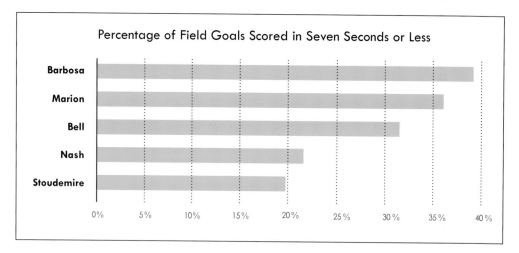

Percentage of Field Goals Scored in Seven Seconds or Less

The key to the Suns' renaissance was Coach D'Antoni's "seven seconds or less" credo. This team thrived on speed, surprise, and ingenuity, dominating by rarefied means of production. The shot clock was the enemy; the longer Phoenix took to get off their shots, the more defenses could settle in and bludgeon them into indignity. "Seven" was the mantra, shorthand for everything the team stood for. This was the first principle from which all of D'Antoni's other designs followed.

Not every play lives up to the principle. Some baskets take eight seconds, some nine seconds, some even ten or longer. But to the extent that the Suns fulfill their own edict, it is Barbosa, their sixth man, who matters most. Steve Nash may lead the break, and Shawn Marion may be lightning with the putback, but it's Leandrinho who sinks the greatest share of his own baskets (almost 40 percent) before the shot clock strikes 16. Others may score more frequently, but none with such consistent speed. It is Barbosa above all others who makes the Suns the Suns.

A Man and His Speed

Number of baskets Barbosa has scored in 7 seconds or less in his career:	**383**
Number of baskets Barbosa has scored in 3 seconds or less in his career:	**96**
Number of baskets Barbosa has scored in 1 second or less in his career:	**9**
Total number of points scored by Barbosa in 3 seconds or less during the 2006–07 season:	**90**
Total number of points scored by the Houston Rockets in 3 seconds or less during the 2006–07 season:	**97**
Most points scored by Barbosa in 7 seconds or less in a single game (March 31, 2006, vs. Toronto):	**18**

Stats compiled from November 2003 through April 2007

If Barbosa Ruled the World

Just how fast is Leandro Barbosa? The typical NBA player uses 13.3 seconds to put up a successful shot; on possessions where Barbosa scores, the Suns use an average of only 10.7. This 2.6-second difference may not seem like much on paper, but to a careful student of fastness, it's an unprecedented margin. Indeed, were Barbosa any less unique a quantity—had the world known many Barbosas, instead of just one—just imagine how history could have been rewritten.

3 Number of years it took Ferdinand Magellan and his crew to circumnavigate the globe.

2.4 Number of years it would have taken a crew of Barbosas to circumnavigate it.

20 Number of years it took 50,000 Egyptian slaves to build the Great Pyramid at Giza.

16.8 Number of years it would have taken 50,000 Barbosas to build it.

116 Number of years it took the French army to defeat the British in the Hundred Years' War.

93.3 Number of years it would have taken an army of Barbosas to defeat them.

EURO
FOR BEGINNERS

Well before Austrian hackles were raised over Turkey's prospective entry into the EU and the very idea of what it meant to be European crept east of the Mediterranean, our fair Association employed a definition of "Euro" so broad, so inclusive, as to make it both meaningless and profound.

As no less an arbiter of geopolitical subtleties than Donyell Marshall himself once noted (when his new Mongolian teammate, Mengke Bateer, demanded Marshall pay him to exchange jerseys so Marshall could have his favored number 42), "Boy, those Europeans sure know how to negotiate."

In short, if a player is white and foreign, he is a Euro. If a player is European, he is a Euro. If a player is seven feet tall and has a name that the average American finds difficult to spell, he is occasionally a Euro. As of yet, no African player has been described as a Euro.

Distribution of Foreign NBA Players
All seasons through 2006–07

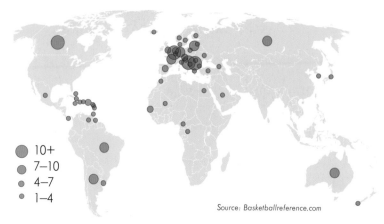

- 10+
- 7–10
- 4–7
- 1–4

Source: Basketballreference.com

FRANCE

Population:
60,656,178

Example:
Boris Diaw

Style of play: Elegant, skittish, and somewhat annoyed.

Notable anecdote: Passing on Queens-bred star Ron Artest in the 1999 NBA draft, the Knicks instead selected 7'3" French center Frederic Weis, who never made it to the NBA and is best known for being literally jumped over by Vince Carter in the 2000 Summer Olympics.

Additional notes: Most French NBA players were actually born in the French Caribbean islands.

Do they have black people? A better question is, do they have white people? All French NBA players (with the exception of the aforementioned Frederic Weis) are black.

ARGENTINA

Population:
39,537,943

Example:
Andres Nocioni

Style of play: Scrappy, fearless, reckless, and prone to flopping.

Notable anecdote: Of the play of Argentinean icon Manu Ginobili, Denver Nuggets head coach George Karl said, "I'm going to put it on tape and show my son how to play basketball . . . just put your head down and run into people, I guess that's a new brand of basketball."

Additional notes: All Argentinean NBA players are actually of Italian heritage.

Do they have black people? No, you must be thinking of Brazil.

EURO

SORT OF EURO

NOT REALLY EURO

NOT EURO

GERMANY

Population:
82,431,390

Example:
Dirk Nowitzki

Style of play: Dirk.

Notable anecdote: Shortly after a playoff loss to the Spurs in 2003, Dirk and then-teammate Steve Nash got hammered at a nearby pub, an event documented with photos that ended up plastered across all corners of the Internet.

Additional notes: Dirk was trained by an eccentric guru whose methods included saxophone lessons, acrobatics, and long walks in the Black Forest. All of which pretty much makes him the poster boy for postwar Germany.

Do they have black people? Yes, but only that guy in all the Fassbinder movies.

SERBIA & MONTENEGRO

Population:
10,829,175

Example: Vlade Divac

Style of play: Tough and rugged, yet with a high level of finesse.

Notable anecdote: While playing for the Kings, Divac and Peja Stojakovic were able to improvise at such a high level—using what Divac calls "Serbian telepathy"—that he began calling Peja "Special Boy."

Additional notes: Serbia & Montenegro has produced the most NBA players of any European nation to date.

Do they have black people? Despite the misleading name, there are no black people in Serbia & Montenegro.

BOSNIA & HERZEGOVINA

Population:
4,025,476

Example:
Nedzad Sinanovic

Style of play: Dedicated, soldier-like discipline and work ethic.

Notable anecdote: During a Blazers practice, the 7'4" Sinanovic once got into a fistfight with 7'3" Korean teammate Ha Seung-Jin, who left shouting, "I'll sue! I'll sue!" Seung-Jin later came back with a wooden pole and began swinging it at Sinanovic before he was restrained by coaches.

Do they have black people? No, but they have Muslims.

LITHUANIA

Population:
3,596,617

Example:
Arvydas Sabonis

Style of play: Do all the little things with surprising grace and feeling—and an iron will to win.

Notable anecdote: Zydrunas Ilgauskas was once spotted trolling the Cleveland suburbs in a stretch Excursion. He stopped to watch a child hit a piñata and then made his way to his friends' nearby house, where he proceeded to keep the neighbors up by drunkenly reveling in *Appetite for Destruction* and *Licensed to Ill*.

Do they have black people? No, but they name a lot of their male children "Darius," which has already caused a great deal of confusion around the league.

RUSSIA

Population:
143,420,309

Example:
Viktor Khryapa

Style of play: Demonstrate far more heart than other Eastern Euros, making their relative absence in the NBA surprising.

Notable anecdote: Russia's most notable NBA player, Andrei Kirilenko, has fourteen different nicknames, including "Electronic," a reference to the Russian kids' film *Adventures of the Electronic*, in which there appears a robot double of the boy Sergei Syroezhkin.

Do they have black people? Viktor Keirou, the "Black Russian," is an up-and-coming NBA prospect of half-Russian, half–South African heritage.

GEORGIA

Population:
4,677,401

Example:
Nikoloz
Tskitishvili

Style of play: A wussier, slightly disinterested version of the Lithuanian style.

Notable anecdote: Skita and his then Warriors teammates Andris Biedrins (Latvia) and Zarko Cabarkapa (Serbia) once pulled up to an NYC club in a horse-drawn carriage.

Additional notes: When asked on draft night about his rumored "ballet training," Skita defiantly replied that it was actually a form of Georgian national dance.

Do they have black people? No. For the millionth time, it's not that Georgia.

Chapter III

Lost
Souls

Outsiders Wandering the Periphery of Greatness

Beautiful and outlandish, the Uncanny Peacocks may be discovered years from now or may be forgotten like they never happened. Then there are the players who, while no less mysterious, are consigned to a much less glamorous form of limbo. The Lost Souls stalk the parameters of NBA purgatory, where men become ghosts and ghosts ply their moon-songs down a lonely road toward history. They defy labels, answers, even our attempts at empathy. The Lost Souls are beyond truth and falsehood—they occupy, some might say, a moral universe unto themselves.

The question is not whether hope remains for these Lost Souls to be found and redeemed, both by themselves and by the wider world of sport. Rather, it is how they may be seen. Their careers stake out a territory that is all too often dismissed as either useless or confounding. But in these Lost Souls, we see not only fascinating studies in human perplexity but also proof that, even in a life of wandering and unease, there is the unmistakable glimmer of might.

LAMAR ODOM

Like Job, with No Psalms to Follow

Literary scholars of varying races, creeds, and sexual orientations have determined that Langston Hughes's poetic invocation of the "dream deferred" is actually an exact prediction of Lamar Odom's career trajectory. Odom's is a tale of begrudgingly strengthened shoulders. He has carried a lifetime full of lifetimes on his back, not because he chose to, but because he was chosen to. He does not question his path, does not even recognize it as potholed and slippery. He simply remains dutiful and patient. Odom represents every one of us: flawed and good. His life has been a series of near-misses, malignant lumps, breaths of mountain air followed by spoonfuls of dirt. He endures all that is possible for man to endure and faces every test so that others may thrive and live a less complicated life. It would be fitting to call the drama that Odom enacts a tragedy, but his story is far too real for theater. Odom is not Achebe's Okonkwo, nor is he the Hughes brothers' Anthony Curtis. He is simply an exemplar of the human condition, sad as it apparently is. Blameless and upright he travels the earth.

It is fitting that Odom claims as his two best friends in the league the angelic Elton Brand and the diabolical Ron Artest. With these two figures perched on his shoulders, Odom exemplifies the ambiguity of well-taught Sunday school principles. Full of travail and tragedy, Odom's life appears prototypical of "the athlete's story," yet it is ongoing and infi-

WHAT HE GIVES US:
The history of the world encapsulated in a flightless aircraft.

WHAT HE STANDS FOR:
The pain and perseverance of every living creature.

WHY WE CARE:
Because he thanklessly and tirelessly has done so much for us.

nite, and therefore lacks the narrative trajectory essential to a Chris Connelly–narrated, piano-trickled ESPN profile.

Odom grew up fatherless, lost his mother when he was twelve, and as an adult lost his six-month-old son Jayden to sudden infant death syndrome. As a high school standout, he would prefigure his nomadic pro career by playing for three teams in four years. At UNLV, where he played college ball, the university punished him for taking $5,600 from a booster. In the wake of the scandal, the school also fired his coach, Bill Bayno, and the NCAA put UNLV on probation for four years. Odom soon transferred to Rhode Island, where he spent only one year before being whooshed away by the winds of fortune.

He was drafted fourth overall by the Los Angeles Clippers and in his second season there received a suspension for twice violating the league's drug policy. He broke down in tears upon admitting to this offense. For the standard athlete, the emission of tears is generally reserved for situations involving the death of a loved one or a national disaster such as a hurricane; for Odom, they indicated that he had been storing for too long all of the world's pain in the pit of his gut. The man simply wanted to play in the NBA.

After receiving his suspension, Odom seemed to undergo a realization: a few thousand under-the-table collegiate bucks and the buzz from some cannabis were impermanent luxuries; basketball, on the other hand, could provide immortality. He came back renewed, but destiny has ever since remained just out of his lanky arm's reach.

In 2003, Odom finally found a home with the Miami Heat, where he joined in a triumvi-rate with the fledgling Dwyane Wade and the gutsy Caron Butler. The trio was disbanded after one promising season. Wade remained with the Heat, becoming a postseason legend while playing alongside the league's Jupiter, Shaquille O'Neal. Butler caromed to Washington and reached All-Star status alongside his Wizards teammates. Odom, on the other hand, became an icon of silence and duty on his new team, the Los Angeles Lakers.

The Lakers brought Odom west to complement their star, Kobe Bryant. But in place of blue skies and mountain peaks, the Lakers constructed for Odom an asbestos-coated ceiling. Instead of freedom and trust, they gave him guidelines and boundaries. Odom was stringently relegated to second option on the Lakers, which on a Kobe-helmed team meant being sent to the dungeon. Odom went from being hailed as the do-it-all prototype player for the New NBA to the league's forgotten man. Even as he labored to carry the team through Kobe's various injuries, the Jack Nicholsons and Dyan Cannons of Staples Center never embraced him, never even acknowledged him. When Pau Gasol joined the team to much acclaim, Odom flourished— and yet his contributions were ignored more roundly than ever.

This stifling of Odom as a public figure and as a player has shaped his game in novel and fantastical ways, but also in ways that can permanently alter a man's posture. Odom leads armies across continents, yet to the common observer of the game, he is merely a lonely serf. Only the attentive enthusiast could see that so many of his teammates succeed because Odom refuses to outdo them.

A similar fate confronted Odom on 2004's

doomed United States Olympic team. This disappointing assembly of men met with international derision as they bumbled their way to a bronze-medal finish. While coach Larry Brown clashed with players and Carmelo Anthony complained about lack of court time, while the team missed three-pointers and failed to defend the painted area, Lamar Odom displayed a wild amalgam of skills and flaws drawn from a dozen players, from Iverson to Duncan to Marbury. Like a blending of all the colors of the spectrum, this transformation only served once again to render Odom invisible.

Odom's style of play encapsulates all positions: the post game of a center, the rebounding tenacity of a power forward, the defensive versatility of a small forward, the long-range shooting of an off-guard, and the passing game of a point guard. He waddles the painted area and basks behind the three-point arc. In a single possession, he might laser a perfect chest pass, lasso a rebound, and punch the ball through the hoop with jackhammer force. On defense, with arms that extend from the Indian Ocean to the Pacific and can plumb the Mariana Trench, Odom guards both giants and dwarfs until they implode with frustration. He moves with the lightness of a willow when he dashes after a guard and bodies forwards up like a human sandbag.

Just as Odom possesses Everyman's skill, he also embodies Everyman's emotion: persistence in overcoming injury, penitence in admitting wrongdoing, acceptance in continuously joining new teams, deference in playing alongside those deemed greater than he. Such emotions are expressed by a face

NAME: Lamar Joseph Odom
BORN: November 6, 1979
HEIGHT: 6 ft 10 in (2.08 m)
WEIGHT: 230 lb (105 kg)
HOMETOWN: South Jamaica, Queens

SPIRIT ANIMAL: Mantid-fly

PLAYER COMPARISON: Smoked-out, maxed-out, inner-peaced-out Magic in the 1980 finals, or an even more depressing KG.

NOTABLE REMARK: "I lead my team in rebounding and assists from a point forward position, and sometimes that might not be good enough for people. If I had averaged twenty points, once you get to that twenty mark, people would think I'm good. If I would average twenty-four points and three rebounds, people would say I had a good year but I wouldn't be helping the team."

INNER VOICE: Despite—or perhaps as a release from—all of his hardships, Lamar Joseph Odom loves to sing.

CAMEOS: Odom appears in both Jadakiss's "Knock Yourself Out" video and National Lampoon's *Van Wilder*. Like both of these works of art, Odom is highly underrated.

that is at once innocent and assured of its knowledge. In both agony and victory, Odom squints, and even the most perceptive among us never knows quite why.

This miscellany of talent and sentiment has produced the NBA's most fatherless, motherless, sonless, friendless, teammateless, directionless, homeless being. He exists as a sideshow, a role player, a conundrum, an "almost," a tempting flash of brilliance, a martyr, and a fall guy so that other players can make All-Star Teams and receive MVP awards. A being of this epic un-belonging appears biblical. Yet while so many players try to perform the role of Christ, feigning death for the sins of others, Odom is better seen as some perpetual Job figure, facing hardships in the name of a divine power. The day the Lakers' 2007 season opened, Odom (beginning the season inactive because of a surgically repaired shoulder) suffered a concussion in a two-car accident that he apparently caused and that left another driver seriously injured. For most athletes, this would have constituted an eye-opening near-death experience; for Odom, it was his daily dose of destiny. Odom has become this character not because he has learned to be, but because he must be, and this responsibility endured bares itself in each wincing smile.

HEART ON HIS SLEEVE

Though many NBA players are known for their expressive ensembles, few can match Lamar Odom, for whom every sartorial choice alludes to a life fraught with loss and grief.

After his mother died Odom was raised by his grandmother. He wears the number 7, his grandmother's favorite number, in her honor.

After his infant son Jayden died on the anniversary of his grandmother's death, Odom inscribed both their names on his sneakers.

After nearly losing his life in a robbery, Odom started his own clothing line, Son of Man, which featured Jesus Christ in all his defiant afro-realness.

After a disappointing 2006–07 season, Odom shaved several stars into the back of his head to help motivate him to become an All-Star in 2007–08.

(He didn't.)

A Basketball House Divided

Much like his spirit animal the mantid-fly, Odom's nature is cumbersomely—or perhaps casually—schizophrenic. The standard guard or big man specializes in the stats proper to his role and size, with occasional blips to the contrary. Odom, on the other hand, churns out a well-rounded diet of basketball acts.

SMALL-MAN STATS
- 3-Point Field Goals
- Assists
- Drives & Jumpers
- Post Points & Tip-Ins
- Offensive Rebounds
- Blocks

BIG-MAN STATS

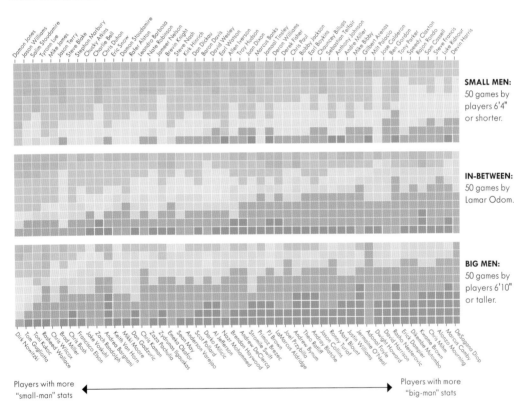

SMALL MEN: 50 games by players 6'4" or shorter.

IN-BETWEEN: 50 games by Lamar Odom.

BIG MEN: 50 games by players 6'10" or taller.

Players with more "small-man" stats ← → Players with more "big-man" stats

We began with a random sample of 50 games from Odom's 2003–2007 seasons, color-coding his first 10 plays according to the various big- or small-man stats. The stats associated with larger plays are represented by various hues of green, while the small man's doings shine forth in orange. This same procedure was then applied to a random sample of various players' big- and small-man games. The resulting arrays reveal the startling range of Odom's performances: diminutive in some games, gigantic in others, with the majority in between styles, committed equally to both. Compare this to the traditional small forward, who ekes out a living in a no-man's-land between these two spheres with drives, jumpers, and a smattering of boards. Like a rainbow, Odom's departure from positional convention is so bold it's unsettling. He is indeed the mantid-fly, a living, breathing study in disjunctive beauty.

Facial Action Coding

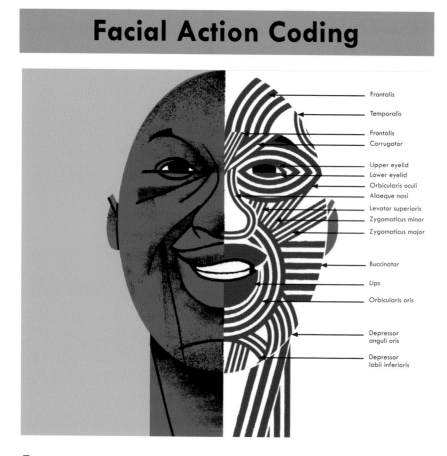

Frontalis

Temporalis

Frontalis
Corrugator

Upper eyelid
Lower eyelid
Orbicularis oculi
Alaeque nasi

Levator superioris
Zygomaticus minor
Zygomaticus major

Buccinator

Lips

Orbicularis oris

Depressor
anguli oris

Depressor
labii inferioris

I t has been said that there exists no English-language equivalent to terms such as the German *schadenfreude* or the Sanskrit *mudita*. This statement implies that not all emotional states are easily translatable. For Lamar Odom, emotional states supersede linguistic representation altogether and are comprehensible only through a careful analysis of his facial expressions. Here we have employed a well-validated psychological technique to classify Odom's affective states. Different action units are identified through detecting specific patterns of facial-muscle activity. These action units are then analyzed accordingly to taxonomize Odom's specific expression. Part of the responsibility of being Everyman is to convey the joy, suffering, and neutrality of all people. For that, we thank him.

Emotional expression analysis adapted from the Facial Action Coding System (Ekman & Friesen, 1978).

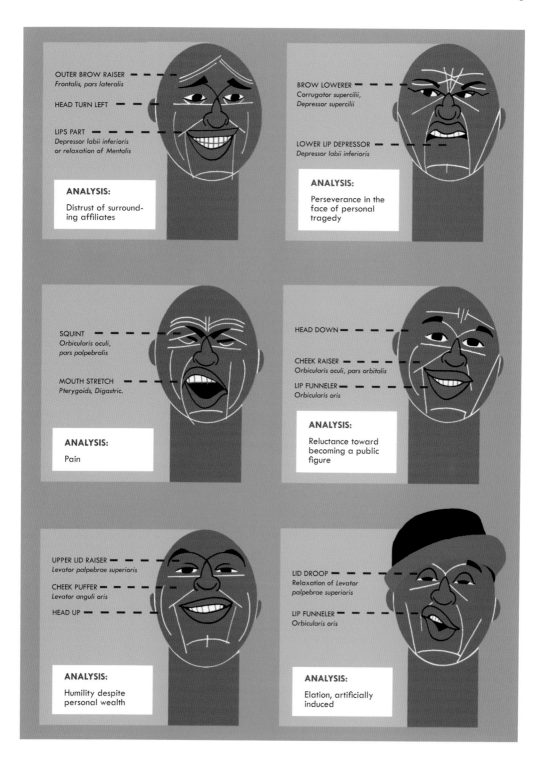

OUTER BROW RAISER
Frontalis, pars lateralis

HEAD TURN LEFT

LIPS PART
*Depressor labii inferioris
or relaxation of Mentalis*

ANALYSIS:
Distrust of surround-
ing affiliates

BROW LOWERER
*Corrugator supercilii,
Depressor supercilii*

LOWER LIP DEPRESSOR
Depressor labii inferioris

ANALYSIS:
Perseverance in the
face of personal
tragedy

SQUINT
*Orbicularis oculi,
pars palpebralis*

MOUTH STRETCH
Pterygoids, Digastric.

ANALYSIS:
Pain

HEAD DOWN

CHEEK RAISER
Orbicularis oculi, pars orbitalis

LIP FUNNELER
Orbicularis oris

ANALYSIS:
Reluctance toward
becoming a public
figure

UPPER LID RAISER
Levator palpebrae superioris

CHEEK PUFFER
Levator anguli oris

HEAD UP

ANALYSIS:
Humility despite
personal wealth

LID DROOP
*Relaxation of Levator
palpebrae superioris*

LIP FUNNELER
Orbicularis oris

ANALYSIS:
Elation, artificially
induced

STYLE

GUIDE

1

Seeing he has a bigger defender on him, Odom takes off toward the basket.

STYLE: **Racehorse**

Speed, gallops from the starting gate

2

Ducks his body and quickly turns the corner, beating the first defender.

STYLE: **Mercury**

Orbits larger bodies quickly

3

As a second defender picks him up, he takes off for an easy dunk.

STYLE: **Rising Sun**

Beginnings, optimism, ascension

4

Realizes he's too far under the basket and isn't going to be able to dunk.

STYLE: **Headless Chicken**

Herky-jerky, terrified

5

Manages to rotate and reposition himself in midair for a new shot.

STYLE: **Snowflake**

Singular in design, melts on impact

6

Heaves up an awkward left-handed floater.

STYLE: **Cross**

Blind faith, occasional miracle

7

Touches down and watches the ball rattle in.

STYLE: **Parachute**

Emergency landing, relief

TRACY McGRADY
Effortless Agony

The career of Tracy McGrady will be forever tinged with disappointment. T-Mac is a seven-time All-Star, two-time scoring champ, and one of the game's most sublime offensive forces. Yet many maintain that he's fallen short of his initial promise. And while McGrady has frequently played on winning teams, his playoff track record is a study in Sisyphean despair. In seven tries, McGrady has yet to advance past the first round.

But these isolated disappointments obscure a larger theme of loss, even doom, that's pervaded his life and added depth to his on-court shortfalls. He exudes wisdom and experience, a survivor where there are supposed to be merely winners and losers.

Somehow, the high-flying, tensile McGrady never seems wholly invested in the catharsis of raw action. He's been called lazy, in part because of his vaguely preternatural walleye, baritone Florida drawl, and loose-limbed gait, and even at his most ferocious gives the impression of semislumber. But there's too much pop in that first step, in those dunks, in the way his threes rip through the net. He moves like one of those single-stroke Japanese sketches: raising up and releasing his shot in a single languorous motion or using his length to hasten his progress to the basket. When he leaped over 7'6" Dallas center Shawn Bradley in the 2005 playoffs, it was straight-up *Planet Earth*: a soft-focus osprey snapping necks in midair.

Sonny Vaccaro, the behind-the-scenes operator who invented modern high school hoops, was once asked who his favorite

WHAT HE GIVES US:
A superstar who can't catch a break.

WHAT HE STANDS FOR:
Basketball's most sympathetic and profound letdown.

WHY WE CARE:
He plays with feeling, even those feelings whose existence sports denies.

athlete was. His answer: "I don't want to go there because there's so many kids, but I'll tell you the one who I think is the most naturally gifted is Tracy McGrady. Tracy doesn't work as hard—and you should put this in your story—as some of the others. Tracy was given more ability than anybody. He didn't always use it." That's a harsh assessment, but certainly the oft-injured T-Mac never fulfilled his vast potential. The curious mix of fate and thwarted will makes him both agonizing and frustrating to fans.

McGrady began his career with the Raptors, where he teamed with distant cousin Vince Carter. In 2000, McGrady forced a trade to Orlando, where he promptly evolved into a freewheeling, buckets-gettin' virtuoso and the league's Most Improved Player. His Magic may have inhabited a piss-poor Eastern Conference, but they faced a dangerous enemy: their own perilously thin roster. In 2004, against eventual champs Detroit, Orlando took the first three games, and all of a sudden hope stirred. McGrady went ahead and remarked how divine it was to "finally be in the second round" of the playoffs. Then the Pistons promptly came lurching back and took the series, and McGrady got called a choker and a braggart. Anyone paying close attention knew he was just a little too eager for release.

He was traded to the Rockets in 2004, paired with franchise center Yao Ming in a surefire bid for contention. Yet the playoff woes continued, with T-Mac playing the role of hero until the deciding loss, when his coat turned goatish. Following a particularly hard-fought (and -lost) 2007 series with Utah, McGrady walked away from a postgame press conference with tears on his face. So is all this his fault? Certainly, he's gotten close enough often enough that it makes sense to question his resolve. T-Mac clearly understands this; before the Utah series he stated defiantly, "If we don't win this series, it's on me." And in the end, it was on him: The Rockets lost that Game 7 because McGrady didn't call forth his full game-changing fury.

This should have been the nadir of McGrady's career, or at least the point at which he lapsed into irrelevance. But the earnestness of the moment, a fusion of bravura and raw honesty, made it into a summation of T-Mac's contribution to the game. Tracy McGrady cares that much about basketball, and invests so much in this kind of loss, because he simply can't keep the full range of his emotions from flooding his athletic identity. He has no choice; they're far too prevalent in his life, too foundational, for him to imagine caring without them.

Many professional athletes come from bad neighborhoods and have friends dead or locked up. Even by this standard, Tracy McGrady's had to deal with a lot. In McGrady's first seven seasons in the league, seven of his relatives or close friends passed away. He started 2005, his second year in Houston, a shell of his usual self. During All-Star Weekend, McGrady revealed that he'd been wrestling some undisclosed personal issues; it eventually came out that he'd lost another string of loved ones. It had taken a toll on his game, affected his will even to walk out on the court each night. McGrady, the NBA's very own Psychological Man, publicly admitted he'd seen a therapist to deal with his pain.

When Michael Jordan's father was murdered in 1998, His Airness retired, tried out a career in baseball, and then returned to win another title. Instead of celebrating, he collapsed, weeping, on the locker room floor and dedicated this Bulls ring to his late dad. Kobe Bryant spent much of the 2003–04 season under the cloud of a rape trial; sometimes arriving minutes before tip-off, he responded with some of the most focused play of his career. These tales are consistent with the usual relationship between sport and life: Competition provides a sanctuary and at best a kind of salvation. We want our heroes to overcome, to subject their personal ordeals to the tidy narratives of sport. Tracy McGrady reminds us that sometimes, it's not that easy. Not only can life refuse to imitate sport—sport can also, in certain wrenching cases, be every bit as rough, uneven, and confusing as the lives we hope to leave behind with it.

After the dismal 2007 playoff exit, coach Jeff Van Gundy left, replaced by Rick Adelman and his quick-hitting system of cuts and passes. At first, the team was slow to absorb his lessons, but around the New Year everything clicked. The Rockets launched into a winning streak of historic proportions, one that continued even after Yao went down. That was when T-Mac stepped in, suddenly playing some of the best basketball of his career.

For anyone who had sensed the pathos in McGrady's game, this was an almost overwhelming experience. This wasn't just winning on a grand scale, a refutation of the critics, and a form of professional redemption. This was pure, unadulterated joy of an almost existential variety. With McGrady, the lows had come to feel especially low and cavernous. Now, when he hit a sustained high note, it was the beaming opposite of mourning.

NAME: Tracy Lamar McGrady Jr.
BORN: May 24, 1979
HEIGHT: 6 ft 8 in (2.03 m)
WEIGHT: 223 lb (101 kg)
HOMETOWN: Auburndale, FL

SPIRIT ANIMAL: Monitor lizard

PLAYER COMPARISON: Scottie Pippen on a rampage; alternatively, Scottie Pippen in the rain.

NOTABLE REMARK: "I'm still not out of it. Regardless of how we played, I've got a lot going inside my head."

HOPES & DREAMS: McGrady was also serious about baseball as a youth and has suggested he'll try MLB pitching when his hoops days run out.

DISTINGUISHING MARKS: A wobbly right eye subject to many interpretations.

CREATION MYTH: McGrady only started playing basketball after seeing what Magic star Penny Hardaway could do with the game.

HOBBIES: T-Mac is a world-class homebody. Mike Miller, his best friend in Orlando, once revealed that McGrady wouldn't go outside at all in rainy weather.

McGrady's Feats

T he reputation of NYC playground legend Earl "the Goat" Manigault relies heavily on the story that he once "made change": leapt so high he was able to grab a dollar bill off the top of the backboard and leave change in its place.

Tracy McGrady's name will always prompt awe because of his similarly outlandish, John Henry–esque displays of skill. One such display was his off-the-backboard dunk against his former team, Toronto, in 2003, which became a signature of his. Another was his fourth-quarter explosion against San Antonio in 2004, in which he unleashed 13 points in the final 35 seconds to win the game. Other NBA greats have had comparable bursts of scoring, but T-Mac's feat is all the more impressive because it came from a supposedly lethargic player, and without the added adrenaline of the postseason.

Rockets 81
Spurs   80

December 9, 2004

■ McGrady
░ Rockets
■ Spurs

0:01.7 Dribbling up the full length of the court with the clock winding down, McGrady launches a fourth 3-pointer to win the game, 81–80.

0:07 McGrady steals the ball under the Rockets' basket.

0:11 Despite stifling defense from Bruce Bowen, McGrady makes yet another 3 to bring the Rockets within 2.

0:24 Eleven seconds later, McGrady hits a second 3, is fouled by Tim Duncan on the play, and makes the following free throw.

0:33 With just over half a minute left, the Rockets down by 8, and the game seemingly out of reach, McGrady hits a 3 to make the score 71–76.

80 Pts

75

70

65

60

11:35 McGrady hits two quick jump shots to begin the fourth quarter, evening the score at 58–58, but he is then held scoreless for the next eleven minutes as the Spurs build a sizable lead.

55

FOURTH QUARTER

12   10   8   6   4   2   0

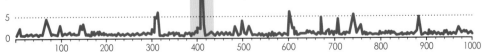

25 Pts

20

15

10

5

0

100   200   300   400   500   600   700   800   900   1000

McGrady's scoring average per minute for 1,000 consecutive minutes of the 2003–04 season

December 9, 2004: During those 35 seconds against the Spurs, McGrady was scoring at a clip of nearly 25 points a minute, almost 4 times his rate at any other point that season.

1 Streaking down the court, T-Mac sees an opening to the basket.

2 Unexpectedly he lobs the ball over the defender's head.

3 As the ball ricochets off the backboard, he prepares to leap.

STYLE: **Idle Rapids**
Seemingly aimless, but powerful forward motion

STYLE: **This Is Not a Pipe**
Surrealism, the treachery of images

STYLE: **Swiss Watch**
Pristine timing, spring-loaded

4 Fully extended, he snatches the ball with both hands.

5 Pulls the ball straight down from on high and into the basket.

6 Swings off the rim and gives a defiant roar.

STYLE: **Frog**
Great leaping and catching ability

STYLE: **Hammer of Thor**
Divine fury

STYLE: **Bull Horn**
Loud, commanding

A Life in Sleep

Tracy McGrady has a truly profound relationship with sleep. Not the realm of dreams, in which new realities unfold before quavering consciousness, but with the pure fact of shut-eye. McGrady sleeps a lot, a quality that in any mere mortal would be taken as evidence of laziness or exhaustion. Yet McGrady thrives on this condition, enriched by it well past the normal bounds of physical replenishment.

In fact, T-Mac is such a diligent practitioner of the nocturnal arts that he has turned it into a form of spiritual duty. For McGrady, sleep is not a break from waking life. It is nothing less than the locus of his being, the hearth from which his life's meaning emanates.

To understand this man's sleeping career is to peer into his soul. Thus, we have juxtaposed the evolution of his sleep orientation with the four life stages outlined in Hinduism's ashrama system. This reveals that McGrady's journey from slumbering teenager to socially aware insomniac is nothing less than the very life cycle of mankind itself.

1 BRAHMACHARYA
The Student

The young student leaves home to live with a guru, acquiring knowledge, practicing self-discipline, learning to live a life of dharma, and practicing meditation.

1997–2000: The 18-year-old McGrady is drafted straight out of high school by Toronto. He plays limited minutes, but adds 15 pounds of muscle after hiring a personal trainer and, rumors suggest, sleeping over 12 hours a day. "You can be sure I slept a lot in Toronto, because the weather was terrible and I hardly ever leave home," McGrady later stated. "All I did was sleep."

2 GRIHASTHA
The Householder

The ideal householder's life is spent selflessly carrying out one's duties to family and society, serving the saints, and diligently pursuing gainful labor.

2000–2002: McGrady is traded to Orlando and promptly leads the league in scoring. He earns the nickname "the Big Sleep" after he scores 41 points in a game before which he had been found dozing in the locker room. "He sleeps all the time," said his then-teammate Darrell Armstrong. "He sleeps when we come in from shoot-around, in the locker room, on the plane. ALL the time."

3 VANAPRASTHA
The Retiree

After the completion of one's householder duties, one gradually withdraws from the world and prepares for the complete renunciation of worldly involvement.

2003–2006: McGrady officially retires his nickname after the birth of his first child in 2003. "No more 'Big Sleep,'" he stated in a *New York Times* interview. "Now I've got a daughter that keeps me up." McGrady is later traded to Houston, where he becomes even more reclusive. "I really, really don't like to leave the house. I'm a prisoner of my own home—by choice," he admitted at the time.

4 SANYASA
The Ascetic

The final stage is a complete withdrawal from the world. Shelter and material possessions are discarded, and one retreats to the wilderness in pursuit of the purely spiritual.

2007: Prompted by African teammate Dikembe Mutombo, McGrady visits a Darfur refugee camp. While there he is forced to sleep in tents overrun with maggots, frogs, and rats, and reportedly wakes several times a night in tears. Having finally forsaken the pleasures of sleep for a heightened social awareness, McGrady claims he has been forever changed by the experience.

No Rest for the Weary

Over an 82-game season, even the most iron-legged scorer requires a few days' rest between games to truly play his best. Yet when Tracy McGrady first entered the league, his commitment to sleep was so profound, so uncompromising, that what most men need the vacation for, he could accomplish in one night. The graph below shows that between 1997 and 2002, T-Mac shot the same high percentage in back-to-back games as he did on several days' rest. But after the birth of his daughter in early 2003, T-Mac could no longer get his 12-hour fix, and like any other mortal, his performance suffered in proportion to his fatigue.

TRACY McGRADY'S FIELD GOAL PERCENTAGE

■ 1997–2002   ■ 2003–2007

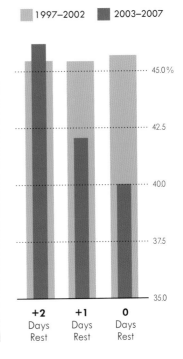

	45.0 %
	42.5
	40.0
	37.5
	35.0

+2 Days Rest   **+1** Days Rest   **0** Days Rest

JOE JOHNSON

Remain Anonymous

Joe Johnson began the summer of 2005 as a promising young player on the Phoenix Suns, one whose contributions were vital to a run to the Western Conference Finals. But by the end of those hot, hot months, he was the new face of the Atlanta Hawks, with a max contract and a mandate to save a decrepit franchise.

The real Joe Johnson lies somewhere between these two extremes, in a purgatory of his own making. As talented as Johnson is, he is ultimately a slow-burning star, a paradox that Johnson positively embodies. He's too talented to be stuck with the "role player" tag but lacks that ineffable quality that makes one a superstar. His game bears no obvious flaws and features enviable all-around ability, but he lacks the majesty of LeBron or the non-stop ruthlessness of Kobe.

Johnson arrived in Atlanta on a mission: to save a team that had won only thirteen games the season before. Only twenty-four years old, he instantly became the team's best player, leading the Hawks in a remarkable six statistical categories: points, assists, steals, games and minutes played, and three-point field goal percentage. On paper, Johnson appeared to be among the league's elite, one of just three players (along with Allen Iverson and LeBron James) to compile more than 40 points and more than 10 assists in multiple games that season. Yet despite such lofty numbers, Johnson's lack of team success kept him from joining Iverson and James at the 2006 All-Star Game.

Being named an All-Star is the kind of individual recognition Johnson felt he would never get in Phoenix. Throughout his

WHAT HE GIVES US:
An attractive all-around game with absolutely no quirks.

WHAT HE STANDS FOR:
The lost brotherhood of only children.

WHY WE CARE:
He humbly reminds us of the limits of human potential.

professional career, he had always been the odd man out. After wasting his first few years playing with the likes of Antoine Walker and Stephon Marbury, Johnson found himself on the 2004–05 Phoenix Suns, without question the most exciting NBA team of the past decade. Led by the newly signed Steve Nash and then-unknown coach Mike D'Antoni, Phoenix unleashed a running game on a league that had been dominated for at least a decade by methodical half-court offense and oppressive physical defense. Nash was rewarded with the first of back-to-back MVP awards for turning around a team that did not even make the playoffs the season prior. That year also marked the emergence of 6'10" manchild Amare Stoudemire and the evolution of the uniquely gifted Shawn Marion. Lost in the shuffle was Joe Johnson, who was overshadowed even by Quentin Richardson, who made his own mark on the season by shooting an absurd 631 three-pointers and getting engaged to R&B sensation Brandy.

Amid the magical passing of Nash, the bizarre jump shot of Marion, and the supernatural bounciness of Stoudemire, Johnson's comparatively pedestrian swingman game failed to stand out. However, it was exactly that all-around game that allowed the other Suns to thrive. In addition to playing at both wing spots, Johnson also was Nash's only capable backup at the point. When Johnson suffered a broken eye socket in Game 2 of the 2005 Western Conference Semifinals, it effectively ended the Suns' run for a championship, and the team fell to the Spurs 4–1. Johnson was unsatisfied being a vital role player, the kind praised by basketball cognoscenti but ignored by casual fans. He yearned for more.

The Hawks had the money to buy a franchise player, and Johnson was eager for a chance to play the role. Since the Suns knew they couldn't pay Johnson and also keep Amare, they agreed to a sign-and-trade deal where they exchanged Johnson for the struggling Frenchman Boris Diaw and two future first-round picks. Freed from his struggles for recognition in Boston and Phoenix, Johnson was ready to finally achieve his dream of being a bona fide NBA superstar. This dream was temporarily deferred when the Hawks' NBA governor Steve Belkin refused to approve the deal, believing that the team was giving up too much to sign Johnson, who, after all, had been the fourth-best player on a team that didn't even make the finals.

Although Belkin's legal maneuvering and general smugness made him look like a complete douchebag, it is hard to argue with his point. It's been three years since the trade, and the Hawks have managed only to sneak into the 2008 playoffs as a lowly, doomed eighth seed. Despite back-to-back All-Star appearances for Johnson, he has merely elevated his position from role player on a title contender to the slightly loftier perch of centerpiece of a lottery team. Ironically, Johnson's current situation in Atlanta bears some striking similarities to the one he left behind in Phoenix. He still sometimes finds himself struggling for attention on the court, with his primary rival being Josh Smith, a raw, explosive player who manages to combine elements of Johnson's former teammates Marion and Stoudemire. Like Marion, Smith is a wing player who uses his athleticism to outrebound power forwards and block more shots than most centers. Yet, he also brings to mind

Amare with his raw power and jaw-dropping leaping ability. Another young Hawks teammate, the bullish center Al Horford, has also garnered comparisons to Amare, while forward Marvin Williams is reminiscent of Joe Johnson himself, not in terms of his skills, but in his similarly quiet demeanor and versatile on-court production.

But Johnson has been unable to assume the role of Steve Nash for this team, either as pre-eminent star or as point guard. After initially using Johnson to run the show—and passing on both Chris Paul and Deron Williams in the process—the Hawks finally gave up on the experiment and traded for Mike Bibby in February 2008. Off the court, Johnson has also failed to capture the public's imagination like the floppy-haired Canadian floor general. This has as much to do with Johnson's prosaic personality as it does the Hawks' lack of wins. While someone like Gilbert Arenas, who is a similarly neglected NBA superstar, has leveraged his way into the conversation through sheer force of will, Johnson demonstrates none of Agent Zero's captivating personality. Johnson is so laid-back that when a reporter asked him to name his favorite activity, he said it was sleeping. Even a groupie who claims (unverifiably) on an online message board that Johnson infected her with herpes must concede that "JJ is a very nice [person] and he is quite humble."

On a team with a Smith, a Williams, and a Jones, Johnson's name stands out as the most boring. Perhaps his mother should have followed the lead of the parents of Aeneas Williams and bestowed upon him a grand name from ancient mythology. It would have been fitting, since his story contains familiar

NAME: Joe Marcus Johnson

BORN: June 29, 1981

HEIGHT: 6 ft 7 in (2.01 m)

WEIGHT: 235 lb (107 kg)

HOMETOWN: Little Rock, AR

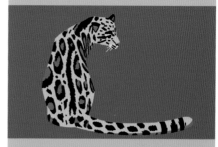

SPIRIT ANIMAL: Clouded leopard

PLAYER COMPARISON: A less elite Grant Hill or a sturdier Penny Hardaway.

NOTABLE REMARK: Joe Johnson has never said anything notable.

HOPES & DREAMS: Johnson is a simple man with simple dreams: "I want to win. I don't just play for myself. I'm repping Atlanta. I'm repping my family. That's important to me. I have to represent [family] every day."

DISTINGUISHING MARKS: Johnson has some word tattooed on each wrist, which signifies something.

OTHER GREAT JOE JOHNSONS:
Joe Johnson (snooker player)
Joe Johnson (baseball player)
Joe Johnson (football player)
Joe Johnson (Australian footballer)
Joe Lee Johnson (NASCAR driver)
Joe Johnson (British motocross star)

themes from Greek tragedy. Just as Oedipus was sent far away from Thebes only to return to meet his certain destiny, Johnson left behind a secondary role on a championship contender only to find himself again striving for recognition on a lesser team. Fortunately for Johnson, he still has his eyes and the opportunity to accept his fate and revel in it. It is Johnson's humility that will save him from making the same mistake twice. As the young players around him continue to improve, he must allow them room to grow, even at the expense of his own personal glory, for that is the only way the Hawks can win.

Actually, maybe Mama Johnson should have named him Phaeton, after the half-mortal son of Apollo who impetuously seized the reins to his father's chariot to prove his divinity and then drove the earth into drought and famine. The NBA is a world where the superhuman is commonplace, and gods walk the court among mortals. But Johnson shows us that there is a place for demigods in this universe. While he may not be able to command the sun all alone, he can certainly nudge it once in a while.

Nobody Knows My Name

Toiling for a forgotten franchise, with a game that's just shy of eye-popping, Joe Johnson might be one of the least-big big names in the league. In fact, when you compare his relative visibility to that of his peers in the 2007–08 All-Star Game, a truly stark picture emerges: One in which, on all fronts of media and chatter, Johnson is systematically ignored and neglected. You can conjure up the chicken, and I'll bring the egg, but one thing's for certain: This All-Star's level of recognition is at odds with the level of accomplishment he brings to the court each night, even if it falls slightly below that of Bron or Wade. It's like he's being punished for failing to measure up to this most exalted yardstick.

VISIBILITY INDEX
National profile of 2007–2008 All-Star shooting guards

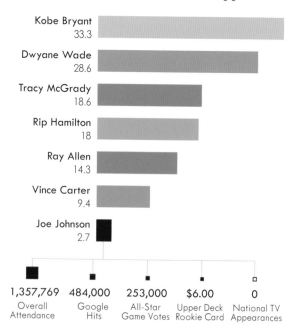

Kobe Bryant 33.3				
Dwyane Wade 28.6				
Tracy McGrady 18.6				
Rip Hamilton 18				
Ray Allen 14.3				
Vince Carter 9.4				
Joe Johnson 2.7				

1,357,769	484,000	253,000	$6.00	0
Overall Attendance	Google Hits	All-Star Game Votes	Upper Deck Rookie Card	National TV Appearances

Visibility Index = (2007-08 Overall Attendance + Google Hits + 2007-08 All-Star Votes + [Upper Deck Rookie Card Price × 100,000] + [2007-08 National TV Appearances × 1,000,000]) ÷ 1,000,000

A Great Day in A-Town

A snippet of fan fiction, written for the stage by an anonymous scribe.

FADE IN:

ATLANTA CAPITOL BUILDING, EXTERIOR. DAY.

Mayor Shirley Franklin takes the stage, accompanied by T-Boz, Hulk Hogan, and Ted Turner. All are wearing Johnson #2 jerseys. Gladys Knight and the Pips' "Friendship Train" is blaring in the background. T-Boz, Hogan, and Turner take seats while Mayor Franklin takes the podium.

FRANKLIN

We are congregated here on this day, May 3, 2008, to commemorate a momentous occasion. It is on this day that we can proudly say that our Atlanta Hawks have miraculously beaten the Boston Celtics three times in the playoffs. On a similar stage one hundred years ago, the great Booker T. Washington noted that "In all things that are purely social, we can be as separate as the fingers, yet one as the hand in all things essential to mutual progress." Yet over the past week, Zaza Pachulia, Josh Smith, and Al Horford existed not as separate fingers but as one tightly closed Eastern European-American-Dominican fist, straight to the collective jaw of the Boston Celtics. The brass knuckle of that fist is the man that we have come here to honor, the man who willed us to victory in these three games. That man's name is Joe Johnson. Today and for all days forward, May 3 in the city of Atlanta will be known as Joe Johnson Day.

The audience cheers as Johnson takes the stage, his eyes harboring a well of secrets and his slow saunter encapsulating the care and order that he puts into his game. The Morehouse College marching band plays Usher's "Yeah!" as Johnson waves to the crowd. Mayor Franklin walks over to award him the key to the city, and Johnson motions to the crowd that he is going to begin speaking.

JOHNSON

My friends. We are at a critical point in this city's history . . .

A prolonged silence comes as Johnson reaches for a glass of sweet tea. He sips it with the calm of an elk that suckles the pure water from a Canadian brook during springtime.

JOHNSON (cont'd)

My teammates and I, we . . .

Johnson looks across the crowd, a single bead of sweat falling from his forehead. A cirrus cloud briefly cloaks the sun, while the crowd begins to shuffle and stir slightly. Jimmy Carter turns to Alice Walker and offers a confused but pleasant shrug. Walker responds with a polite, knowing smile. Overhead, a brown thrasher flits as Johnson's silence continues. He surveys the audience, taking steady breaths but still saying nothing. Eventually, he leans in to the microphone, emitting an audible exhalation of humility and honor.

JOHNSON (cont'd)

I just want to thank you all so much for everything you have done.

Johnson leaves the stage to thunderous applause and cheers. People are overwhelmed by his greatness as he walks off the stage and into quiet oblivion.

There's a War Between Us

Although the U.S. Civil War was fought well over a century ago, the North and South remain very different places. If that weren't true, we wouldn't be able to explain the career of Jeff Foxworthy or the comic strip *Kudzu*. Joe Johnson has felt this disunity firsthand, as his career has flourished while playing south of the Mason-Dixon Line and suffered at the hands of fast-talking Yankees.

THE NORTH

1 Steve Belkin
NBA Governor, Atlanta Hawks

The Boston businessman refused to approve the sign-and-trade deal that brought Johnson to Atlanta in the summer of 2005. Of all the members of the Atlanta Spirit LLC group, which owns the Hawks, Belkin was the only one not based in Atlanta.

2 Chris Wallace
General Manager, Boston Celtics

Wallace selected Johnson with the tenth overall pick of the 2001 NBA draft, expecting him to be a cornerstone of a rebuilt Boston team. Although Johnson started 33 of the first 38 games, Wallace abruptly traded him to the Suns midway through his rookie season.

3 Stephon Marbury
Point Guard, New York Knicks

Hailing from Brooklyn, Marbury is the prototypical New Yorker: provincial, arrogant, and rude. Two of the three seasons Johnson played with Marbury ended in losing records. After Marbury left and headed back north, Phoenix won 62 games and advanced to the Western Conference Finals.

THE SOUTH

4 Little Rock
Arkansas

Johnson starred at Little Rock Central High School, site of the historic standoff between Orval Faubus and the National Guard over the integration of public schools. When Johnson signed with Atlanta, he announced, "I wanted to come back down South, which is home for me."

5 Mike D'Antoni
Head Coach, Phoenix Suns

Although his home state of West Virginia was part of the Union, no one would ever mistake the heavily accented D'Antoni for a Yankee. Johnson credits the Suns coach with developing his game at a key stage in his career. Also, Phoenix is located in the part of Arizona that used to be Confederate territory.

6 Nolan Richardson
Head Coach, University of Arkansas

Johnson was an All-SEC performer at Arkansas, playing on one of the last teams Richardson coached before leaving the university amid claims of racial discrimination and intolerance. Richardson said of his treatment by the university: "My great-great-grandfather came over on the ship. Not Nolan Richardson. I did not come over on that ship."

WHERE THEY ARE NOW
A PAPER TRAIL REVELRY

Only 450 NBA roster spots exist. This painfully finite number has forced scores of the world's greatest athletes to exit the hallowed Association. But where do these players go? By the grace of the Freedom of Information Act, we were able to research the lives of thousands of former ballplayers and have discovered an impressive array of documents that shed at least some light on the whereabouts of those beloved ballers. Here we present a sampling of some of our most interesting finds.

2008 Battle of the Bands Application

June 5th 6:00 p.m. / Riverton City Park at 12800 So. 1450 W.

Rules
*Each band will have 30 minutes stage time. This includes set up and brake down. The quicker you are the more play time you will have.
* Judging will be based on crowd and crowd participation, original music, cover music, creativity, and all over performance.
* Band members cannot be older than 40 years old.
*You must have your own crew to handle your equipment.

Winners
*Will receive $300.00 Cash Prize

Applications
*Applications can be dropped off at Riverton City Office buildings in the Recreation Department.
Or mailed to R.A.F.1233 West 13140 South Riverton, UT. 84065
If you have questions call Camie 580-7200

Band Name _The big three_

Band Members _Gilbert Cheaney, Ed O'Bahnon, Tony Delk_

Substitute Members _Bobby Hurley, Aye Earl_

Type of Music _Barbershop quartet_

Original Song 1 _Makin Love in the morning Hours"_

Cover Song 2 _Mr Sandman_

Optional Song 3 _For the Longest Time_

Contact Name _Big Ed-O_ Phone _Unlisted_

Address _Hit up my car dealership Findlay Toyota and Scion_

Email _TheBig3hree@aol.com_ Alt. Phone _NA_

U.S. STUDENT GRANT APPLICATION

COUNTRY (applying to): **Saudi Arabia**

DATE OF BIRTH: **03/09/69** ☑ MALE ☐ FEMALE

NAME: **Jackson Abdul-Rauf Mahmoud**
Last *First* *Middle* *Maiden*

PRESENT ADDRESS: *Street* **Gulfport, MS, Atlanta, GA**

City **Mecca** *State* *Zip* *Country* **The Earth**

CITIZENSHIP(S) 1) **NA** 2)

SOURCE OF CITIZENSHIP **Hoodwinking, bamboozling** *Country of Birth* **AmeriKKKa**

CURRENT ACADEMIC RANK/PROFESSIONAL STATUS **Imam** (See Instructions)

CURRENT ACADEMIC OR PROFESSIONAL AFFILIATION: **School of life** *Since* **2000**

PREVIOUS FULBRIGHT GRANTS: **No** *Country* *Since* **Birth**

ACADEMIC DEGREES

Degree **Master of Freethrows** *Date Received or Expected* **1990** *Institution* **Louisiana State University** *Country* **U.S. of KKK**

FELLOWSHIPS, Honors, Publications, Exhibitions, Extracurricular Activities (Do not attach additional sheet nor write on reverse)

Most improved player award

FUTURE PLANS (Upon return to the U.S.)

Write a book about basketball as a metaphor for spiritual enlightenment and the NBA as a symbol of institutionalized oppression; build more mosques out of crackhouses.

ABSTRACT OF PROPOSAL (Do not attach additional sheet nor write on reverse)

Based on Rushdie's reading of Sartre's reading of Benjamin's reading of the 1001 Arabian Nights, the political unconscious has certain resemblances to the discussion of colonial discourse in postcolonial history. Based on this notion, I seek to invert the male gaze and operate as the other within the sphere of the other by playing basketball in Saudi Arabia for Al Ittihad and chronicling my experiences.

I will present this as a hermeneutical problematization of basketball as simultaneously the transformation of identity and the solidification of...

STARBUCKS COFFEE   APPLICATION FOR EMPLOYMENT

Starbucks Coffee Company is an equal opportunity employer, dedicated to a policy of non-discrimination in employment on any basis including race, color, age, sex, religion, national origin, the presence of mental, physical, or sensory disability, sexual orientation, or any other basis prohibited by federal, state, or provincial law.

Please complete entire application to ensure processing.

Social Security/Social Insurance Number _____   Date (M/D/Y) _____

PERSONAL INFORMATION (Please print)

Name — Last **RIDER**   First **ISAIAH**   Middle **J.R.**

Other names you are known by **THE EAST BAY MACK**

Have you been convicted of a crime in the last seven (7) years? Yes ~~☒~~ No ☒
If Yes, list convictions that are a matter of public record (arrests are not convictions). A conviction will not necessarily disqualify you for employment.

U.S. Applicant Only: Are you legally eligible for employment in the U.S.? Yes ☒ No ____
(All new hires will be required to provide proof of eligibility to work in the U.S.)

Present Address — Street **SKID ROW / SOME DUDE'S CAR**   City **LOS ANGELES**   State/Province **CA**   Zip Code/Postal Code **90013**

Permanent Address — Street **NEAR SMOKEHOUSE IN BERKELEY... BUT I'M IN OAKLAND, CA**   Zip Code/Postal Code **94705**

Referred By **HAROLD MINER**

Phone Number — Daytime **(510) 555-3640**   Evening **BEEPER**

EMPLOYMENT DESIRED

Position **CASHIER**   Location/Department **HOLIDAY FAVORITES**   Salary Desired **$75,000**   Date You Can Start **NOW →**

Specify hours available for each day of the week: Sunday / Monday / Tuesday / Wednesday / Thursday / Friday / Saturday — **ALL — I'M USUALLY AWAKE AROUND 4AM – 6AM**

Are you able to work overtime? **NO**   Which store/department? ____

Have you ever worked for Starbucks Coffee Company? **NO**   If yes, when? ____

EDUCATION

	Name and Address of School	Circle Last Years Completed	Did You Graduate?	Subjects Studied and Degrees Received
High School	**ENCINAL HIGH SCHOOL**	1 2 3 (4)	(Y) N	**POTTERY (STUDENT AWARD)**
College	**ALLEN COUNTY COMMUNITY COLLEGE**	(1) 2 3 4	Y (N)	**BASKETBALL**
Post College	**MORE JUCO**	(1) 2 3 4	Y (N)	**HOOPS**
Trade, Business, or Correspondence School	**UNLV**	(1) 2 3 4	Y (N)	**TARKOLOGY, BALLIN**

SKILLS For Office/Administrative positions only

List skills relevant to the position applied for **CROSSOVER, MID-RANGE JUMPER, DUNKING**

Typing WPM: **8**   10-Key: ☒ Yes ☐ No

Computer Proficiency: ☐ Word for Windows ☒ Excel ☐ Others: ____

Have you ever visited a Starbucks Coffee location? Where? Describe your experience. **IN FRESNO ON A MULE TRIP. I ORDERED 3 VENTI MOCHACHINOS — TWO TO KEEP ME AWAKE, AND ONE TO THROW AT THE MANAGER'S FACE. I THINK I HIT ONE UP LAST NIGHT.**

What do you like about coffee? **IT'S FROM THE EARTH.**

Why would you like to work for Starbucks Coffee Company? **I THINK I REALLY CAN MAKE A CONTRIBUTION TO THIS TEAM.**

Describe a specific situation where you have provided excellent customer service in your most recent position. Why was this effective? **MY GUY THIS ZAPP AND ROGER RECORD FOR HALF PRICE. IT WORKED BECAUSE HE NEEDED THE RECORD AND I NEEDED THE MONEY. I SOLD**

SKU #1938

U.S. Department of State

OMB APPROVAL NO. 1405-0
EXPIRES: 09/30/2010
ESTIMATED BURDEN: 1 HOUR
(See Page 2)

APPLICATION FOR IMMIGRANT VISA AND ALIEN REGISTRATION

PART I - BIOGRAPHIC DATA

INSTRUCTIONS: Complete one copy of this form for yourself and each member of your family, regardless of age, who will immigrate with you. Please print or type your answers to all questions. Mark questions that are **Not Applicable** with "N/A". If there is insufficient room on the form, answer on a separate sheet using the same numbers that appear on the form. Attach any additional sheets to this form.

WARNING: Any false statement or concealment of a material fact may result in your permanent exclusion from the United States.

This form (DS-230 PART I) is the first of two parts. This part, together with Form DS-230 PART II, constitutes the complete Application for Immigrant Visa and Alien Registration.

1. Family Name
TABUSE

First Name
YUTA

Middle Name

2. Other Names Used or Aliases (If married woman, give maiden name)
JORDAN OF JAPAN

3. Full Name in Native Alphabet (If Roman letters not used)
田臥勇太

4. Date of Birth (mm-dd-yyyy)
10-5-1980

5. Age
28

6. Place of Birth
(City or town)
YOKOHAMA

(Country)
JAPAN

7. Nationality (If dual national, give both)
JAPANESE

8. Gender
☒ Male
☐ Female

9. Marital Status
☒ Single (Never married) ☐ Married ☐ Widowed ☐ Divorced ☐ Separated
Including my present marriage, I have been married _____ times.

10. Permanent address in the United States where you intend to live, if known (street address including zip code). Include the name of a person who currently lives there.
BASKETBALL HALL OF FAME
SPRINGFIELD, MA

Telephone number:

11. Address in the United States where you want your Permanent Resident Card (Green Card) mailed, if different from address in item #10 (include the name of a person who currently lives there).
STEVE KERR'S HOUSE

Telephone number:

12. Your Present Occupation
G.O.A.T. ANAHEIM ARSENAL

13. Present Address (Street Address) (City or Town) (Province) (Country)
MOTEL ROOMS
(FORT WAYNE TO BAKERSFIELD)
Telephone number: Home   Office

14. Name of Spouse (Maiden or family name)
CURRENTLY SEARCHING.
Date (mm-dd-yyyy) and place of birth of spouse:
Address of spouse (If different from your own):
ASU GIRLS WHO DIG FROSTED TIPS
GET AT ME!

First Name   Middle Name

Spouse's occupation:

15. Father's Family Name
NAISMITH

First Name
JAMES

Date of marriage (mm-dd-yyyy):

16. Father's Date of Birth (mm-dd-yyyy)
1939

Place of Birth
A PEACH BASKET

Current Address

17. Mother's Family Name at Birth
EDWARDS

18. Mother's Date of Birth (mm-dd-yyyy) Place of Birth

First Name
TERESA

Current A

If deceased, giv

DS-230 Part I
10-2007

THIS FORM MA

GANIC FARMER
ERS ASSOCIAT
APPLICATION (2(

blue ink. Application
harge for resubmitte
inal fee from MOFGA
you download your ap
ual and its Appendice

shon Leonar

uld be one of the r
ration in our da
ce

Country: US

above:

g address) SAME

_____ State _____ Zip _____
n-Profit ☐ Corporation ☒ Cooperative
ner: _____
fication)

873 Pleasant St.
State ME Zip 04614

arcels of land on which crops or livestock are produced, you
s and submit landowner affidavits.

APPLICATION TO DISCHARGE INDUSTRIAL WASTEWATER TO A PUBLICLY-OWNED TREATMENT WORKS (POTW)

This application is for a wastewater discharge permit for a discharge of industrial wastewater to a publicly-owned treatment works (POTW) as required by Chapter 90.48 RCW and Chapter 173-216 V It is designed to provide the Department of Ecology with information on pollutants in the waste str materials that may enter the waste stream, and the flow characteristics of the discharge.

Information previously submitted to Ecology that applies to this application should be referenced appropriate section. Ecology may request additional information to clarify the conditions of this discharge.

SECTION A. GENERAL INFORMATION

1. Applicant name: Robert "Tractor" Traylor
Traylor's Trailers

2. Facility name:
   (if different from applicant
   1234 West 8 Mile Road

4822

FORM NOTICE OF PETITION
AN APPEAL INVOLVING A HOMELESS CHILD OR YOUTH

9. List address of child's/youth's last permanent residence:

THE TRAILER FROM THE PARADE MAGAZINE ALL-AMERICAN HIGH-SCHOOL BASKETBALL PHOTOSHOOT... OR MAYBE THAT CONDO ME AND TROY BELL SHARED IN TURKEY.

10. Prior to becoming homeless, DEANGELO COLLINS (child's/youth's name) was attending, or entitled to attend, the NBDL ~~District~~ ~~school~~ on a tuition-free basis.

11. Describe the circumstances causing child/youth to become homeless: (Attach any relevant documents and add additional pages if necessary.)

NBA TEAMS ARE SCARED OF ME BECAUSE I BASHED THIS DUDE'S SKULL IN WHEN I WAS IN HIGH SCHOOL. DUDES LIKE BOB LEY TRIED TO PSYCHO-ANALYZE ME SO I GOT A BUM DRAFT POSITION. THEN I HAD TO GLOBETROT AND GET ON SOME BIG BIRD IN CHINA SHIT. LATELY I'VE BEEN GETTING THAT NBDL MONEY, TRADING ELBOWS WITH RICK RICKERT. BUT IT HASN'T KEPT A ROOF OVER MY HEAD.

12. Since DEANGELO COLLINS (child's/youth's name) became homeless, he/she has attended the following school districts. (If known, list the approximate dates of attendance at each school district listed.) I AM A STUDENT OF THE GAME. GOT MY SCHOOLING WITH THE RED BULL BARAKO IN THE PHILIPPINES, DARUSSAFAKA ISTANBUL, THE YUNNAN HONGHE RUNNING BULLS, SOME ARGENTINE REC LEAGUE, AND THE FLORIDA FLAME (PAT RILEY: HOLLER AT ME!)

13. List names and address(es) of child's/youth's parent(s) or legal guardian(s):

LORETTA TAYLOR IS MY MOM. BUT J.R. SMITH IS MY SPIRITUAL GUIDE

MP-3 (Rev. 9/13/2002)

TEXAS DEPARTMENT OF PUBLIC SAFETY
MISSING PERSONS CLEARINGHOUSE REPORT FORM

BE VERY SPECIFIC AND COMPLETE:

Alias/Nickname **Tree**

Name of Missing Person **Keon Clark**   Social Security Number **NA**

Date of Birth **4/16/75** Age **33** Drivers License Number **Revoked**   Eye Color **Brown** Hair Color **Bald**   Build **Kelvin Cato-esque**

Race **Black** Sex **M**   Height **6'9"** Weight **221 lbs**

Unique Characteristics (Scars, Limp, Tattoo, Jewelry, Glasses, Etc.) **Extremely skinny legs, 40-inch vertical,**

Six-pack of Amstel Light, tattoo of someone's face on his chest

Dental Records Available? Yes **X** No ___   Medical Records Available? Yes **X** No ___   Fingerprints Available? Yes **X** No ___

Blood Type **THC**   Medical Problems? Yes **X** No ___   Type of Problem **Sore Knees**

Prescription **Self-prescribed**

Mental State (Depressed, Suicidal, etc.) **Chillin**

Location Last Seen: City **Salt Lake City** State **UT** County **Delta Center** Zip **84104**

Date/Time Last Seen **2004**   Possible Destination (City, State) **Salt Lake, UT**

Last Seen Wearing **Toronto Raptors 2001 Eastern Conference Semifinals commemorative T-Shirt**

Hobbies & Interests **Golf, Firearms**

Associations & Hangouts **Septuagenarian Golf buddies, Vlade Divac**

Vehicle Year **2003** Make **Mercedes** Model **Benz** Color **Black** License Number & State **Removed (sold on Ebay)**

Other Identifying Characteristics of Vehicle **Lost Boyz "Music Makes Me High" maxi single in CD Player, multiple dents and cup holders**

IF APPLICABLE: In Company With **Greg Ostertag**   Alias/Nickname **"Tag"**

Relationship: Noncustodial Parent **X** Relative ___ Abductor ___ Friend ___

Address **The Backwoods** City ___   State **TX** Zip ___   Phone Number **NA**

Social Security Number ___

Date of Birth **4/6/73** Age **35** Drivers License Number ___   Eye Color **Blue** Hair Color **Buzzy** Build **Shawn Bradley**

Race **White** Sex **M** Height **7'2"** Weight **280 lbs**

Unique Characteristics (Scars, Limp, Tattoos, Jewelry, Glasses, Etc.) **Squirrel-skin cap**

Vehicle Year **1984** Make **El Camino** Model **7-footers customized for** Color **Rust** License Number & State **Expired**

Other Identifying Characteristics of Vehicle **Wild Turkey-stained upholstery**

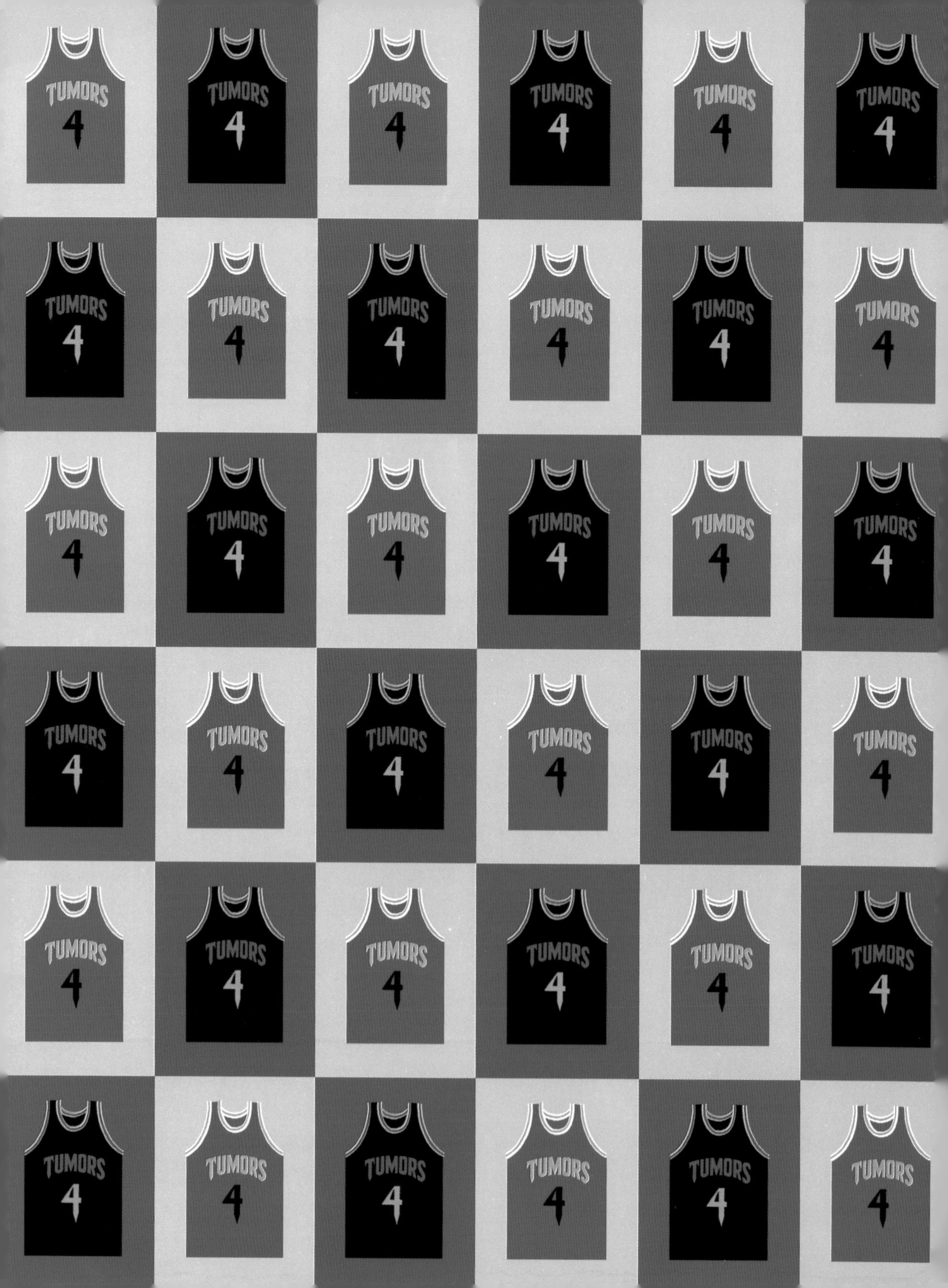
TUMORS
4

Phenomenal Tumors

One-Man Rot and Its Deleterious Ways

Who knows when precisely a player becomes deserving of the appellation of "cancer"? It can be a single play or a confluence of off-court events. But once the gavel has landed, its imprint made, life is never the same. However high his level of skill, he is deemed to do more harm than good for the clubhouse he inhabits. For some, the mark can fade, sometimes becoming endearing proof of human fallibility. But for others, this epithet closely stalks their name until they have nothing left with which to disprove it. We come not to judge these men, but to understand how it is that they fell into the chasm of wholesale damnation.

Just as each cancer of the human body is unique, so do these players have their own haggard, strangely proud stories to tell. They are, like the disease whose name they bear, functions of both themselves and the context they have stumbled into. May we learn from them, if not with an eye toward prevention or extermination, then maybe with something else: the cool lens of scientific appreciation.

RON ARTEST

Madness in a Cup

By the time you read this, Ron Artest might be dead, playing in Poland, or out of basketball entirely, selling skulls on eBay. Artest plays for that same dream others play for: capturing the Larry O'Brien trophy. But even if he never gets it, his indelible influence on the league should serve as a satisfactory consolation prize. One single, unforgettable image of him has stained the annals of American history: Artest, the neckline of his Indiana Pacers jersey stretched slightly below his nipples, being escorted off the basketball court at the Palace of Auburn Hills by Indiana assistant coach Chuck Person. That was the day the NBA stood still.

This is what happened: In the closing seconds of a game against the Detroit Pistons, Artest endured a flagrant shove from Ben Wallace. To avoid an altercation, he laid down on the scorers' table during the ensuing time-out. Harmless enough—but what happened next would permanently transform Artest's image from meathead to all-time menace. An intoxicated moron of a Detroit fan lofted a cup of beer at the precise arc that would send it caroming off of Artest's chest and onto the parquet. Righteously enraged, Artest rushed into the stands to obtain violent justice, his teammate Stephen Jackson behind him, pummeling fans along the way. Team captain Jermaine O'Neal threw a punch at a fat man rushing the court. At the periphery of this scene of madness stood backup center David Harrison, lofting a metal folding chair toward no one in particular. A full-

WHAT HE GIVES US:
The continual dry-humping of the apocalypse.

WHAT HE STANDS FOR:
Drinking and smoking and staying out past curfew for the first time ever.

WHY WE CARE:
The violin-strung tension that follows Artest night in and night out.

scale riot ensued, marking one of the most shameful days in modern sports.

Artest, credited with starting the whole thing, subsequently received a seventy-two-game suspension from Commissioner Stern—the longest non-drug-related penalty in league history. Appearing on the *Today* show shortly after the incident, a nonchalant Artest used the opportunity not to apologize but to promote the new album by female R&B group Allure, which had been recently released on his record label, Tru Warier.

The tragedy of Ron's story is that all of his strife and mischief has overshadowed the fact that he is one of the greatest talents ever to play the game (note: greatest "talents," not greatest "players"). The first bit of testimony for Artest's greatness is his spectacular physique. The man is broadly built to the point of being pyramid shaped, with a sturdy base of muscular legs supporting a brick-solid torso, capped off with a pointy noggin. Like Charles Oakley or Kevin Willis, he is immovable, yet at a mere 6'7", normally the height of a tweener forward, he is also swift and flexible. And though Artest primarily plays the small forward spot, he can shift shapes to fit whatever on-court situation he encounters. He may not be a multifaceted performer like Kevin Garnett or Lamar Odom, but he is always the man that the moment needs him to be.

Offensively, Artest is a bucking bronco, capable of charging uninhibitedly into the lane and suddenly shifting momentum to step back for the jumper. He can post up and bowl opponents over, or he can go straight to the hoop. His buckets rarely look easy, much less pretty; instead, they are frantic pileups of multiple juke moves, gyrations, and off-kilter

extensions of the body. Never aspiring to be the alpha dog on any of his teams, he nonetheless maintains a high scoring average. Points simply seem to accumulate around him.

By far the most striking and singular aspect of Artest's game is his defense. He has won the NBA's Defensive Player of the Year award for the 2003–04 season and has made the All-Defensive Team multiple times. But these league-sanctioned awards do not begin to capture his defensive prowess. Simply put, Artest is the lockdown defender of his era. The feisty Ben Wallace is a worthy contender, using his small hands and undersizedness to create havoc down low. Bruce Bowen is the purist's favorite; Dikembe Mutombo and Alonzo Mourning long controlled the painted areas of various NBA arenas. But if you need one player to slow an opponent's best guy, no matter who that best guy is—if you need a concrete wall to provide indisputable stoppage—Artest is your man.

Defense, the roundball sages say, is the hardest facet of the game to master. From a young age, children are taught by failed community-college coaches at basketball camps across the land to value defense like a sickly firstborn son. "Defense wins championships" is the "Ask not what your country can do for you" of the sporting world. While offensive greatness is seen as an automatic outgrowth of one's basic nature, defense takes determination, courage, nerve, and desire. Strip away the clichés, and these words delineate the most difficult task humans are given to perform: the exercise of will. On the defensive end, Artest imposes his will like nobody else. This is how we know that Artest is "there," as in the opposite of "not all there."

The stereotype has persisted that guys who focus on defense are the good guys of the league, the guys who, as Artest would say, "eat Cheerios": the saints who would work out in the cornfields, dripping sweat and getting their hands dirty. Artest is the biggest head case in the league and yet plays defense like virtually no one else in his generation. And head cases aren't supposed to be great defenders—they supposedly lack the willpower to get through endless drills of prolonged crouching, squatting on underdeveloped glutei maximi, and life-draining back arches. Dennis Rodman defied that notion years before Artest, but he specialized in havoc-wreaking rebounds, body-abasing hustle, and unhinged application. Artest, by contrast, is disciplined, focused, and obsessed with his craft.

Artest could steal the ball from a back-from-the-grave Wilt Chamberlain to win an NBA title, and his legacy would remain one of recklessness, lawlessness, and mindlessness. The brawl, taken alongside Artest's pattern of trade demands and trade refusals, an absurd request for time off from the NBA season to promote his rap career, a history of domestic violence charges, a grab bag of flagrant fouls and subsequent suspensions, and a penchant for smashing cameras and furniture—this is Ron-Ron's vacant offering to basketball fandom. Without the distraction and interruption that has plagued him throughout his career, without all of the bouncing from team to team, suspension to suspension, and question mark to question mark, Ron Artest could have been the toast of his generation. Instead he is a complicated miscreant.

Despite his goodwill trips to Kenya and his self-sponsored charity game in his old

NAME: Ronald (Ron) William Artest Jr.

BORN: November 13, 1979

HEIGHT: 6 ft 7 in (2.01 m)

WEIGHT: 248 lb (112 kg)

HOMETOWN: Queensbridge, NY

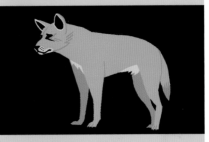

SPIRIT ANIMAL: Dingo

PLAYER COMPARISON: Jose Canseco on reality television with Scottie Pippen's skill set; the hip-hop Rodman; a super-stupid Michael Cooper.

NOTABLE REMARK: On his season-long suspension in 2004: "I'm trying to be positive. I'm a big fan of the Nobel Peace Prize."

NOTABLE RAP LYRIC: "David Stern! Damn, David Stern. I gotta teach you 'bout the ghetto, there's some things you should learn."

HAIRSTYLES: Short, trapezoidal Afro; high-low (as a child); TRU WARIER engraved in the back of his head; KINGS shaved into his head; Mohawk.

REAL RECOGNIZING REAL: Ron-Ron knows his place in the rap world of professional ballplayers. "I'm not the best rapper in the NBA," Artest once said. "Elton Brand is better than me. Stephen Jackson is better than me. Troy Hudson is nice. Hudson has fire."

Queensbridge neighborhood, few fans can muster the sympathy to see him as "simply misunderstood" or as "just a big kid." Yes, Ron does seem childlike at times, excitedly attuned to the wonder of the world around him. But in fact he is a grown-ass man, and as such is eligible to be tried as an adult for the crime of killing Ron-Ron, the most dominant player of our time.

With his talents, he could have proved to the world that ineptitude and needless aggression do not triumph over all, that small forwards truly matter, that defensive skill and offensive skill need never be inversely correlated.

Artest need not be blamed for any particular crime against the Paul Pierces of the world, against his family members, against the teammates who supported him, the league that birthed him, the cities that he has Godzilla'd, the fans that he has enraged. He can only be held accountable for the waste that he has become, for his poor judgment and wanting morals.

Artest's strange ways will never change. He will never be able to harness all of his skills to be the player he could become. Only this is certain: His future will defy our expectations.

From the Mixed-Up Files of Ron W. Artest.

I, Ron Artest, Social Security # 866-77-5842, of the County of Queens, State of New York, declare this to be my will, and hereby revoke any former Wills and Codicils made by me. All assets and properties that I have accrued over my life shall be distributed by means of the below-detailed game of MASH, which will employ the product of my jersey numbers, 15, 23, 91, and 93 (heretofore referred to as the "magic number"), as the number for tallying these outcomes. Please proceed using the following categories:

VALUABLES
- Complete Big Noyd collection on CD-R
- Aviator shades (game worn)
- Vern Fleming Pacers throwback
- Komodo dragon
- *In Search of Excellence* (autographed by Peters and Waterman)

AUTOMOBILES
- Promotional Tru Warier custom-painted van
- 1967 Aston Martin (never driven)
- Solar-powered school bus
- Tank

RESIDENCES
- Mansion
- Apartment
- Shack
- House

FAMILY
- Kimsha (wife)
- Ron-Ron
- Diamond Clear
- Sade
- Jeron

AWARDS
- Platinum plaque for album *My World* (certified 1,000,000,000 sold in Denmark)
- NBA Defensive Player of the Year trophy, 2004
- Regional Cable Ace Award for Best Guest Appearance (joust with American Gladiator Hawk on *Best Damn Sports Show Period*, FSN)
- *Don Diva* magazine Man of the Year award, 2004
- Student "mathlete" award, St. John's Mathematics Department, 1998

Tango on the Tundra

How some of the league's best offensive players fared against Artest from 2002–2003 through 2007–2008.

4/15/06 Carmelo Anthony, 0.385, 15pts 4/18/07 Kobe Bryant, 0.632, 34pts 2/23/06 Kobe Bryant, 0.519, 36pts 3/29/03 Paul Pierce, 0.238, 16pts 2/13/08 Tracy McGrady, 0.250, 10pts 2/23/07 Vince Carter, 0.625, 26pts 3/25/04 Paul Pierce, 0.435, 27pts 4/1/03 Paul Pierce, 0.524, 27pts 12/15/03 LeBron James, 0.625, 27pts 3/6/06 Vince Carter, 0.364, 21pts 11/30/03 Kobe Bryant, 0.400, 12pts 11/3/04 LeBron James, 0.421, 28pts 12/15/03 LeBron James, 0.625, 27pts 12/1/07 Tracy McGrady, 0.467, 40pts 11/5/04 Paul Pierce, 0.357, 15pts 1/4/07 Kobe Bryant, 0.524, 42pts 1/6/04 Tracy McGrady, 0.519, 43pts 11/4/03 Carmelo Anthony, 0.077, 2pts 2/6/04 Vince Carter, 0.412, 18pts 2/23/07 Vince Carter, 0.625, 26pts 3/1/06 LeBron James, 0.333, 19pts 4/8/07 Tracy McGrady, 0.500, 40pts 11/11/03 Paul Pierce, 0.389, 19pts 1/31/06 Carmelo Anthony, 0.588, 24pts 12/8/07 Carmelo Anthony, 0.313, 14pts 3/12/04 Paul Pierce, 0.368, 21pts 1/10/03 Tracy McGrady, 0.409, 23pts 3/29/03 Paul Pierce, 0.238, 16pts 1/31/04 Paul Pierce, 0.611, 24pts 12/12/07 Paul Pierce, 0.467, 26pts 2/20/07 Paul Pierce, 0.533, 26pts 3/14/04 LeBron James, 0.545, 26pts 3/9/08 Kobe Bryant, 0.389, 26pts 4/11/03 Tracy McGrady, 0.344, 35pts 3/24/08 Tracy McGrady, 0.313, 17pts 1/6/04 Tracy McGrady, 0.519, 43pts 3/19/03 Paul Pierce, 0.333, 40pts 2/13/07 Tracy McGrady, 0.423, 28pts 1/9/07 LeBron James, 0.538, 34pts 12/30/03 LeBron James, 0.450, 22pts 3/23/04 Paul Pierce, 0.235, 9pts 12/26/07 Paul Pierce, 0.333, 16pts 1/13/07 Tracy McGrady, 0.387, 37pts 12/17/03 Tracy McGrady, 0.421, 21pts 3/24/03 Paul Pierce, 0.625, 21pts 1/22/08 Vince Carter, 0.692, 21pts 4/1/08 Tracy McGrady, 0.387, 32pts 12/30/03 LeBron James, 0.450, 22pts 3/19/03 Paul Pierce, 0.286, 14pts 11/7/03 LeBron James, 0.444, 23pts 4/2/04 Vince Carter, 0.421, 21pts 3/25/04 Paul Pierce, 0.435, 27pts 4/1/03 Paul Pierce, 0.524, 27pts 12/18/07 Vince Carter, 0.417, 15pts 11/24/05 LeBron James, 0.300, 19pts 11/3/04 LeBron James, 0.421, 28pts 2/6/04 Paul Pierce, 0.278, 20pts 3/11/07 Carmelo Anthony, 0.458, 29pts 2/3/07 Carmelo Anthony, 0.280, 20pts 3/5/03 Kobe Bryant, 0.346, 20pts 2/13/07 Tracy McGrady, 0.423, 28pts 11/22/02 Tracy McGrady, 0.550, 28pts 1/4/07 Kobe Bryant, 0.524, 42pts 3/7/04 Carmelo Anthony, 0.500, 29pts 1/2/04 Paul Pierce, 0.421, 18pts 3/9/04 Vince Carter, 0.500, 28pts 3/22/06 Kobe Bryant, 0.316, 13pts 3/21/03 Paul Pierce, 0.278, 14pts 1/27/06 Paul Pierce, 0.438, 18pts 4/18/07 Kobe Bryant, 0.632, 34pts 1/11/05 Vince Carter, 0.615, 18pts 3/14/06 Kobe Bryant, 0.429, 30pts 3/4/08 Kobe Bryant, 0.385, 34pts 12/26/07 Paul Pierce, 0.333, 16pts 3/2/07 Kobe Bryant, 0.455, 30pts 12/23/07 Carmelo Anthony, 0.524, 30pts 1/17/03 Paul Pierce, 0.414, 31pts 4/7/04 Vince Carter, 0.316, 15pts 1/22/07 Vince Carter, 0.364, 8pts 2/23/06 Kobe Bryant, 0.519, 36pts 3/27/03 Paul Pierce, 0.476, 37pts 3/17/04 Vince Carter, 0.412, 18pts 4/1/07 Kobe Bryant, 0.429, 19pts 12/1/07 Tracy McGrady, 0.467, 40pts 4/8/07 Tracy McGrady, 0.500, 40pts 4/4/07 Carmelo Anthony, 0.500, 31pts 11/5/04 Paul Pierce, 0.357, 15pts

The Lunacy

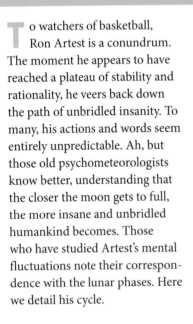

of Ron Artest

T o watchers of basketball, Ron Artest is a conundrum. The moment he appears to have reached a plateau of stability and rationality, he veers back down the path of unbridled insanity. To many, his actions and words seem entirely unpredictable. Ah, but those old psychometeorologists know better, understanding that the closer the moon gets to full, the more insane and unbridled humankind becomes. Those who have studied Artest's mental fluctuations note their correspondence with the lunar phases. Here we detail his cycle.

NEW MOON (RIGHT)

MARCH 9, 2003: Artest receives the first automatic suspension of his career for his sixth flagrant foul of the season, on the Trailblazers' Bonzi Wells. (Artest would receive two more that season.) Later, as a teammate of Wells's on the Sacramento Kings, Artest playfully threatens to kill Bonzi if he doesn't re-sign with Sacramento, stating, "Unless he wants to die, he's got to stay [with the Kings]." Months later, Wells signs with the Houston Rockets.

CRESCENT (RIGHT)

JANUARY 30, 2003: Artest is suspended four games and fined $84,000 after he gets into a confrontation with Miami Heat head coach and basketball legend Pat Riley. Artest confronts Riles first to argue about a foul call against him. Riley orders, "Don't talk to me." Later, the warring continues as Artest walks toward the Heat bench with arm flexed, bumping against Riley, which elicites a shove from Riles in response. Artest culminates his night by flipping the bird to the Miami crowd. Truly a masterful final act.

FIRST QUARTER

JANUARY 4, 2003: After a close loss against the Knicks, Artest hurls a television monitor in anger and smashes a $100,000 high-definition camera. He is suspended for three games for the incident, fined $35,000, and asked to pay the difference for the camera.

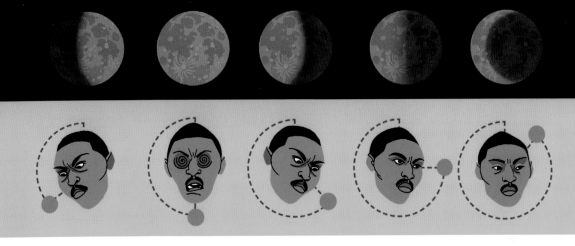

WAXING GIBBOUS

SUMMER 1999: Just prior to his rookie season with the Chicago Bulls, Artest applies for a job at a local Circuit City, listing "NBA player" as his last job and Bulls president Jerry Krause as a reference. All so he could get a discount on home electronics—and because, as Artest notes, "I had a friend who worked there."

FULL MOON

NOVEMBER 19, 2004: The Motor City is burning. The Artest-inspired melee between the Pacers and the Pistons may be the all-time most absurd event in sports history. Months after the incident, Artest appears on the cover of *Penthouse*, offering to engage in a boxing match with Ben Wallace on pay-per-view.

WANING GIBBOUS

MAY 25, 2002: One of Artest's baby-mamas accuses him of grabbing her around the neck and arm during a dispute, yet declines to file charges. Four months later, another girlfriend, Kimsha—later his wife—calls the police complaining of being hit and scratched during a fight with Artest. In 2007, Artest is arrested for domestic violence, again following complaints from Kimsha that he slapped her and pushed her to the floor, attempting to prevent her from calling 911.

LAST QUARTER

SUMMER 2004: Ron records a country song, "This Is My Song," with his 78-year-old neighbor, Doris, from Zionsville, Indiana. Artest explains that they developed a relationship when Doris baked him a cake to welcome him to the neighborhood. Of the song, Artest stated, "I'm not rapping, I'm like, singing, but really like, screaming, like, 'The pain...'"

CRESCENT (LEFT)

FEBRUARY 15, 2004: Ron-Ron wears mismatched sneakers throughout the 2004 All-Star Game, in hopes of landing a shoe deal. The next year, he becomes the only NBA player to be sponsored by the German shoe company k1x (kay-one-ex).

VINCE CARTER

Heartbreaker

In 1999, Michael Jordan, the NBA's consummate winner, showman, and marketing asset, retired for the second time. Jordan had been the ultimate symbol of the NBA's boom in popularity during the 1980s; while Magic Johnson and Larry Bird had started the ball rolling several years earlier, Jordan was the culmination. His departure was a critical blow to a league that had just begun to understand how to sell itself.

The hunt had already begun for the Next Jordan, a designation that could describe either on-court style (Harold Miner) or crossover appeal (Grant Hill). But on the eve of MJ's second retirement, providence arrived in the form of rookie Raptors guard Vince Carter. Like Jordan, Carter had attended the fabled University of North Carolina. Like the young MJ, Carter could leap and dunk in ways that had previously seemed unimaginable. He had that same coarsely balletic quality to his play, those sweeping motions that were at once polished and violent. And with his shaved head and forced scowl, even Carter's appearance was an acceptable facsimile of Jordan's.

The Greek chorus of the league loudly agreed. Raptors teammate Jerome Williams raved, "Every day I go to work, it's like, 'I saw something today you'll never believe. You won't even understand it.' It's just one of those things where he just has a God-given talent to be very creative with a round object." T-Wolves coach Flip Saunders stated bluntly, "I want to see somebody better than Vince Carter. He single-handedly beat us." And Jason

Kidd gushed, "That's the next coming. Michael Jordan hasn't done that, nobody's done that. I think everybody sitting here, even myself as a teammate, enjoyed watching a player like that."

But there was one key problem: While Michael Jordan lived to play basketball, Carter always seemed to embrace his calling reluctantly.

The NBA is littered with big men who find employment simply by virtue of their bigness. Seven-footers like Erick Dampier and Elden Campbell have always lacked in motivation or engagement; Adonal Foyle, a well-liked journeyman with a nose for political activism, plays professional basketball only because he can. Those with a Jordanesque skill set—jumpers, leapers, game-changing scorers—tend to overplay, asserting themselves too much and falling victim to the "selfish" label. While he may bear a superficial resemblance to Jordan, Carter fits more into that archetype of big man passivity than into the mold of the ball-hogging game changer.

To paraphrase *The Wire*, Carter just ain't built for shit. The irony, of course, is that every fiber of his physical being is. He seems immune to the norms of athletic and competitive culture, despite fitting innumerable criteria for the role of modern superstar. Vince Carter has left a trail of destruction and disappointment in his wake, one that seems to mean nothing to him at all. One might go so far as to call him a sociopath, were it not for the fact that off the court, he's a perfectly well-adjusted, well-meaning, and convivial human being.

Carter's actual career has been a strange admixture of apathy, insecurity, and disappoint-ment. The league's 1999 Rookie of the Year, he became a household name in that year's dunk contest—an event synonymous with Jordan's ascent. The dunk was, and still is, the crack cocaine of the NBA, for players and fans alike: a sharp thrill not necessarily conducive to success in the daily grind. Carter's performance rivaled MJ's finest moments in that arena. It was so hair-raising in its perfection that, in effect, it pulled the heart out of the contest, crippling it for years to come. When Carter gave a throat-slash gesture after his last go, it was more than that year's competition that was over. He'd actually succeeded in supplanting the all-time king of the event.

The irony here was that this contest is, at best, an experimental lab for moves that will one day be unleashed in games, or a rep-building showcase designed to strike fear into the hearts of colleagues. Carter's performance was so crystalline, so choreographed, that it bore little resemblance to any conceivable in-game situation. His most famous in-game dunk came in the 2000 Olympics, when Carter rather conspicuously grew out a mini-fro and unleashed some hidden wellsprings of aggression. The USA cruised to the gold, but there was at least one indelible highlight: Vince leaping entirely over the head of 7'1" French center Frederic Weis on the way to a ferocious dunk. Carter screamed like a gladiator, and yet he might as well have been employing a prop under the Vegas lights. (Drafted by the Knicks, Weis left American basketball the next season.)

The Jordan parallels continued. Tracy McGrady arrived to play the Scottie Pippen role, and a 2000 playoff appearance signaled an end to a culture of losing. However,

McGrady soon left for Orlando, leaving Carter to carry the team. The next season, Vince's Raptors met Allen Iverson's Sixers in the second round of the playoffs. Iverson's white-hot motivation, diminutive stature, and pit bull resolve couldn't have been further from Carter's accidental brillance. Yet for seven memorable games, the two exchanged monumental scoring figures and bouts of pure competitive fury, as Carter looked for once like a man at home in his own skin.

But then came a moment that would forever seal Carter's fate and spell the end of his time in the NBA's elite. Honoring a promise he had made to his mother, Carter had been working to finish his degree at UNC. It just so happened that the graduation ceremony was the morning of a crucial game, possibly the most important of his career. Vince opted to take the short trip south to Chapel Hill, going down the night before and returning in time for pregame preparations. Fittingly, the game came down to a single Carter shot—which clanked out, sending the Sixers ahead to the Eastern Conference Finals.

The backlash was swift: For outraged fans, the graduation jaunt was to blame for Carter's miss, having placed unnecessary fatigue on his body and possibly distracted him. Others took it as proof that Carter saw there was more to life than basketball—or, even if they didn't want to say so, that their star player could be only so interested in this moment of utmost athletic tension. It was around this time that MJ washed his hands of Carter, "he's dead to me" style—as if to make a public statement that, for all the similarities, Carter had missed the point.

His career since has been a steady slide into

NAME: Vincent Lamar Carter
BORN: January 26, 1977
HEIGHT: 6 ft 6 in (11.98 m)
WEIGHT: 220 lb (99.8 kg)
HOMETOWN: Daytona Beach, FL

SPIRIT ANIMAL: Eagle ray

PLAYER COMPARISON: Strike in Spike Lee's *Clockers*, DaVinci's Tim Thomas, rec-league Antichrist.

VERY REVEALING HOBBY: Carter played saxophone in his high school band and has continued to dabble. He favors the smooth jazz stylings of Najee and Mike Phillips, and had Brian McKnight perform at his 2004 wedding.

NOTABLE REMARK: "I'm going to make a lot of people eat their words when it's time."

NICKNAME: "Half Man, Half Amazing," bestowed upon him by Kenny Smith after the 2000 Dunk Contest. In recent years, it's taken on a decidedly inhuman connotation. Same for "Vinsanity," which now sounds like a form of neurosis.

BENTLEY, ESCALADE, OR COUPE: Grown-ass Benz.

irrelevance. From that fateful game on, Carter never again glowed like a leading man. While a superstar would've taken it upon himself to lift up the team, Vince seemed to wait around for someone else to catalyze things or step up only when things happened to swing Toronto's way anyway. His injuries became more and more frequent, leading many to question his toughness—or commitment.

In 2002, he missed months due to something known as "jumper's knee"; during his absence from the team, he appeared onstage dancing at a Nelly concert. He dunked less and less, severing that visceral tie with the community. In 2003, he suggested the team trade the fourth pick in the best draft ever for "some veteran help"; they ended up with versatile big man Chris Bosh, who gladly accepted the role of franchise player. It made perfect sense when, in 2004, Carter was shipped to New Jersey for pennies on the dollar. The Raptors had come to see him as a ghost, of the kind that occasionally chipped tiles or flooded sinks, while the Nets could use him as an accessory to point guard supreme Jason Kidd. Of course, Carter's utter disinterest in staying with the Raptors gave them little to no leverage, meaning he screwed them even on the way out.

With most active players, our fandom depends on seeing the character in their game. Each man plays with a unique style, one that

A Day in the Life of Vince Carter's Graduation

When a student-athlete opts to finish his degree, he's hailed as a man of integrity and maturity. It's thus ironic that one of Vince Carter's most infamous moments came when, in 2001, he flew to Chapel Hill to walk in his graduation ceremony the morning of the Eastern Conference Semis' decisive Game 7. Vince played well but missed a go-ahead shot at the buzzer. Did the travel itself take a toll? Was it a distraction from basketball? Or was it something else that day? Finally, science can tell us just how much of an effect this episode had on Vince's physical and mental basketball capacity.

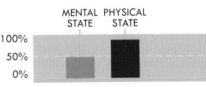

MENTAL PHYSICAL
STATE   STATE

100%
50%
0%

4 p.m. Saturday: Carter, accompanied by his mother, his agent, Raptors owner Larry Tanenbaum, and general manager Glen Grunwald, departs Toronto aboard Tanenbaum's private jet bound for Chapel Hill, NC. He has a fear of flying, but the seats are comfy.

10:30 a.m.: Jostled by autograph hounds as he reflects on what's happened, Carter departs campus.

12:05 p.m.: Arrives at Philadelphia International Airport. The runway has potholes. Grunwald's now humming Mahler.

12:20: Arrives at Raptors' hotel. Stubs toe while trying to find a towel.

12:30: Attends a team meeting. Remembers that his team needs him; Antonio Davis hugs him and it doesn't hurts.

1:25: Gives Keon Clark the last sandwich on the catering tray. He doesn't need seconds.

reflects both his professional experience and something of his personality. In Carter's case, this model simply doesn't apply. In fact, the opposite seems true.

Compare Carter's slightly creepy presence in the league with that of his cousin Tracy McGrady. T-Mac, awash in pain and humanity, disrupts the usual separation of life and sport. But in T-Mac's case, all his real-life travail comes rushing back into his game. Carter, on the other hand, is distracted from basketball by something either more important or simply more real. His game is a glassy-eyed harlot, a beautiful black hole that threatens everything that makes the NBA so profound. This is the kind of thing that makes fans call T-Mac "bottomlessly soulful" and Carter "without a soul," and makes us feel that watching McGrady is more than just an exercise in aesthetics and entertainment.

Vince Carter does have a soul; he's a devoted father, and he wept openly when asked to speak at the dedication of the high school gym that bears his name. Unfortunately, it remains hidden from us as fans, at least when we watch him perform. And that such overpowering, sublime play could be so empty is enough to cause any basketball lover a crisis of faith. You could never convince Carter that his career has been tragic, but it has visited anguish upon nearly everyone who finds meaning in this great American game.

4:30: Glen Grunwald sits next to Carter and won't stop humming Herb Alpert.

5:30: Arrives at Raleigh-Durham Airport, flooded with memories and relieved to land.

5:55: Arrives at his hotel in Chapel Hill. Takes a bath, watches a really sad episode of *Martin*.

8:30 a.m. Sunday: Departs hotel and arrives on North Carolina campus, signs autographs and takes pictures. He's got butterflies.

9:30: Participates in graduation ceremonies, receiving a ceremonial undergraduate degree in African-American studies. He cries, mom cries, and basketball disappears from his mind.

3:45: Carter departs hotel with the team en route to the First Union Center. The adrenaline starts flowing, but maybe he could've used that extra sandwich.

4:00: Arrives at First Union Center with the team. He dodges the press, who are on his ass about the trip, and finds some olives in the trainer's office.

4:35: Puts on deodorant. Vince hates odor. Too bad sweating releases toxins, and most antiperspirants plug your pits.

5:35: Carter is introduced with Raptors' starting lineup. Bumps chests, remembers what a tear he's been on, stretches a little extra.

CONCLUSION: Carter experienced many ups and downs over that 24-hour period. However, he was at 100 percent by all accounts during the team meeting. Anyone looking for a scapegoat needs to focus on the time between the team meeting and tip-off.

STEPHON MARBURY

Hategoat

The greatest American tragedy of the individual is not River Phoenix, nor Len Bias, nor Duane Allman, nor any of a parade of coked-up teenage strumpets depositing their talents at the rehab clinic gates. That distinction goes to Stephon Marbury, the lone cub slowly losing his mental faculties as a result of the scars the NBA bestows on young, unequipped individuals.

Marbury has endured the most awkward career of his generation and emerged with the status of the league's lone "star" journeyman. Contaminating seemingly everything that he touches,

WHAT HE GIVES US:
The pitiless misery of post-millennial New York.

WHAT HE STANDS FOR:
Turning one's own oblivion into notoriety.

WHY WE CARE:
Because nobody else does.

he has been tossed from team to team—hindering squads on the rise, diminishing the status of near-contenders, and destroying teams' dreams at the apex of hope.

Marbury entered the league in 1996, during the waning years of the Isiah-Magic-Stockton era of point guard dominance (only Stockton was still playing), with the stage seemingly set for his rise. But it was not to be. Within a few years, Jason Kidd, Steve Nash, and even Sam Cassell emerged as likelier candidates for PG supremacy. Although these six-footers fought no bloody turf wars, Marbury mounted a personal struggle to be first among his peers—one that would eventually contribute to his undoing.

Marbury is the ultimate individual in a league that preaches the sanctity of team play. He has been tarred with the title of "shoot-first point guard"—widely interpreted as a synonym for "me-first douchebag." *His* starting spot, *his* playing time, *his* financial earnings, and *his* shots have always held primary importance for him, and for this prioritization he has always been unapologetic. He has become the face of that archetypal spoiled athlete that the Mitch Alboms of the world love to admonish. He demonizes Commissioner Stern, despite avoiding legal trouble or accruing technical fouls on the court. Marbury values comfort in his own strange eccentricity more than playoff wins, and in a league that seeks to champion collectives over constituents, Marbury takes his abuse with maniacal pride.

Marbury's missteps toward insanity began with the Minnesota Timberwolves, who drafted him in 1996. Playing alongside long-time friend Kevin Garnett on a rising team seemed an ideal situation, but it was one that Marbury would soon spoil. The great Garnett once said, "If you don't like Shaquille O'Neal, there's something wrong with you," and it's fair to adapt his phrase to state, If you don't like *Kevin Garnett*, you have some serious frontal lobe damage. Garnett has been known across the NBA universe as the ultimate teammate and mensch, yet Marbury spurned him in an autistic act of betrayal. The promising young point guard wanted out of Minnesota, after delusionally pining for the same monumental money KG received.

Marbury was flipped to New Jersey, where he began to wither, and in a hummingbird's wink found himself on a flight to Phoenix in exchange for Jason Kidd. While Kidd resurrected the Nets franchise, Marbury stagnated in Phoenix. Amid the burgeoning talents of Amare Stoudemire, Joe Johnson, and Shawn Marion, Marbury played the drug-pushing high-schooler poisoning the seventh-graders' minds and relieving them of their innocence. Realizing that Marbury's talents would get them nowhere, the Suns bounced him to the New York Knicks, in exchange for salary cap relief (which, as with NJ, would ultimately net Phoenix their own franchise savior, Steve Nash). Marbury was to breathe manna-infused oxygen back into the city of dreams, and the Knicks would provide a glorious homecoming for Coney Island's finest. For the first time in years, a human smile supplanted Marbury's perma-scowl.

Whatever honeymoon period there was in New York, however, quickly deteriorated toward marital estrangement. Marbury failed to secure a single playoff victory or .500 record. Despite hiring the legendary Larry Brown as head coach, New York continued to lose with Marbury at the helm. Brown often criticized Marbury's play and the two feuded publicly. In 2006, the Knicks fired Brown, and the embattled general manager Isiah Thomas took over head coaching duties as a last-ditch effort to guide Marbury and the Knicks back to respectability.

With Isiah front and center, things for the Knicks and for Marbury became ever more tumultuous. A sexual harassment lawsuit against Thomas by a former Knicks employee landed Marbs in the witness box, where he, a married man, admitted to having steamily fornicated in an SUV with a young Knicks intern after a quick jaunt to a Westchester strip club. As the trial played out, Marbury, perhaps embarrassed by being thrust in front of cameras under such odd circumstances, did himself one worse by threatening Isiah Thomas with blackmail over playing time. "Isiah has to start me," Marbury reportedly warned. "I've got so much [stuff] on Isiah and he knows it. He thinks he can [get] me. But I'll [get] him first. You have no idea what I know." During the 2007–08 season Isiah banned an injured Marbury from Knicks home games altogether, the metaphorical exclusion of Marbury, no longer possessing anthropoid mental capabilities, from the tribe.

Insanity now envelops all of Marbury's daily words and deeds. He recently discussed his hopes for ending his basketball career playing in Italy. He has hosted his own sports talk show, complete with promos in which he mockingly impersonates journalist Stephen A. Smith (a longtime Marbury detractor). He has openly beefed with LeBron James over sneaker prices and has subliminally dissed

James in stating, "I'm not the dude on the ESPYs, getting carried on a throne. I'm not him. I'm the good guy, not the bad guy. I don't want to be carried on the throne . . . I just want to walk among the people." He has ranted bizarrely on WNBC's *Mike'd Up* show, stating that the Knicks can "steal the trophy" and calling his wife his "better ho." He has claimed to have found God. And he has penned a schizophrenic blog on the *New York Post* website, responding to commenters with couplets such as:

> *You don't know about me.*
> *You don't know my life.*
>
> *You heard about me.*
> *You heard about my life.*

Perhaps the most defining and damning moment in Starbury's career was the day he told the world what he thought of himself. Just prior to a 2005 game against his playoff-tested contemporary Jason Kidd, Marbury stated, "I love Jason Kidd, he is a great point guard . . . [But] how am I comparing myself to him when I think I'm the best point guard to play basketball? That makes no sense. I can't compare myself to somebody when I already think I'm the best." Reiterating, Marbury said, "I'm telling you what it is. I know I'm the best point guard in the NBA." It was an outlandish statement and an invitation to criticism from experts and casual fans alike. Few stopped to appreciate this rare display of honest confidence from an athlete.

There was no well-groomed "thanks to all my teammates" or eye-roll-inducing "I just care about winning" rhetoric. This has never been Marbury's way. Whether spouting the ridiculous or the insightful, Marbury has never uttered a fraudulent word, nor has he held his tongue. Unfortunately for his legacy, as he has descended into madness, such freakish soundbites now eternally brand him instead of his good deeds, which include developing an affordable sneaker brand and donating thousands of pairs to public schools, as well as an emotional response to victims of Hurricane Katrina. These endeavors will be long forgotten after sports historians pore over the insanity that has gripped Marbury over the past few increasingly bizarre years. One can only hope that some day, some child finds strength in Marbury's story and emulates him as a man who spoke from the heart, even to his detriment.

NAME: Stephon Xavier Marbury
BORN: February 20, 1977
HEIGHT: 6 ft 2 in (1.88 m)
WEIGHT: 205 lb (93 kg)
HOMETOWN: Coney Island, NY

SPIRIT ANIMAL: Prairie vole
PLAYER COMPARISON: Isiah Thomas with less creativity and even fewer friends; a delusional Andre Miller.

Marbury Parcheesi

The game of Parcheesi accurately captures Marbury's career, from his explosive birth in Georgia to his homecoming in New York. He has been granted multiple opportunities to prove his worth, and yet he casts out pawn after pawn, only to meet capture or blockade. Even upon reaching his fated destination with the Knicks, Marbury quickly fell from favorite son to *New York Post* whipping boy. Here we detail the various travels he has taken throughout his strange career.

NEST

Steph was a standout at Georgia Tech (perhaps Marbury's only happy place), where he spent only one year and averaged 18.9 points and 4.5 assists per game. As a Yellowjacket, he was full of flair and smiling promise, showing no signs of what was to come in the NBA.

BLOCKADE

Where it all went terribly awry. As a rookie, Marbury joined forces with his boyhood friend Kevin Garnett for what was certain to be the dominant NBA duo of the 21st century. But once KG signed a monster contract with the Timberwolves that designated him as the Wolves' clear alpha dog, Marbury and his delusional selfishness forced a trade out of Minnesota, pitting the karma gods against him for years to come.

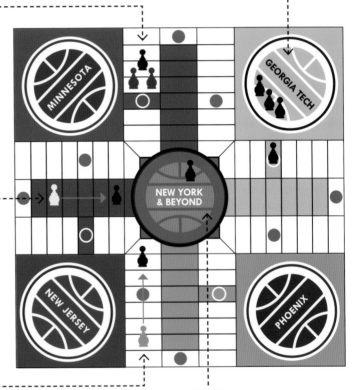

CAPTURE

From Minnesota, Marbury was traded to New Jersey, claiming he wanted to be closer to home. Marbs spent three dismal years as a Net, failing to advance to the playoffs and getting robbed of a $150,000 necklace during his tenure there.

CAPTURE

Marbury flourished as the ostensible leader of the young talent surrounding him in Phoenix; it was the first time he had been granted such a role. Still, the team had little success during his reign at point guard, and the year following Marbury's departure, Phoenix achieved the best record in the Western Conference.

HOME

Even home does not feel like home for the Coney Island native. Since Marbury arrived, he and Isiah Thomas have been blamed for comprising some dual aura of negativity that will doom the Knicks franchise for eternity. With the New York masses clamoring for his departure just as loudly as they first welcomed him, Marbury will proceed elsewhere, just as he has done so many times. Will it be to another NBA team, an Italian franchise, or the galaxies above? Only time will tell.

The All-Time Greatest NBA Cancers

tephon Marbury has a reputation as a bad influence on teams. But where does he rank all-time, and who else can claim this ignominious distinction? Throughout the NBA's entire history, only seven players have had a higher cumulative "cancer effect" for their careers: that is, only seven players in NBA history have made their new teams worse—and, by their departure, made their old teams better—than Stephon Marbury. Some of the players on this list are predictable, others shocking, but in each case, their malignancy is indisputable. This is not revisionism; rather, it allows us to discern an evil that all too often hides in plain sight.

Rank and Player	Trade Period		Cancer Effect
1 Cadillac Anderson	1987	1997	150
2 Stromile Swift	2000	2006	118
3 Tony Massenburg	1990	2004	114
4 Juwan Howard	1994	2006	97
5 Junior Harrington	2002	2006	96
6 Tim Legler	1989	1999	89
7 Zendon Hamilton	2000	2005	84
8 **Stephon Marbury**	**1996**	**2006**	**80**
9 Vladimir Stepania	1998	2003	70
10 Jo Jo White	1980	1980	70
11 Richard Anderson	1982	1989	65
12 Ben Warley	1962	1969	64

The Cancer Effect

During his first ten years in the league, Marbury was traded three times. In each case, Marbury's old team's record improved dramatically while his new team plummeted in the standings. The chart below shows the change in wins for both teams following the trade, based on the increase or decrease in wins from the previous season. For mid-season trades, the change in wins is based on Marbury's first full season with the new team.

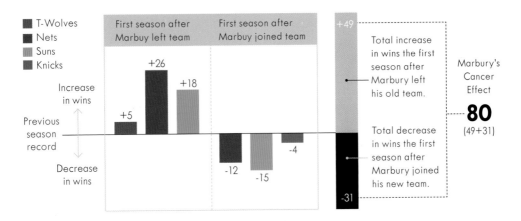

THE 2000 NBA DRAFT

A Legacy of Ruin and Evil

When Y2K descended upon the computerized world, the millennial masses dropped their champagne, grabbed a bunch of canned food, and ran for their sandbagged bunkers. Moments later, an air of calm fell over the land, as the earth's citizens realized there would be no apocalyptic ruin—at least not yet. Civilization would maintain itself through that winter and into the spring. Then came June, and the 2000 NBA draft, a dispersion of the most useless, vile, and dastardly group of ballplayers ever selected in a single year. These young villains ranged from cancerous ball hogs to crumpled nonentities, personifications of boredom, criminals, and guys who were just plain bad at basketball. With all due respect to festering second-rounders Marko Jaric, Brian Cardinal, Jabari Smith, and Khalid El-Amin, here we detail the best of the worst: the most hellish first round in the annals of the NBA.

1 | **KENYON MARTIN** | Cincinnati

A goonish power forward closely identified with exhortative power dunks, flagrant fouls, and decay of knees and legs, Martin came to blows with teammate Alonzo Mourning after mocking Zo's kidney transplant and demanded his college jersey be unretired when Cincy deposed longtime coach Bob Huggins. Was once challenged to a Don King–sponsored boxing match by fellow fuck-up Tim Thomas, who called Martin a "fake thug" and "fugazy."

2 **STROMILE SWIFT** LSU

The classic "what if" player, Swift has never been able to translate his jackrabbit athleticism and ferocious shot-blocking into sustained production, or even a steady job. His refusal to learn basketball has discouraged such notable coaches as Hubie Brown and Jeff Van Gundy for almost a decade now. Is believed to be poisoning Tyrus Thomas's career by proxy.

3 **DARIUS MILES** East St. Louis High School

Scrawny, striking, and vaguely guardlike, this high school All-American was supposed to approximate Kevin Garnett and save the Clippers. Instead, he got famous for banging his fists on his forehead after baskets, and for a Nike commercial granted on cult appeal alone. He then disappeared into a vortex of inflated contracts, declining youth, and most recently, a blown-out knee that made him get fat.

4 **MARCUS FIZER** Iowa State

Taken despite the presence of Elton Brand on the Chicago roster, Fizer has spent his career floating in and out of the NBA without ever definitively proving he sucks. But there must be something wrong with the dude—otherwise, he'd have found his footing at some point. Often confused with Lonny Baxter, another unlucky PF who eventually ended up licking shots at the White House.

5 **MIKE MILLER** Florida

For a long time the pick of this runt-littered litter, Miller won the ignominious 2001 Rookie of the Year award and was the only rook to not miss a single game that season. However, his propensity for making buddies has made him a peculiar kind of cancer; his friendship with Tracy McGrady made it very difficult for their team to trade Miller in 2003.

6 **DERMARR JOHNSON** Cincinnati

Johnson's presence barely registered in the league until 2002, when his Benz hit a tree and his neck broke. Instead of never walking again, he had himself back in playing shape for 2003. Johnson must be a real asshole, though, since despite his miraculous comeback and above-average play, no one wants to keep him around. Or maybe they've got him mixed up with DeShawn Stevenson.

7 **CHRIS MIHM** Texas

(To Cleveland) A seven-footer once fantastically considered the top pick in the draft, he plays about two inches shorter than he is. Any team with Mihm at center knows it's in a transition period.

8 JAMAL CRAWFORD — Michigan

(To Chicago)

Through no fault of his own, Crawford structurally fucks up teams from the inside out. The Bulls learned the hard way that he'll never be a point guard; at the same time, his flurries of scoring marked him as an undersized shooting guard, the positional equivalent of a black sheep. That he emerged as the best player on the 2007–08 Knicks, a team defined by its dysfunction and suffering, kind of makes him the king of the cockroaches. Or the one smart guy on *Survivor*.

9 JOEL PRZYBILLA — Minnesota

(To Milwaukee)

The third player in a row to get traded on draft night, "the Vanilla Gorilla" parlayed a strong 2005–06 season into a decent-size contract with the Blazers. While not exactly a cancer, he's never developed any kind of consistent usefulness, making him into a periodic annoyance for those fond of scouring salary situations.

10 KEYON DOOLING — Missouri

(To Clippers)

The poor man's Jamal Crawford, but not good enough to warrant shooting guard consideration. After an okay rookie campaign, he missed most of the 2001–02 season with ankle problems, while the point-guard-starved Clippers continued to hold out hope that he could contribute. Eventually he ended up in Orlando, where, during a meaningless 2006 Magic-Sonics game, he exchanged punches with NBA model citizen Ray Allen, which is kind of like shanking Oprah at a cocktail party.

11 JEROME MOISO — UCLA

This Frenchman's failure to capitalize on his combination of height, perimeter skills, and athleticism has let down a nation. Although Moiso was only the second French player to ever be selected in the NBA draft, he no longer plays for his national team, even though Frederic "the Human Dunk Contest Prop" Weis does. Moiso is also shunned by his countrymen Tony Parker and Boris Diaw, who refuse to let him go to wine tastings with them.

12 ETAN THOMAS — Syracuse

If those earnest, politically conscious slam poets annoy you at the coffee shop, just imagine what it must be like to have one as an NBA teammate. Being in the league is supposed to be about nailing groupies, driving expensive cars, and playing video games all day, not signing petitions and playing bongos. Brendan Haywood, Thomas's teammate on the Washington Wizards, finally decided to take a stand, leading to a series of fierce locker room brawls between the two, including one in which Haywood ripped out one of Etan's signature dreadlocks.

13 COURTNEY ALEXANDER — Fresno State

(To Dallas) Although he started out in the basketball-pure ACC, Alexander was kicked off the team at UVA for allegedly assaulting his girlfriend. Having few other options, he turned to the dark side, transferring to Fresno State to play for Jerry Tarkanian. Despite a few scoring outbursts, injuries have derailed his career, and he hasn't played an NBA game in five years.

14 MATEEN CLEAVES — Michigan State

Cleaves is widely regarded as a great teammate and leader, but it's exactly this quality that causes all the problems. A team's leader cannot average 1.0 point per game, as the disconnect between talk and action leads to an awkward locker room environment. Teams finally recognized this and sent him down to the D-League, where he can lead as much as he wants.

15 JASON COLLIER — Georgia Tech

(To Houston) Collier's premature death from an enlarged heart at the age of 28 proves what a breeding ground for Satan this draft really is.

16 HEDO TURKOGLU — Turkey

At 6'10", he has played every position from point guard to power forward during his NBA career, which sounds pretty awesome, but is really just annoying. Turkoglu is like the smart friend that never does his homework but still manages to get an A on the test. He's finally hit his stride with the Magic and proved himself to be the hands-down best player from this draft, but Kings fans have to be wondering what took him so damn long.

17 DESMOND MASON — Oklahoma State

The former slam dunk champion's athleticism and interest in fine art say "franchise player," but his production says "frustrating bench player." Mason irritates teammates by making them come to his gallery openings and by turning the locker room into figure-drawing class. That might be cool in Oklahoma, but it doesn't fly in Brew City.

18 QUENTIN RICHARDSON — DePaul

Although he has shown flashes of vast potential, Q is best known for selling his soul to the devil along with former Clippers teammate Darius Miles, an alliance they surreptitiously announced by constantly pointing to where the invisible devil horns sprout from their heads. Since his halcyon Clipper days, life has brought only woe for Young Quentin, from a failed engagement to Brandy Norwood to his incurable back problems.

19 JAMAAL MAGLOIRE — Kentucky

Magloire is an unremarkable big man who takes everything too seriously. The best example of his humorless approach to the game is his workmanlike 19 points and 8 rebounds in the 2004 All-Star Game, which threw off the curve and made everyone else look like the lazy, dunk-happy players most casual sports fans already thought they were. Thanks a lot.

20 CRAIG "SPEEDY" CLAXTON — Hofstra

Claxton missed his entire rookie year after suffering a devastating knee injury during the preseason. Since then, the only somewhat speedy point guard has averaged just 47.4 games a season. As a tribute to Claxton's maddening innocuousness, celebrity nobodies Rob and Big named their turtle after him.

21 MORRIS PETERSON — Michigan State

Mo Pete had the longest tenure with the Raptors of any player in the team's history, dooming the franchise's emergence from NBA middle-of-the-roadness with his mind-numbing inconsistency and speckles of genius. When the Raptors finally resurfaced as a playoff-caliber team in the post–Vince Carter era, Peterson bitched about playing time, whining, "They want me to sacrifice and not start to help the team . . . and that's affecting me."

22 DONNELL HARVEY — Florida

Harvey holds the distinguished honor of being the only player to provide absolutely no help to five NBA teams (Orlando, New Jersey, Dallas, Phoenix, Denver), a CBA team (the Sioux Falls Skyforce), and a Euroleague team (Banvitspor, Turkey). If only the NBDL was around when Harvey was playing, he could have contaminated a fourth league.

23 DESHAWN STEVENSON — Washington Union (CA) HS

DeShawn entered the league under treacherous circumstances, getting beat up by his high school teammates on draft night and turning himself in on a statutory rape charge of having sex with a 14-year-old during his rookie season. Later, D-Stev would embarrassingly spat with LeBron James, calling him "overrated" and a Jay-Z fanboy, and claiming a monopoly on sub-chin facial hair, warning, "Tell LeBron to cut that beard off and stop copying me."

24 DALIBOR BAGARIC — Benston Zagreb (Croatia)

Bagaric's tumorousness emerged only overseas, where he clashed with legendary Croatian coach Jasmin Repesa and ditched the yearning Croatian national team in 2006. Although only Croatian-language news outlets have documented this conflict, a rough translation of one report reveals, "Centre Gyros, Dalibor Bargain with overpast crop had into a jostle with Repešom when had a menu relation Bagarica FIBA—plus because had self-willed desert to prepare then first into a tomu is required to seek the reasons otkazivanja."

25 IAKOVOS TSAKALIDIS — AEK (Greece)

Tsakalidis's shittiness began prior to his NBA career, when he literally jeopardized the life of his Greek agent, Gus Polites. As Tsaka fled AEK for the NBA, furious Greek fans blamed Polites's influence and began sending him death threats. The Suns ended up drafting "Jake" with the expectation that he would one day battle Shaq in the post, yet the guy couldn't even beat out Chris Dudley and Daniel Santiago for playing time.

26 MAMADOU N'DIAYE — Auburn

Although N'diaye may be the first Senegalese player ever to play in the NBA, he has brought shame to his native country for holding the least awesome name of any Senegalese-born player in the league; he is a millennially distant fifth, behind Pape Sow, Saer Sene, Boniface N'Dong, and Cheikh Samb.

27 PRIMOZ BREZEC — Olimpija (Slovenia)

With Brezec's teams longing for the oversized Slovenian to show some passionate aggression, Brezec's only evidence of fire came when he walloped the Orlando Magic's mascot, Stuff the Magic Dragon. Brezec then reportedly uttered to the mythical beast, "Fuck you. I'll fuck you up."

28 ERICK BARKLEY — St. John's

During Barkley's overwhelmingly underwhelming rookie campaign, he ill-fatedly promised, "I guarantee in a year or two, I'll be starting on somebody else's team." Perhaps a more ominous quote comes from Cancer Emeritus Stephon Marbury, who promised that Barkley would "be a top-five [NBA draft] pick, easy."

29 MARK MADSEN — Stanford

Madsen twice reached into the lowest depths of NBA excrement, once in a shameful act of unashamed tanking, when the offensively challenged center hoisted seven three-pointers in the Timberwolves' last game of the 2005–06 season to secure favorable draft positioning. The other instance came when the bullish Madsen collided with the adorable T. J. Ford, almost paralyzing Ford and sidelining the diminutively cuddly guard for an entire season.

Chapter V

People's Champs

Stars Stuffed with the Gravity of the Masses

Fans, crowds, dollars, loyalty . . . without masses and masses of people, sport is but a pantomime. And basketball is certainly dependent on the eyes and wallets of the many. But even beyond this bottom-line populism, it produces figures who have a unique bond with the masses, adored to the degree that the Master Builders are worshipped. These People's Champs, avatars of mortality in a game crowded with perfection, are the kind of celebrity we relate to. (This despite the fact that none of us could ever score once on any of them in a game of one-on-one.)

Of course, this being a business, popularity can be manufactured and true human magnetism co-opted. Yet what makes these players so notable is the way their relationship with fans seems strangely independent of the basketball-industrial complex, the machinery of marketing that drives the construction of the modern athlete. So endearing, so seemingly approachable are these players (at least in spirit) that they create a grassroots magic all their own. No matter what Madison Avenue thinks, or what the mainstream scribes write, these are the guys who will always inspire the warmest feelings among the real fans. They may not change the game, but they bring you and me that much closer to it.

CARMELO ANTHONY
Charm City Graduate

In 1996, Allen Iverson wrecked the league—for some—by bringing in braids, hip-hop, oceans of ink, and a remarkable honesty about growing up hard. The timing couldn't have been worse; Michael Jordan, the NBA's one and only model for an individual savior, was on his way out, and the people who sell basketball for a living were in a panic. Was the street game finally going to invade their high-walled (and highly profitable) preserve? Then, in 2003, came the miraculous entrance of high school phenom LeBron James, amid a storm of biblical imagery, marketing heft, and sublime basketball powers. They called him the next Jordan—because he was good, of course, but also, and as importantly, because he had the gravitas to brush aside Iverson.

Five years on, the two men represent the opposing halves of a basketball dichotomy: When an athlete starts to matter, the conventional wisdom says, he needs to choose between his inner Iverson and the beckoning Jordan role. But there's an exception: Nuggets forward Carmelo Anthony, who serves as both partner in Bron's New NBA and heir to Iverson's mantle of authenticity. Throughout his time in the league, Anthony has struggled with these two parts of his soul. Today, he's the antihero made whole for the King James era.

Coming into the 2003 draft, Anthony was part and parcel with LeBron. In fact, 'rows and tats aside, he was in some ways more reputable. While James had made himself a billion-dollar corporate entity just out of high school, Melo had opted to attend Syracuse University, where, in one short year, he'd brought in an NCAA title. He lacked Bron's flash and apocalyptic ability, instead

WHAT HE GIVES US:
The game's most elegant scorer and most eligible cool kid.

WHAT HE STANDS FOR:
Expertise filtered through subversion.

WHY WE CARE:
No one's "made something of himself" quite like Carmelo Anthony.

relying on sound shooting and smart, team-mate-friendly conduct. If James was magnificent and a little seedy, Anthony was a proven winner who also struck most as down-to-earth. The two harked back to the arrival of Magic and Bird, twin horsemen who augered a new era of prosperity.

True, Anthony came into the league with a winner's pedigree, a Magic-like megawatt grin, and a baby-faced charm that actually made basketball youth seem pleasant and, well, youthful. Yet he's also brought an updated version of Iverson's street cred. While Iverson's fans struggled to relate to the urban-rural weirdness of their hero's hometown, Newport News, Virginia, Anthony's Baltimore was hand-delivered to the masses in the form of the HBO series *The Wire*. The contrast is telling. Iverson was a gruff, defensive pioneer; Anthony—and, more precisely, his public relations people—feel that Melo's upbringing can be a strength.

The strongest evidence of this came in 2006, when Melo conceived of a Nike ad that transformed *The Wire*'s dystopic Baltimore into a symbol of uplift. Underneath police helicopters and what looked like eternal night, Anthony strolled through a bombed-out landscape. Along the way, he encountered esteemed (and non-hood) basketball icons like Syracuse coach Jim Boeheim and Hall of Famer Bernard King, whose game Melo sometimes echoes. Instead of Bodymore, Murderland, Anthony's shoes announced the slogan "B.More." To Anthony, the place he came from represents both roots he won't forsake and the motivation to never stop striving.

None of this would be possible were it not for Iverson's efforts, or for Melo's own discretion when it comes to constructing his public persona. Anthony has had his missteps. Most notoriously, he performed in the street DVD *Stop Snitchin'*, which strongly discouraged cooperating with police investigations. While Anthony appeared in only a single "scene" and had no lines, he had been filmed hanging out in the company of those who condoned gunning down witnesses. Melo has also been busted with someone else's weed, beaten down a fellow clubgoer who'd heckled his fiancée, and sunk into a depression that earned him the media label "moody."

Unlike Iverson, though, he's anything but a rebel on the court. After weathering a sophomore slump, Anthony matured into one of the NBA's most potent offensive weapons. And it's not just that he puts points on the board; any number of less vaunted players can do that. It's the way he does it. Despite his deceptive athleticism, strength, and speed, Anthony's ultimately a gigantic basketball nerd. He deploys moves, works through possessions like logic puzzles, and thinks about solutions, not dominance. Certainly he's aggressive, as he outwits a defender with footwork, utilizes his post game on smaller opponents, or picks just the right moment to take someone off the dribble. But the satisfaction you feel watching him is anything but ecstatic. It's cool, head-nodding, and lives up to his inevitable nickname.

By 2006, the Melo/Bron comparisons were a thing of the past. Anthony had discovered his own niche: on-court classicist, with a touch of the hood credibility that forever evades LeBron. A necessary force for the future, but not square enough to stand up and wave his arms about it. As that season started, you could've made the argument that Anthony was more popular than James—at least in the same way that while Kobe always led in jersey sales, Iverson couldn't walk down a crowded street without provoking faints.

Then came the MSG Brawl. With Denver in town to take on the lowly Knicks, and the score gulf rapidly widening, New York coach Isiah Thomas started to fume. Instructions may have been given, warnings may have been relayed. What's certain is that when Anthony protégé J. R. Smith uncorked a prodigious slam on a fast break, diminutive firebrand (and former college defensive back) Nate Robinson made a solid tackle on his man. This prompted fisticuffs and mass migrations; at some point, Anthony open-hand assaulted Knick Mardy Collins and then ran away, smack-dab into a fifteen-game suspension. It was a relatively minor event that, because it was Melo and because it was New York, turned into a firestorm of controversy.

Much was made of his supposed cowardice, his rekindled thuggishness, and the blow Melo's immaturity had dealt the Nuggets' season. In one night, he'd gone from an MVP candidate who led the league in scoring to a player who put the whole league back in crisis mode. The sinkhole had opened beneath Melo's feet, and once again, the mainstream's acceptance of him, and all he stood for, was in jeopardy. And then the Nuggets pulled off a coup for the ages: They acquired none other than Allen Iverson, who was being shopped furiously by the Sixers. From a public relations perspective, this was pure gold. It swept the brawl off of the radar, replacing it with a delectable question—"Can they coexist?"—that the media savored in every form imaginable.

NAME: Carmelo Kyan Anthony
BORN: May 29, 1984
HEIGHT: 6 ft 8 in (2.03 m)
WEIGHT: 230 lb (104 kg)
HOMETOWN: Baltimore, MD

SPIRIT ANIMAL: Sun bear

PLAYER COMPARISON: Bernard King with a stylist; Alex English with cash in a boxing gym.

NOTABLE REMARK: "I respect everything that AI do, just for the simple fact that he came from the same place—not technically, but he came from the same place I came from. Which is the grimy . . . the streets, put it like that. So for somebody to stay true to themselves and not care about what nobody else thinks, then you get a following. You get people to start respecting you on a whole totally different level when they see that you real."

ADVENTURES IN CASH: Despite his numerous charitable donations to worthy causes, Anthony is no ascetic; he has also sponsored an Indy car team alongside Kiss letch-ball Gene Simmons.

More subtly, it allowed for a lot of wide-angle coverage of the two men, softening Iverson's hard edges and reinforcing the sympathetic view of Melo. Anthony could state, "We've kind of been through the same things . . . he's a guy who feels my pain more than anybody in the NBA," while AI could follow with "A lot of times people think that we're not human and we don't make mistakes like everybody in everyday life. But we do. It's just important for guys to try not to make that mistake twice." It was about the MSG Brawl, and yet it wasn't. It made Iverson into an elder statesman at the same time as he sided with his younger teammate.

With this trade, the Denver Nuggets effectively neutralized the thug cliché. And while it helped save Melo, it was also an extension of his life's work. In 2007–08, the Nuggets were a murderer's row of racially charged NBA stereotypes. In addition to Iverson and Anthony, there was the brutish Kenyon Martin; J. R. Smith, a high school draftee lacking in focus, troubled off the court, and forever bewitching with his potential; and Marcus Camby, a veteran of the badass Knicks teams of the late 1990s. They even had Brazilian big man Nene rocking braids, perhaps the most salient example of pan-African bonding in the league. These Nuggets were beautiful, no matter what people said. That they fell somewhere between pretenders and contenders mattered less than the fact that, finally, such a bunch had to be taken seriously as legitimate working athletes.

Whenever Iverson insisted in the press that "This is Carmelo's team," that's exactly what he meant.

A Prince Among Givers

In 2006, only seven celebrities gave more in public charitable donations than Melo; he came in right behind Tiger Woods, Rosie O'Donnell, and Martha Stewart, and was the only NBA player in the top thirty.

CELEBRITIES (Entertainers & Athletes) Charitable donations, 2006		ATHLETES OR SPORTS-RELATED FIGURES Charitable donations, 2006	
1. Oprah Winfrey	$58,300,000	1. Tiger Woods	$9,500,000
2. Geoffrey Beene	$44,000,000	2. Carmelo Anthony	$4,282,000
3. Jack & Marie Lord	$40,000,000	3. Dwayne "the Rock" Johnson	$2,000,000
4. Barbra Streisand	$11,750,000	4. Arnold Palmer	$2,000,000
5. Tiger Woods	$9,500,000	5. Andre Agassi	$1,070,000
6. Rosie O'Donnell	$5,700,000	6. Tiki & Ronde Barber	$1,000,000
7. Martha Stewart	$5,000,000	7. George Steinbrenner	$1,000,000
8. Carmelo Anthony	$4,282,000	8. Tony Stewart	$1,000,000
9. Pat & Shirley Boone	$3,000,000	9. Mike Sexton	$560,000
10. LeRoy Neiman	$3,000,000	10. Lance Armstrong	$500,000

Source: "The Giving Back 30 List of Largest Charitable Donations"

STYLE GUIDE

Defender's Steps   **Melo's Steps**

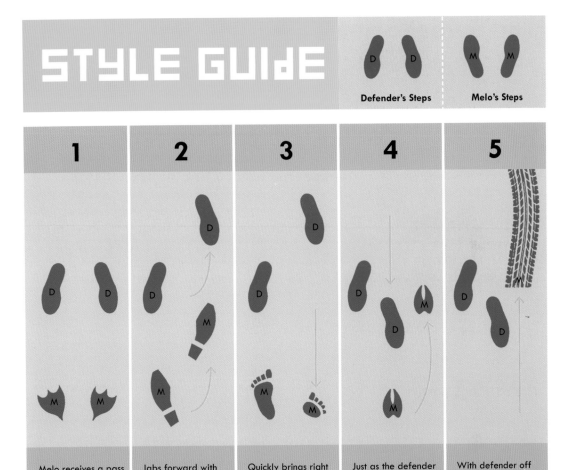

1
Melo receives a pass and squares up with his defender.

STYLE: **Duck**
Appears round and flat-footed, but can actually fly

2
Jabs forward with non-pivot foot as defender steps back.

STYLE: **Salsa**
Fast synchronized steps with a partner in a tight space

3
Quickly brings right foot back before defender can react.

STYLE: **Baby Steps**
Spry and confusing, doesn't always go in a forward direction

4
Just as the defender does react, Melo springs forward.

STYLE: **Deer**
Skittish, lithe, agile, bounds forth as if upon clouds

5
With defender off balance, Melo drives straight to the hoop.

STYLE: **Motocross**
Powerful straight-ahead speed over any sort of terrain

The Sweet Science's Badass Song

In addition to his on-court brilliance and magnetic personality, Carmelo Anthony will be forever associated with the wobbly sucker punch he threw during the 2007 Knicks-Nuggets brawl. Hardly the stuff great boxing is made of. But Melo is actually quite an aficionado, training during the off-season and stoked to pose for photos with fighters like Miguel Cotto. Here's how the boxing universe has influenced Anthony's identity as a player:

OFFENSIVE FOOTWORK—ROBERTO DURAN: "Manos de Piedra" was an attacking machine, using his ferocious pressure to break down his challengers. Duran used his bobbing, darting footwork to get inside and create spaces where he alone could operate. A fearless body destroyer, he never took a backward step or avoided taking on opponents far larger than himself.

Highly advanced in the post, Melo's footwork allows him to get perfect positioning and reliably get points when his jumper isn't falling. A mark of maturity that sets him apart from other high-scoring wings.

THE JAB—LARRY HOLMES: The "Easton Assassin" held the heavyweight championship for one of the longest periods in history, making many defenses of his title. Holmes often won fights almost exclusively with the jab. His style was heavily dependent on this long, metronomic, and consistent punch, which contrasted sharply with the dynamism of the previous champ, Muhammad Ali, and the explosiveness of the following one, Mike Tyson. He would often throw the jab two or three times consecutively, leaving his opponent so distracted he would miss the power punches that followed.

Carmelo's jab-step is renowned throughout the league. It's consistent with a patient, methodical approach to scoring that makes him something of a throwback.

NO DEFENSE—ARTURO GATTI: "Thunder" Gatti was one of the most popular fighters of recent years, despite never being among the sport's true elite. Highly entertaining, he rarely bothered with even the rudiments of defense. Gatti participated in several fights of the year, during which he was content to let his opponent score as many blows as they pleased until he was able to respond in kind. By the end of his career he had needed so much cosmetic surgery to repair his cuts and facial injuries that he looked like a catcher's mitt atop shoulders.

Anthony is a tremendous talent, but he won't be garnering All-Defensive honors anytime soon.

OVERSHADOWED—MIKE McCALLUM: "The Bodysnatcher" was a truly great fighter cursed with bad timing. Too good for his own good, McCallum was born in Jamaica and lacked a loyal nationalistic group of fans to make him a box office star. Though his accomplishments were tremendous, he was overshadowed by the legendary contemporaries of his day: Duran, Hearns, Leonard, and Hagler. Though potentially competitive with any of them, he never got to test himself on the grandest stage.

Anthony came into the league with LeBron and Wade, both of whom have gone on to achieve far greater notoriety and playoff glory. By contrast, at this point Melo's almost underrated in his ever-developing game.

CRAFTINESS WITH THE BALL—BERNARD HOPKINS: The loquacious Hopkins emerged from the mean streets of Philadelphia and a five-year stint in prison to become the longest-reigning middleweight champion of all time. Not blessed with any particular gifts other than his extraordinary toughness, Hopkins had to rely on craft and guile as he fought well into his forties. Low blows, holding, feints, banging to the hips, intentional head butts, sneaky lead rights—"the Executioner" knows every trick in the book.

Even before Melo made leaps and bounds in his physical conditioning, he could beat his man off the dribble through sheer attention to detail. Smart and resourceful, Anthony's drives have always been the opposite of reckless abandon.

SMOOTHNESS—SALVADOR SANCHEZ: The Mexican featherweight fought like a man dancing to violins. Always on his toes, with erect posture and flowing combinations, he was as much a performer as a fighter. Sanchez never lost his bouncing, liquid movement, even in the final rounds of his most difficult contests. Despite his punch-flattened nose, he had the sweet face of a Spanish prince.

If you had to describe Melo's game in one word, it would most likely be "smooth." It's how to keep things polished and professional while maintaining that all-important swagger.

RICAN PRIDE—WILFRED BENITEZ: Though he had a short peak, Benitez was one of boxing and Puerto Rico's first great heroes. A natural, he became a contender at only fifteen years old and, at seventeen, the youngest champion in any weight class. Raised in a boxing family, he was called "Radar" because he was so aware of his opponent's movements. Benitez was an electric and elusive fighter who never went into the ring without his trademark thin moustache.

Melo's father, who died of cancer when he was two, was Puerto Rican; this Hispanic heritage was largely unknown at first, but has now become an integral part of his image and appeal.

YAO MING

Big Human

In Chinese culture, the firstborn son bears a heavy burden, with tremendous familial responsibilities and the expectation that he will achieve great things. Among the generation of Chinese men now entering adulthood, no one carries a heavier burden than Yao Ming. At 7'6", with the intelligence and smoothness that can make a man who happens to be tall into advanced basketball weaponry, Yao has been hailed as the first Chinese player with a real chance to excel in the NBA. There have been a handful of others, most notably Wang Zhizhi, a seven-footer whose main role on the Dallas Mavericks was to hit meaningless threes, drive the score up, and deliver free chalupas into the arms of adoring fans. But Yao was the chosen one, the athletic face of a nation—like Hank Greenberg was for the Jews or badminton player Taufik Hidayat is for Indonesia.

Shanghai, Yao's hometown, is the center of Chinese capitalism and a symbol of the nation's gradual move toward the modern West. But Yao's journey to America had nothing to do with the free market and everything to do with the state's athletic apparatus. His first pro team, the Shanghai Sharks, was under the thumb of the nation's basketball program, which lived in fear that its best players would leave for America and never come back. When, in 2002, rumors swirled that Wang, even then a less important player than Yao, might defect to the U.S., the Chinese government sent two military officials to ensure that he returned to China. Yao's own move to the NBA was

WHAT HE GIVES US:
A trip back to the future in a Geely Chengbao.

WHAT HE STANDS FOR:
Globalization that we can all believe in.

WHY WE CARE:
Despite his mighty burden, he remains light of heart.

postponed several times by the Chinese government, largely out of concern over this sort of incident.

For many Americans, Yao represented their first genuine exposure to the realities of modern China. From afar, he looked like an Asian Ivan Drago, created in a Cold War basketball laboratory from the genes of the nation's most exceptional players. His height alone made him an imposing curiosity. But Yao had already demonstrated in international play that he was no mere novelty. Stronger than Shawn Bradley, more fluid than Romanian giant Gheorghe Muresan, Yao entered the NBA as perhaps the most talented man standing taller than 7'4" to ever play the game. He combined his physical gifts with a very solid jump shot, outstanding passing ability, and a strong all-around basketball knowledge. In Yao, roundball observers found all the cherished big-man fundamentals that American youth had supposedly discarded in favor of indulgent dunking and ill-advised threes.

When Yao arrived in the U.S., it became quickly apparent that he was anything but a nationalist robot. Instead, fans discovered a big-hearted, shrewd young man. Even when employing a translator, Yao's sense of humor was bountiful, combining all-out goofiness with intentionally cryptic one-liners. When asked about Dallas Mavs PA announcer "Humble" Billy Hayes repeatedly saying Yao's name in a mocking Chinese accent during a game, Yao responded that "there are lots of branches on the tree and many kinds of birds." His quest to earn a U.S. driver's license became something of a running joke, given his massive size and proclivity for hitting parked cars. Notorious cutups like Cuttino Mobley

and Steve Francis instantly took to the big guy. On the court, he became a foil for Shaquille O'Neal, whom he once aptly described as "a wall of meat." Seeing this mysterious, gigantic foreigner so readily absorbed into the locker room and watching him blossom into one of the league's most quotable figures did wonders for the average American's perception of urban Chinese citizens.

Yao's first showdown with Shaq Fu also had the unexpected effect of unifying the Asian-American community behind him. When asked during Yao's rookie year if he had a message for Yao, Shaq responded by giving an offensively cartoonish imitation of the Chinese language. Asian-Americans of all nationalities were outraged. After Yao stood his ground against the Diesel in their first meeting, Pinoy pundit Emil Guillermo wrote proudly of how Yao blocked a shot from Shaq, whom he likened to "an oversized, over-cooked pot sticker." Before the NBA draft, much had been made of the possibility that Yao would go to the Golden State Warriors, since the Bay Area is home to the nation's densest population of Chinese-Americans—roughly 2.5 million citizens with no athletic hero to call their own. But with the Rockets, Yao has established himself as an individual talent and personality, with an appeal that transcends national boundaries. He has truly become a global icon, ecumenically shilling for everything from Visa cards to Reeboks.

Of course, if Yao had been a bust—if he'd mimicked Wang's career average of 4.4 points per game—then none of this would matter. But Yao was solid even as a rookie, and his first three NBA seasons showed signs of steady improvement. By 2005–06, he had begun to dominate, averaging over 22 points and 10 rebounds a game. Alas, as the ancient Chinese proverb states, "There is no life without pain, just as there is no art without submitting to chaos." Each of Yao's past three seasons has been shortened by injury, making Bill Simmons's description of him as "the next Bill Walton" seem depressingly prophetic. During the 2005–06 season, Yao broke his left foot—the same one that he broke twice as a teenager in China. After recovering from surgery, Yao began the 2006–07 season averaging 26.8 points, 9.7 rebounds, and 2.3 blocks a game, looking like a legitimate MVP candidate—and then was sidelined by yet another injury, this time breaking his right knee. In February 2008, in the midst of a twelve-game Rockets winning streak, Yao learned that he had yet another stress fracture in his left foot, one that would again require surgery. When Yao has been able to play, he has been stellar. But it's hard not to think that his left foot may keep him from ultimately fulfilling his vast potential.

Even if Yao never plays a full season again, he will still have exceeded all expectations and will go down in hoops history as the greatest Asian player of all time. Given China's political realities, to call Yao a People's Champ would seem to have an obvious connotation. But "the people" he represents are not those of Little Red Book rhetoric. Yao doesn't represent the will of the people, or what's best for the people, or anything else Mao may have yammered on about. Rather, Yao belongs to the people because they want to claim him as their own, just as they have with all great sports heroes.

NAME: 姚明 (Yao Ming)
BORN: September 12, 1980
HEIGHT: 7 ft 6 in (2.29 m)
WEIGHT: 310 lb (141 kg)
HOMETOWN: Shanghai, China

SPIRIT ANIMAL: Giant moa

PLAYER COMPARISON: A superior Smits or a skinny Sabonis.

NOTABLE REMARK: On having a shot rejected by the five-foot-nine New York Knicks guard Nate Robinson: "I've been blocked by a five-foot-three guy before, so that's not a record."

CULTURAL INTERPRETER: As China's basketball ambassador, Yao evaluates the league's many *hanzi* tattoos. He approved of AI's "loyalty" but was befuddled by Kenyon Martin's, "not aggressive." "Anybody who has seen Kenyon play knows he isn't like that."

BENTLEY, ESCALADE, OR COUPE: Yao drives a BMW 7-series sedan, customized to fit his oversized body.

Incredible Engineering Feats of Modern China

In the narrative of modern China, Yao Ming and his hometown of Shanghai are inextricably linked. Shanghai literally means "on the sea," and it is the place from which China looks outward to the rest of the world. Since economic reforms began in 1992, Shanghai has become the center of finance and trade in China and symbolic of the nation's future as a leading force in the world economy, just as Yao represents China's future as a force in international basketball. Located along the Huangpu River, Shanghai's Pudong district features some of the tallest skyscrapers in the world, and Yao is one of the tallest people in the world.

ORIENTAL PEARL TOWER

BUILT: 1994
HEIGHT: 468 m

This Shanghai landmark and Yao have a lot in common: Both are impressive, unabashedly Eastern in design, and tall. It is the third tallest tower in the world and the tallest in Asia. Likewise, when Yao entered the league standing 7'6", he became the third-tallest player in NBA history and the tallest from Asia. The tower's owners, SMG, also own the Shanghai Sharks, the team Yao led to the 2002 Chinese Basketball Association championship.

BANK OF CHINA TOWER

BUILT: 1999
HEIGHT: 258 m

The building's large base is reminiscent of Yao's solid lower body, which allows him to maintain his position in the post. Yao's strength was a concern when he first arrived in the United States, but he has become sturdy enough to bang with any big man in the league.

JIN MAO TOWER

BUILT: 1999
HEIGHT: 421 m

The fifth-tallest building in the world, it was designed by an American architectural firm and shows a strong foreign influence, while also incorporating elements of traditional Chinese design in its tiered pagoda and its 88 floors, as the number 8 is associated with prosperity in Chinese culture. Yao's game demonstrates a similar blend of Asian precision and discipline with a growing willingness to dominate.

SHANGHAI WORLD FINANCIAL CENTER

BUILT: 2008
HEIGHT: 492 m

Both the SWFC's construction and Yao's career have been marked by a series of starts and stops. The SWFC's foundation stone was first laid in 1997, but the project was soon halted by a fund shortage. Similarly, Yao was initially going to enter the NBA draft in 1999, but did not do so until 2002. Once building resumed in 2003, the structure was seemingly under perpetual construction, just as injuries have left Yao's recent seasons unfinished.

SHANGRI-LA HOTEL EXTENSION

BUILT: 2005
HEIGHT: 180 m

In 2007, Yao married Ye Li, a member of the Chinese national women's basketball team, in a small private ceremony at the Shangri-La Hotel in Shanghai. Though no Rockets teammates were invited, the hotel's extension, made of a larger tower linked to a slightly smaller tower, is strangely emblematic of Yao's relationship with Tracy McGrady, as the two stars must find a way to work together effectively for the Rockets to prosper.

AURORA PLAZA

BUILT: 2004
HEIGHT: 185 m

More than any other building in Pudong, it represents the free-market economy that flourishes there. It has a garish façade of gold reflective glass that becomes the world's largest LED screen at night, broadcasting huge advertisements to the rest of the city. The distance from the Oriental Pearl Tower to the Aurora Plaza replicates Yao's transition from the face of the Chinese national team to global marketing phenomenon.

Presuming the Great Unknown

Although Yao Ming's name was known through the basketball world when the Rockets drafted him first overall in 2002, his quality as a player was still a relative mystery. Caught without substantive information, many members of the media immediately launched into predictions of doom and gloom, some of them with racial overtones. These continued throughout the season's early months but soon slowed to a trickle—and in some cases were grandiloquently retracted. Here we relish the sight of respected professionals falling flat on their faces.

Mark Cuban, Dallas Mavericks owner: "If you put Shawn Bradley next to him doing the same drills he did in the [Chicago] workout, Shawn would look quicker, more athletic, handle the ball better, and inside 18 feet shoot as well if not better."

Ronald Tillery, Memphis *Commercial Appeal*: "They call Yao Ming 'The Next Big Thing,' but he looks more like the 'Next Big Stiff'. . . The Chinese government may want to go to war after Shaquille O'Neal puts a hole in Yao's chest."

Ian O'Connor, *USA Today*: "Think poster dunks along the lines of Vince Carter's Sydney-stopping slam over France's Weis, who still hasn't reported to the Knicks three years after they wasted a first-round pick on him."

Sam Smith, *Chicago Tribune*: "The biggest reason not to draft the big guy is he's not very good. . . I say this with complete confidence, even though I wouldn't know Yao Ming if he were standing next to me."

Bernie Lincicome, *Rocky Mountain News*: "In all my studies of Chinese, I do not recall coming across the word or the character for 'basketball,' never mind 'dribble drive' and 'slam dunk.'"

Jay Mariotti, Chicago *Sun-Times*: "Yao can touch the sky, but offensively, he'll never score more than 12 points a game."

Alan Thayer, *Wyoming Tribune*: "The Rockets are willing to bet millions on Yao. [They're] hoping he's not a Chinese bottle rocket whose flame extinguishes all too quickly."

Bob Wolfley, *Milwaukee Journal Sentinel*: "If you're 7-5 and you're not a shot-blocker or a game-altering defender, then what are you? A bust from a would-be Ming Dynasty is what you are."

Charles Barkley, TNT: "If he gets 19 points in a game, I'll kiss [Kenny Smith's] ass right here." [Barkley subsequently kissed a donkey's rear on national television; the donkey had a "Kenny" sign around its neck.]

The Three Degrees of Aggression

Science tells us that height is the best predictor of man's capacity to dunk. Yet for the tallest of the tall, shot selection is more a function of psychology than physics. Given the choice between laying it in and throwing it down, less aggressive players like Zydrunas Ilgauskas or Tim Duncan tend to favor layups, while more belligerent types like Kenyon Martin or Dwight Howard prefer to dunk. Since Yao entered the league, his own above-the-rim aggression (as measured by his dunk-to-layup ratio) has varied wildly from season to season, from the Herbal Tea level of Brad Miller to the Liquid Meth of Tyson Chandler. What exactly this reveals of Yao's inner contradictions or the struggles that rage within his soul remains a mystery for all to ponder.

Dunk-to-Layup Ratio Among NBA Big Men

Among selected players, this graph includes all seasons from 2003–04 to 2007–08 in which total dunk and layup attempts were greater than 150. The number following each player's name indicates the relevant season; "Ming 04" indicates Yao Ming's dunk-to-layup ratio for the 2004-2005 season.

RASHEED WALLACE
Family Man

Rasheed Wallace is the rare professional athlete known not for his accomplishments or his style of play but for a single emotion: anger. He is seen by many fans as a basketball savage who screams after dunks and chases down referees. And there is some truth to that perception. Rasheed does indeed have a quick temper, one that often manifests itself in flamboyant fouls. Were Sheed's career to come to an abrupt end tomorrow, he would still be immortalized for amassing an ungodly 41 technicals in 2000–01, setting the single-season record. And he does chase down referees, once confronting Tim Donaghy on the Rose Garden loading dock after being ejected from a game in 2003. (Incidentally, Donaghy later resigned from the league after being implicated in a gambling scandal.)

To a great extent, Wallace has no one but himself to blame for his image. In an age where marketing has been elevated to something like the national religion, Wallace stubbornly clings to an old-school belief that hard work will be rewarded and the truth will out. His refusal to play the media relations game has sometimes gone to outrageous extremes. In a press conference during the 2003 playoffs, he engaged in a form of verbal passive resistance by giving the same answer ("Both teams played hard") to every question he was asked, and he has gone stretches where he simply refused to talk to the media at all. Wallace has even gone so far as to decline to sign autographs for his fans, shouting at them to "get away from me!"

WHAT HE GIVES US:
A role player's attitude with a superstar's game.

WHAT HE STANDS FOR:
"It takes five," but in Air Force Ones.

WHY WE CARE:
At some level, everybody wants to strangle somebody else.

On some level, though, his rep seems not entirely deserved. Off the court and away from the media gaze, Wallace is by all accounts a great teammate and a devoted father and husband, and, through his charitable foundation, a very active member of the community. To see how Rasheed Wallace gained his undignified reputation, we need to go where it all started: Portland.

Wallace came to Stumptown as an enigmatic but promising young player. But by the end of his stay there, his fits of rage had him unfairly lumped in with legitimate knuckleheads like Zach Randolph, Darius Miles, and fast-corrupted Bonzi Wells. When he and teammate Damon Stoudamire were busted for weed possession one night in 2002, no one cared that it was just a misdemeanor or that he drove away with only a ticket. The fans were tired of their Jailblazers, and the team had to be blown up. It was an inglorious end for a squad that had come *this* close to being NBA champions. Only two years earlier, Portland had been one of the league's elite teams and, if not for a historic late-game collapse against the Lakers in Game 7 of the Western Conference Finals, would likely have bested the Indiana Pacers for the 2000 NBA title.

That crushing loss brought to light many of the team's problems, most significantly the lack of a go-to player who was capable of basketball transcendence when the situation called for it. Although Wallace and Scottie Pippen were unquestionably the best players on the team, each refused to take control, preferring to play second fiddle to the other. Pippen is well known as the NBA's greatest second banana, but Wallace's deference is no less ingrained. While at North Carolina,

he happily let Jerry Stackhouse get the attention, even if it made the difference between second-team All-American honors and first. Even back at Simon Gratz High School in Philadelphia, Wallace would often play only the first halves of games so that his teammates could get more playing time. And in 2008, in contrast to other so-called stars who whined to the media that they'd been unfairly snubbed by the All-Star voters, Wallace was actually angry that he had been selected to the All-Star Game, since it meant he would have to miss a family trip to the Bahamas that his wife had planned.

Perhaps because of this reticence, Kevin Garnett and Dirk Nowitzki are generally given credit for reinventing the power forward position over the past fifteen years, while Wallace's contributions are overlooked. At a full six feet eleven inches, the incredibly athletic Wallace runs the floor like a guard and possesses an unblockable jump shot, with range out past the three-point line. And unlike many of the big men who have followed in his path, Wallace's skills aren't limited to the perimeter; he has a complete post game with an array of back-to-the-basket moves and is one of the best post defenders in the league. During one *NBA on TNT* broadcast, Charles Barkley and Kenny Smith flummoxed host Ernie Johnson by insisting that Wallace could be one of the top five players in the league if only he really applied himself.

Which, of course, is a strange thing to say about a man so often criticized for excessive intensity. You see Rasheed dunk and scream, shut down the star big man, knock down jumpers with a sneer on his face. He doesn't go into games hoping to posterize someone, but given the opportunity, you'd best believe he will. He's not passive-aggressive, nor an aggressive player lying dormant. Wallace is more like an alpha predator conserving its energy because it's got nothing to prove, then inflicting savagery because that's what it does. Great whites don't nibble; lions lack table manners; crocodiles spend half the day asleep. They're not flashy, but their very makeup entails a certain amount of dramatic action.

Wallace's reluctant dominance made him a perfect fit for the Detroit Pistons, a team of ballsy, hardheaded vets whose swagger was a collective effort. When he arrived there in 2004, having finally been traded from the Blazers, he found a team of kindred souls—a bunch of castoffs with boulder-size chips on their shoulders and enough resources to get them to the Eastern Conference Finals the season prior. Rasheed put them over the top, solidifying their interior defense and finally giving them a dependable offensive weapon in the post. More importantly, Chauncey Billups's early work in cultivating his reputation as "Mr. Big Shot," along with Ben Wallace's bulging biceps and throwback Afro, was more than enough to keep the attention off of Rasheed. When the Pistons pulled off a shocking 4–1 upset of the Lakers to bring home the title and Wallace was celebrated as the missing puzzle piece who had made it all possible, it was a part he enthusiastically embraced. While he may not always be humble or servile, Sheed's greatest pride is reserved for team, rather than individual, success.

Part of the reason that the Pistons thrive while the Blazers failed is that they feature a high-scoring pair of guards, Billups and Rip Hamilton, neither of whom is shy about

NAME: Rasheed Abdul Wallace

BORN: September 17, 1974

HEIGHT: 6 ft 11 in (2.12 m)

WEIGHT: 230 lb (104 kg)

HOMETOWN: Philadelphia, PA

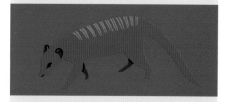

SPIRIT ANIMAL: Egyptian mongoose

NOTABLE REMARK: "Some people say I'm mean and this and that. On one hand that's cool. That keeps away all the riffraff and all the bugaboos."

DISTINGUISHING MARKS: On his right arm is a tattoo depicting Akhenaton, the pharaoh who introduced monotheism to ancient Egypt by worshiping the sun god Ra.

GETTING GEOPOLITICAL: Wallace grew up in a rough neighborhood in North Philadelphia, and he recognizes gulliness wherever he encounters it. On former Pistons teammate Carlos Delfino's Argentinean roots: "Carlos ain't no punk, they kidnap people where he's from." On Darko Milicic's Serbian background: "I'm telling you, Darko is a Serbian gangster. Darko's got some bodies back there."

KNOWLEDGE SEED WITH NO JEWELRY ON: After winning the 2004 NBA title, Rasheed made WWE-style championship belts for himself and his Pistons teammates.

taking a big shot. Granted, when there's a play to be made, Sheed will take the shot without hesitation. It's so much "within the flow of the game" that it's almost stupid. But you'll hardly ever see Wallace force anything or blindly go for self. And because he can do pretty much anything, it behooves the team to let him take it easy. When the Pistons got four All-Stars onto the 2006 All-Star Team, it was a validation of Wallace's worldview as much as his game. For him, the ideal situation is a team of equals where no one has to spend too much time under the spotlight.

Rasheed Wallace represents a number of contradictions about our expectations of professional athletes. We praise on-court intensity but condemn players when it crosses the line into anger. We praise teamwork and unselfishness but criticize players who don't possess a "killer instinct." We praise people for doing charity work and taking care of their families but demonize as thugs players who commit victimless crimes such as drug possession. In the end, it may not be Rasheed who is irrational, but our decidedly grotesque opinions of him.

Rasheed Wallace Plays Better When He's Angry

When Ben Wallace, Rasheed's former teammate on the Pistons, was asked if Rasheed's frequent on-court outbursts bothered him, he replied, "Not at all. When he got excited, I got ready. Sometimes the team didn't get started until he got a T." Often it is Sheed himself who only gets started once he gets a T. After receiving a technical foul, Sheed's per-48-minute averages jump in four statistical categories.

Averages Per 48 Minutes

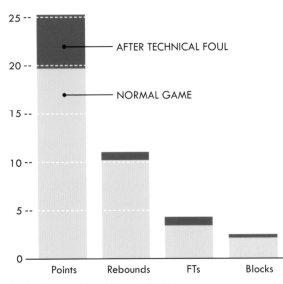

AFTER TECHNICAL FOUL

NORMAL GAME

Points   Rebounds   FTs   Blocks

Regular Season and Playoff Games, 2004–07

Technical Foul Leaders
1996–97 through 2007–08

248	Rasheed Wallace
152	Gary Payton
143	Antoine Walker
126	Karl Malone
126	Steve Francis
121	Allen Iverson
108	Kevin Garnett
104	Shareef Abdur-Rahim
100	Shaquille O'Neal
98	Kobe Bryant

1 Wallace leans back against defender.

 STYLE: **Palm Tree**
Tall, strong, bends but doesn't break

2 Bumps defender back to create more space.

STYLE: **Hard Hat**
Labor, effort, dirty work

3 Turns and dribbles into the space he's created.

STYLE: **Cockroach**
Quickly moves into any nook or cranny

4 Steps back out, turning body toward basket.

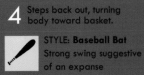 STYLE: **Baseball Bat**
Strong swing suggestive of an expanse

5 Launches a 10-foot turnaround jumper.

STYLE: **Toaster**
Quickly heats and elevates

STYLE GUIDE

Metaphysical Wisdom

1995–1996

Has a frustrating rookie year; stuck playing behind Chris Webber and Juwan Howard.

1996–1997

Traded to Blazers for Rod Strickland; plays well before breaking his thumb and missing a month.

HERACLITUS:

Everything is in flux.

ARISTOTLE:

Teleology, potential has a purpose.

J ust because Rasheed is a man of the people doesn't mean he's not also a deep thinker. In his memoir *A Coach's Life*, Dean Smith lists Rasheed's undergraduate major as philosophy. From the ancients to the Frankfurt School, Rasheed's read them all. That might explain why the arc of his career has reflected the evolution of Western philosophy. In the early years, he was just trying to figure out what it all meant. His years in Portland followed, and while they are now largely seen as a dark period in his career, it was then that he advanced his game and achieved his greatest personal success. Rasheed's championship with the Pistons caused a reevaluation of his earlier work, and now the Flip Saunders years have him questioning whether it is even possible to determine the absolute truth.

2002–2003

Blazers lose in the first round of the playoffs for the third straight season; height of "Jailblazer" criticism.

2003–2004

Wallace traded to Detroit; finally finds a home and redemption as Pistons go on to win the championship.

SCHOPENHAUER:

Pessimistic philosophy that sought to explain why men are not reasonable.

THOREAU:

Living in the woods is great and natural.

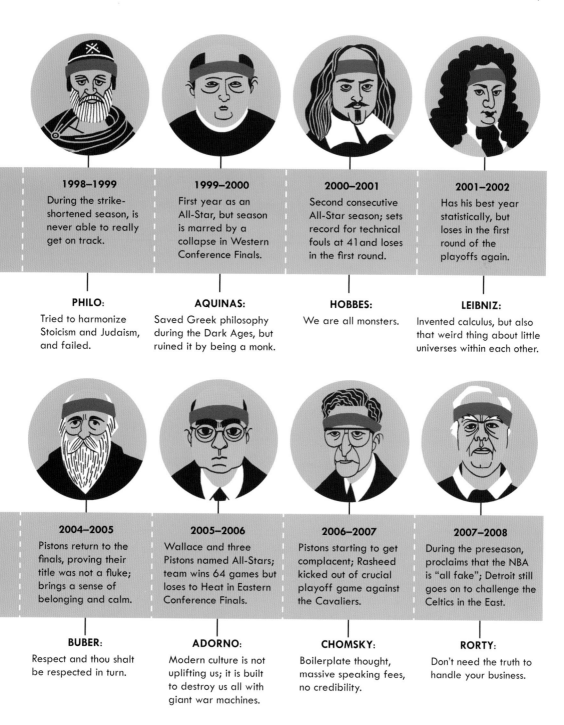

1998–1999
During the strike-shortened season, is never able to really get on track.

PHILO:
Tried to harmonize Stoicism and Judaism, and failed.

1999–2000
First year as an All-Star, but season is marred by a collapse in Western Conference Finals.

AQUINAS:
Saved Greek philosophy during the Dark Ages, but ruined it by being a monk.

2000–2001
Second consecutive All-Star season; sets record for technical fouls at 41 and loses in the first round.

HOBBES:
We are all monsters.

2001–2002
Has his best year statistically, but loses in the first round of the playoffs again.

LEIBNIZ:
Invented calculus, but also that weird thing about little universes within each other.

2004–2005
Pistons return to the finals, proving their title was not a fluke; brings a sense of belonging and calm.

BUBER:
Respect and thou shalt be respected in turn.

2005–2006
Wallace and three Pistons named All-Stars; team wins 64 games but loses to Heat in Eastern Conference Finals.

ADORNO:
Modern culture is not uplifting us; it is built to destroy us all with giant war machines.

2006–2007
Pistons starting to get complacent; Rasheed kicked out of crucial playoff game against the Cavaliers.

CHOMSKY:
Boilerplate thought, massive speaking fees, no credibility.

2007–2008
During the preseason, proclaims that the NBA is "all fake"; Detroit still goes on to challenge the Celtics in the East.

RORTY:
Don't need the truth to handle your business.

WHEN THEY WERE
MAYORS

Marion Barry. Buddy Cianci. Sharpe James. Frank Rizzo. These names may be tarnished today, but there's no denying the sway they once held over the citizenry of DC, Providence, Newark, and Philly. Local politics don't just decide leadership; they let a populace decide what they stand for, what their Facebook profiles should look like. There's a direct line from the hearts and minds of the people to these elected officials.

Some athletes—the ones we see as broadly heroic—have crafted political careers out of states' bland allegiance to their pro franchises. That's where Bill Bradley, Jim Bunning, Jack Kemp, and Lynn Swann come from. Other ones, though, carry within themselves a far more intensive form of civic pride. They maintain their love for the forgotten cities on our map, the ones most desperately in need of recognition, of telling the world "I am somebody." It is this extreme devotion to one's hometown that makes a specific kind of NBA-er an ideal mayoral candidate. The NBA is a league of swagger, and in local politics, swagger is gold. (Marion Barry's swag was *phenomenal.*) Leadership for leadership's sake fills the void created by creaky bureaucracy, widespread incompetence, and varying degrees of corruption that come with city government. In the face of an impossible task, it offers voters the strength to suspend judgment.

In the great tradition of Barry, Cianci, and the others, these players—often People's Champs in their careers—could take a decent shot at the mayorship of the cities they so value. It's not only the logical next step, it's practically inevitable. Perhaps they don't know how to balance a budget, coordinate mass transit, or make nice with rivals. But when you live with a city deep inside you, you've always got its best interests in mind. The Champs are here, and they won't take a fall for no one.

Port Arthur, TX

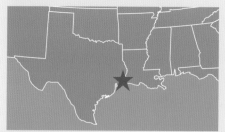

Population: 57,042

Demographics: 43.7% African-American, 25.5% Hispanic, 20.2% White, 5.9% Asian

Major Industries: Refineries, environmental racism, corruption, blight, car customizing

Notable Tragedy: Hurricane Rita, which hit Port Arthur's largely abandoned downtown at 120 miles per hour.

FUN FACTS:

- For a good time, visit Pleasure Island, just off the coast. Built by the Army Corps of Engineers around the turn of the century, it's an oasis of golf and leisure.

- Along with nearby Beaumont and Orange, Port Arthur forms the "Golden Triangle" of Gulf Coast oil production. Not to be confused with the opium-rich Southeast Asian region of the same name.

- Port Arthur experienced white flight as early as the 1940s.

- "Gasoline Alley," the largely African-American west side of the city, has some of the worst air pollution in the country and a high rate of cancer.

Candidate: Stephen Jackson

Résumé: Fought and clawed his way from overseas ball into the league; won a ring with the Spurs, defended teammate Ron Artest against angry fans; was the heart and soul of a Warriors team that pulled off history's greatest playoff upset.

Slogan: "I make love to pressure."

Platform: Bring more megaclubs to historic district; make mentoring a priority; work with gang leadership to keep promising kids off the streets; impose subjective gun control.

Notable Repping: Funds the city's K–12 Stephen Jackson Academy; has a big-ass PAT (Port Arthur, TX) tattoo on his right shoulder.

Campaign Theme Song: UGK's "One Day," or anything by Fushitsusha.

Skeleton in the Closet: Was beloved in the San Antonio clubhouse.

JACKSON FOR MAYOR

I MAKE LOVE TO PRESSURE

Newark, NJ

Population: 281,402

Demographics: 53.5% African-American, 29.5% Hispanic, 26.5% White, 1.2% Asian

Major Industries: Insurance, telecommunications, electric, gas, carjacking, weed, Mafia

Notable Tragedy: In 1967, a riot ensued after a black cab driver, John Smith, was fatally beaten by cops after resisting arrest for a traffic violation. After television broadcasts of the incident, additional riots occurred that took the lives of 26, wounded 1,500, and led to 1,600 arrests and $10 million in property damage.

FUN FACTS:

- Accomplished Jewish gangster Dutch Schultz was killed at the Palace in Newark.

- In 1944, the Office of Dependency Benefits (ODB) hired Constance Baker Motley, who would become the first African-American woman appointed as a federal judge. When she left her ODB job to go to law school, her supervisor said, "Why waste your time doing that? Women don't get anywhere in the law."

- Nicknamed "Brick City"

- On February 26, 2008, a man was shot and killed in Newark. It was the first homicide in 43 days, which marked the longest stretch without a killing in nearly half a century.

Candidate: Eric Williams

Résumé: When he was seven, Williams's uncle died of a seizure as Williams tried to keep a wooden spoon in his mouth. Williams's rolling stone of a father was beaten to death with a sledgehammer, and his mother's boyfriend was fatally stabbed. His best friend was shot and killed while he was away at college, and the mother of his son (incidentally also the lover of Amiri Baraka's daughter) was murdered in 2003. Even as everyone around Williams has tragically died, he has persevered as one of the league's all-time nice guys.

Slogan: "You try to be a professional, but fuck professionalism."

Platform: Plans on instituting a zero-tolerance crime policy and an initiative for the restoration of real estate.

Notable Repping: Had the words "Prince of Newark" tattooed on his back. Has stated, "Even fans that's not rooting for you, but they know I represent New Jersey, they can identify where I'm at, and looking up to an individual like myself who came from the inner city and who made it."

Campaign Theme Song: Pace Won's "I Declare War."

Skeleton in the Closet: Pitched a clothing line devoted to the "Black League Basketball" of the 1920s, '30s, and '40s, yet basketball historians say the league never existed.

Coatesville, PA

Population: 10,838

Demographics: 49.2% African-American, 41.9% White, 10.8% Hispanic

Major Industries: Memories of steel, finance, service, resentment, eminent domain

Notable Tragedy: In the 1960s, Lukens Steel employed 10,000 residents; now, it's closer to 1,000.

FUN FACTS:

- Coatesville is warmly known as "the Pittsburgh of the East."

- Rebecca Lukens, who ran Lukens Steel in the 1800s after her husband's demise, was one of the country's first female executives.

- The 1911 lynching of Zachariah Walker in the city prompted the NAACP to begin its nationwide crusade against what had been a tacitly approved civic practice.

- Essie Mae Washington-Williams, the illegitimate black daughter of segregationist senator Strom Thurmond, was raised here by her aunt Mary.

Candidate: Richard "Rip" Hamilton

Résumé: Was named the NCAA tournament's Most Outstanding Player after helping UConn go all the way; played alongside Jordan on the Wizards without being psychologically scarred by the experience; was traded to the Pistons and became an integral member of their 2005 championship team; wears a face mask for good luck, even though it makes him look weird.

Slogan: "Hopefully, I can talk to someone."

Platform: New Deal–style reform; government-financed health care, even the unnecessary kind; plenty of soup kitchens and basketball courts; seminars on team building.

Notable Repping: Has his own line of "Rip City" jerseys, in tribute to Coatesville; along with ten members of his crew, has "CV FOR LIFE" tattooed on his abs; has "CV" on his jewelry, game shoes, and license plates.

Campaign Theme Song: The Dead Milkmen's "Whities Gonna Pay."

Skeleton in the Closet: Gets a lot of technical fouls for a man of such integrity.

RIP CITY '12

PAID FOR BY HAMILTON '12

Peekskill, NY

Population: 22,441

Demographics: 57.1% White, 25.5% African-American, 21.9% Hispanic, 2.4% Asian

Major Industries: Manufacturing, yeast, Metro-North, the arts, gangs, meteorites

Notable Tragedy: George Washington signed West Point over to Benedict Arnold here.

FUN FACTS:

- The Peekskill Riots of 1949, which used a concert by Paul Robeson as an excuse to go after commies, blacks, and Jews, actually took place in nearby Van Cortlandville. Whew.

- There's acting in the water: Mel Gibson, Pee Wee Herman, and Stanley Tucci were all born here.

- The city was a stop on the Underground Railroad.

- Meadowville, the hometown of 1930s and 1940s comic strip sensation Little Lulu, was based on Peekskill.

Candidate: Elton Brand

Résumé: The epitomic no-nonsense, blue-collar power forward has chosen function over flash throughout his career, even though it has cost him recognition; called "Peekskill's favorite son" by fellow Peekskillian George Pataki; named NCAA Player of the Year at Duke and gracefully dealt with hate mail he received for entering the draft a year early; picked by the Bulls, didn't fret when they decided he wasn't a franchise player and traded him for a pick; has stayed loyal to the Clippers, arguably the worst organization in pro sports; produced a Werner Herzog film.

Slogan: "Each milestone is a big step."

Platform: Using sports to teach math skills; getting movies made in Peekskill; free citywide Wi-Fi and a computer in every home; enhanced civility in government and business.

Notable Repping: Has called Peekskill "a good environmental city"; will talk your ear off about the chicken parmigiana at Highland Pizza.

Campaign Theme Song: Anything from the four albums' worth of hip-hop that Brand has made but refuses to share with the public.

Skeleton in the Closet: Played AAU ball with Ron Artest; was tight with Lamar Odom during Odom's lost years.

BRAND
Each milestone is a big step

Compton, CA

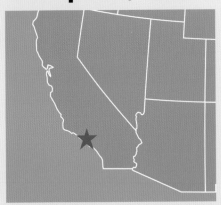

Population: 93,493

Demographics: 40.0% African-American, 56.8% Hispanic, 1.0% White, 1.0% Asian, 1.2% other

Major Industries: Entrepreneurship, gangsta rap, gangbangin'

Notable Tragedy: Early settlers faced heavy rains, and a devastating flood threatened to wipe out the community before it even got started. Rising waters forced town founder Griffith Dickenson Compton and his party to take to high ground.

FUN FACTS:

- Known as the Hub City, because it is located in almost the exact geographical center of Los Angeles County.

- Has a homicide rate almost eight times the national average.

- Compton's first black mayor, Douglas Dollarhide, was elected in 1969.

- Future presidents George H. W. Bush and George W. Bush briefly lived in Compton around 1949–50.

Candidate: Tayshaun Prince

Résumé: Starred at Compton's Dominguez High and the University of Kentucky, but was considered too skinny to be effective in the NBA. After playing only 42 games during his rookie season, he broke through in the 2003 playoffs with tenacious defense and an impressive all-around game, and he hasn't looked back since.

Slogan: "Anything that's more creative is going to be more fun."

Platform: More funding for arts programs in the public schools; more green areas in the city.

Notable Repping: Whenever Prince makes a good play, the Palace's sound system blasts N.W.A.'s "Straight Outta Compton."

Campaign Theme Song: DJ Quik's "Born and Raised in Compton" and Charles Wright and the Watts 103rd Street Rhythm Band's "Comment (If All Men Are Truly Brothers)."

Skeleton in the Closet: Prince is a skeleton everywhere.

Ames, IA

Population: 51,557

Demographics: 87.3% White, 7.7% Asian, 2.7% African-American

Major Industries: Beef, engineering, canning jars, plastic bottles, face painting, seed art

Notable Tragedy: The Blizzard of 1942 showered the city with 24 inches of snow in 24 hours.

FUN FACTS:

- For four years, Ames held an annual Ginkgo Festival, which featured performances by the Taz Band and the Euelenspiegel Puppets.

- Home to master of obesity G. W. "Fatty" Nichols, who weighed 612 pounds at a mere five feet tall and became a sideshow attraction at various county and state fairs.

- In 1953, Mrs. Lilly May Riggs, mother of eight and widow of the Reverend Fred A. Higgs, won Iowa's Mother of the Year award.

- Contains a disproportionate number of pipe organs, both on the Iowa State campus and in various churches.

Candidate: Fred "the Mayor" Hoiberg

Résumé: Dick Vitale nicknamed Hoiberg "the Mayor" of Ames because of his immense popularity while playing college ball at Iowa State. Hoiberg became a three-point assassin in the NBA, especially while playing alongside Kevin Garnett on the Timberwolves, before being forced to retire because of a heart condition.

Slogan: "Even though the risk of something serious happening is very low, there is a risk."

Platform: Progressive Democrat who will promote Iowa's strengths in manufacturing and agriculture. Will push for the addition of a three-point line in high school basketball.

Notable Repping: Became Iowa's Mr. Basketball—then went to Iowa State, for chrissakes! After his career ended, willingly agreed to the dreaded role of successor to Timberwolves GM Kevin McHale, simply so he could have a job closer to home.

Campaign Theme Song: The Mountain Goats' "This Year."

Skeleton in the Closet: Once committed a flagrant foul . . . on Allen Iverson, of all people.

FARMERS FOR FRED
Ames Agricultural Union for Hoiberg in '09

Newport News, VA

Population: 181,913

Demographics: 53.5% White, 39.1% African-American, 2.5% Asian or Pacific Islander

Major Industries: Shipbuilding, warmongering, drug dealing

Notable Tragedy: Newport News has existed in one form or another for almost 400 years, so of course it's screwed over some Native Americans along the way.

FUN FACTS:

- The town was likely originally called New Port Newce, after the English soldier Sir William Newce.

- The Newport News Shipbuilding and Drydock Company was once the world's largest shipyard.

- It's the home of the Thomas Jefferson National Accelerator Facility, whatever that is.

- Newport News native Michael Vick's dog-fighting ring was called "Bad Newz Kennels," although it was based in nearby Surry County.

Candidate: Allen Iverson

Résumé: Won Virginia state championships in both football and basketball as a junior at Bethel High School; in 1994, was sentenced to five years in prison for his role in a brawl at the Hampton bowling alley Spare Times; after being pardoned by Governor Doug Wilder, committed to Georgetown, where he played two years before declaring for the NBA draft. Has been a nine-time All-Star, and in 2001 became the shortest player ever to be named MVP of the league.

Slogan: "Put a murderer in a suit and he's still a murderer."

Platform: Gun-buyback programs; smoking ban in all restaurants; transition to hybrid buses.

Notable Repping: Iverson has "NBN" tattooed on his left forearm; it stands for "Newport Bad News," "because a lot of bad shit happens there."

Campaign Theme Song: Clipse's "Virginia."

Skeleton in the Closet: Iverson has been convicted of assault and drug and gun possession, and publicly kicked his wife out of the house naked. No skeletons left.

Chapter VI

Destiny's Kids

Born to Leave a Throbbing Imprint on the Sport

So much of our investment in sport is based on hope and joyous prediction and the fullness that they bring to our lives. This is especially true of the NBA, which has made a habit of trying to repeat the past and of putting much stock in inchoate youngsters barely of age. But in some cases, these collective aspirations bear fruit, and players emerge whose career trajectories could have been spat from an oracle.

What makes these such awe-inspiring cases is the way that their play itself seems endowed with the promise of a new day. No matter how good they are today, they are still defined by their limitless future, a path tracing all that we yet expect them to achieve. Judging by what has come already, it's a safe bet that they will continue to outdo themselves and amaze us, an outcome that is both utterly predictable and feverishly anticipated. They are the children of divine expectations that have, for once, come to pass.

LeBRON JAMES

Inland Empire

A t this stage in LeBron James's career, the only way for him to cultivate a greater legacy would be to die tragically. He is the NBA's Star of Stars, its new-league ambassador, the post-millennial Face of the Association. But what has he made of this role? Since 2003, when he burst, fully formed, out of high school and into the league, LeBron has hewed to an unyielding script, while a generation of fans longs for the impulsiveness of bygone stars like Barkley, Magic, Bird, and, yes, Michael Jordan.

Pining for past glories is generally a futile and tiresome endeavor. Yet a consideration of the stars of 1980s and 1990s hoops shines a critical light on LeBron. These characters of yesteryear had such personality and fervor that they forever defined their roles: the warrior-god (MJ), the proletarian (Bird), the villain (Barkley), the celebrity (Magic). The best LeBron can do is embody the one NBA archetype that not even MJ fully realized: the emperor.

Does LeBron have style? Yes, insofar as "businesslike" is a style. Rigid and slicked-up, his is a style of caution—the precision of a jacked-up wonderboy so concerned with his entrepreneurial future that he avoids anything remotely controversial or soul-revealing for fear that it could somehow jeopardize an endorsement deal.

Witness James's legendary Nike ad campaign, "The Le-Brons." In it, James reveals four sides of himself: Kid LeBron, Athlete LeBron, Wise LeBron, and Business LeBron. It is the

WHAT HE GIVES US:
The American Dream that most of us are too bashful to even dream of.

WHAT HE STANDS FOR:
People who can ask, with a 95 percent success rate, for women to take their clothes off in a public place.

WHY WE CARE:
We bow out of respect for divinity walking the earth.

latter that rules. As Athlete LeBron reluctantly defeats Wise and Business in a backyard dunking challenge, Business LeBron dismisses the defeat: "Dunk contests," he says, "are bourgeois." This is not just marketing copy; it is an implicit response to the masses who clamor for LeBron to showcase his freakish athleticism, to allow us the pleasure of the frivolous display of his skill—to do *one fucking spontaneous thing* in his life. This statement also comprises a clever and calculated move by James. In denouncing the "bourgeoisie," Business positions himself as the underdog (just *keepin' it real*); yet as an avatar of the LeBron empire, Business has the luxury of making such a statement from the comfort of *Actual LeBron's* trillion-dollar real-life bankroll.

In his narrative, LeBron is only what David Stern allows him to be. Stern has been the Giuliani of the league, sweeping the remnants of unsavory misdeeds (like Micheal Ray Richardson's coke habit) so far from the eyes of sponsors that even the remotest display of badassedness is severely shunned. Save for the odd Stephen Jackson shoot-out or Ron Artest altercation, radicalism—and radical cool—is now rarely associated with the league. People used to literally kill each other over Air Jordans—the ill Air Jordans with the waffle material and the air bubbles. Today, no one would bother shaking down a six-year-old to get a pair of LeBron's astronautically ugly Nike Zooms.

In the early 1990s, even NBA role-players like Tony Campbell were getting shout-outs in the liner notes of *Midnight Marauders* and *Apocalypse 91 . . . The Enemy Strikes Black.* Charles Barkley was appearing in a commercial with Humpty Hump from Digital Under-

ground. By contrast, LeBron hangs out with dorks like DJ Whoo Kid, grown-ass Jay-Z, and Usher. Today's NBA-ers have no urge toward the dangerous, cultish kind of cool. Under Commissioner Stern's regime, they would more likely be found reading *Green Eggs and Ham* to a classroom of preschoolers.

And so, because of personal disposition and the generation in which he has emerged, LeBron is the pinnacle of restraint. With his mind on his money at all times, Bron knows that any tiny grievance toward management, any alteration in personal fashion or hairstyle, any complaint toward the league or the commissioner, any off-court misdemeanor (the closest he has come is a fairly unpublicized speeding ticket and two children born out of wedlock), or any uncharitable act toward the general public could potentially erode the obelisk of dollars he is perpetually constructing.

LeBron's most controversial act? Donning a Yankees hat to a baseball playoff game between New York and the hometown Cleveland Indians. Bron was accused of unsavory hometown betrayal—and perhaps sending a subliminal message to New York fans that his heart was in Gotham and the rest of him would be there soon. In actuality, his choice of lid simply exemplified his daily strategy, to align himself with success, profitability, and empire.

James once said, "In the next fifteen or twenty years, I hope I'll be the richest man in the world. That's one of my goals. I want to be a billionaire. I want to get to a position where generation on generation don't have to worry about nothing. I don't want family members from my kids to my son's kids to never have to worry. And I can't do that now just playing basketball."

Thus, Business LeBron has been a ball-busting pioneer of me-first negotiations. He rejected the Cavaliers' maximum contract extension offer after his third year, agreeing instead—after pacing and posturing interminably while Cavs fans waited in agony—to a three-year, $60 million deal, instead of five years at $80 million. Bron knew that rejecting the maximum contract would put more pressure on Cleveland to form a solid team around him and would give him the flexibility to sign with a bigger-market team in the nearer future, sending his Q value through the roof.

But LeBron's money-mindedness does not necessarily mean he undervalues the game that has brought him such success. He has tirelessly worked toward basketball perfection. In the beginning, his detractors—as though denigrating him for his raw athleticism—loved to point out these "learned-skill" deficits in his game: a certain rookie shakiness from the free throw line in clutch situations and inconsistency from around the perimeter. James quickly silenced those critics, though; he mastered the outside shot in his second year, increasing his field goal percentage from 41.7 percent to 47.2 percent, and has maintained a relatively high tally ever since. Going one step further, he has developed a knack for casually making ridiculously long-range threes with precise form. No less a legendary shooter than Reggie Miller has noted his perfect feet square/shoulders square mechanics. He has also addressed his late-game free throw woes, improving his clutch free throws from 66 percent to 71 percent in 2007–08.

Many questioned James's mental stamina,

NAME: LeBron Raymone James
BORN: December 30, 1984
HEIGHT: 6 ft 9 in (2.06 m)
WEIGHT: 260 lb (118 kg)
HOMETOWN: Akron, OH

SPIRIT ANIMAL: Great horned owl

PLAYER COMPARISON: A Transformer that turns into more than two things. Or, as LeBron prefers, what could have become of Penny Hardaway.

VERY STRANGE NOTABLE REMARK: "I'm the next O. J."

A BUSINESS, MAN: In 2006, *Forbes* magazine named James the top-earning celebrity under 25. His endorsements include Upper Deck, Nike, Sprite, Powerade, and Bubblicious.

PLAYERS WHOSE SOLE PURPOSE IN LIFE WAS TO SHOOT THREES AFTER LEBRON GETS DOUBLE-TEAMED AND KICKS IT OUT: Damon Jones, Donyell Marshall, Daniel Gibson, Jason Kapono, Wally Szczerbiak, Luke Jackson, Jiri Welsch.

NOTABLE PHYSICAL CHARACTERISTIC: Does everything left-handed, except shoot a basketball.

implying that he could have benefited from a few tight 54–53 NCAA tourney games, standing alone at the line while the brass band blared "Louie Louie"; yet after five years in the league, he stands as the worst conceivable argument for the NBA's newly imposed college requirement. His game would have only been softened by attending college. Instead of collecting scalps and pandering to sponsors in NCAA ball, he has spent his four professional seasons hovering about the NBA stratosphere.

LeBron's rigidity and business sense shouldn't distract from his sheer dominance as a basketball player. It is only because his game is so hermetically flawless that even his sickest behind-the-back passes, his most ornate dunks seem as though they were crafted in NASA labs rather than on the playground. This is not vapid style; this is athletic excellence transformed into a power that transcends mere sport. And he has given us glimpses of the unearthly: when he scored 29 of his team's final 30 points in a double-OT win over the Detroit Pistons in Game 5 of the Eastern Conference Finals, or in any number of his high-

Epic of Kings

A round the year 1000, the Zoroastrian poet Firdawsī composed the *Shahnameh*, a mythical history of pre-Islamic Persia. It is an epic work that chronicles the great shahs of this ancient age—and also eerily prefigures certain events in the contemporary NBA. The shahs in Firdawsī's account possessed the essential qualities of royalty that would shape society in the cradle of civilization and hence in the modern world. Like these majestic figures, LeBron was anointed as a king from the day he entered the league. Here, we characterize his sovereignty through the emblematic attributes of each of the *Shahnameh*'s primary figures, from the first king, Keyumars, to the Great Eskandar.

flying chomp-the-backboard dunks, where his mass and acceleration threaten to outduel the earth's magnetic field.

One must wonder what James's ultimate goal is. Is it merely, as he has said, to procure financial security for his descendants, through countless ad campaigns, contract maneuvers, and an eventual and inevitable move to New York City? Or is it to establish himself as the greatest to ever touch leather, one who redefines the game through a rare combination of mechanical force and natural instinct? Finance and athleticism are ultimately indistinct for Bron; he utilizes both to progress toward infinity. His superordinate desire, it seems, is to live up to his moniker, King James, to create and rule his own kingdom of bland perfection. In this he is succeeding. Yet as LBJ's peers stand below him in awe, rather than alongside him as compatriots, he is becoming that empire's lone citizen. He communicates so rarely with the millions over whom he reigns. (Basketball is so *bourgeois*.) For James, there is only implacable ascent, until he smashes every record ever set and finds himself alone in a palace without end.

KEYUMARS – Primacy:
There has never before been a player like him

HUSHANG – Fire:
He burns with the desire for glory eternal

TAHMURAS – Magic:
His big-man passing skills rival those of the old Lakers point guard

ZAHHAK – Demonism:
The evil glare emitted after the legendarily brutal dunk over Damon Jones

DARAB – Valor:
He has brought courage to a city that needed it so badly

BAHMAN – Amazement:
He surpasses even his own expectations

NOWZAR – Heroism:
He is an inspiration to college dropouts everywhere

MANUCHEHR – Vengeance:
The entire Association will eventually know his wrath

KEI QOBÁD – Personal Responsibility: He feasts on one-on-one matchups

KEI KHOSROW – Fame:
He is the American Beatles

JAMSHID – Invention:
The Madison Square Garden one-handed behind-the-back dribble tiptoe-the-baseline dunk

LOHRASP – Trust:
He can enhance the status of any who plays with him (save Larry Hughes)

FEREYDUN – Wisdom:
He has the business sense of a young Bob Johnson

GOSHTASP – Justice:
He punishes those who dare trash-talk him, opponents and fans alike

KEI KAVOOS – Erudition:
He had to suffer playoff failure before defeating his demons

DARA – Exuberance:
He was a fount of youthful impulsivity, which he has learned to harness into positive energy

ESKANDAR – Reign:
He is the personification of dominance in a headband

Keep the Pain on the Inside

T raditionally, game-winning shots are delivered from afar. Think Jordan rising up at midcourt against the Cavs in Game 5, or Reggie Miller killing the Knicks with his trademark
three-point buzzer-beater. Rarely are games won with a drive to the basket—and for good
reason. It's just too easy for defenses to collapse in the paint, provided there's even enough time
for the player to make it there. Yet as with every other aspect of the game, the rules for LeBron
are different. James is quick enough to hit the lane in time, strong enough to absorb the contact,
and has the body control to weave his way right up to the rim. While other superstar scorers are
stuck gunning away from outside, James can set up the highest-percentage shot in the game and
deliver a leisurely final dagger at close range. To wit, consider the following charts comparing
James's game-winning shots with those of his clutch-shooting contemporaries.

Game-Winning Shots Among Clutch Players

Shots taken with 12 seconds or less left and team down by 0–2 points, to win game or force overtime

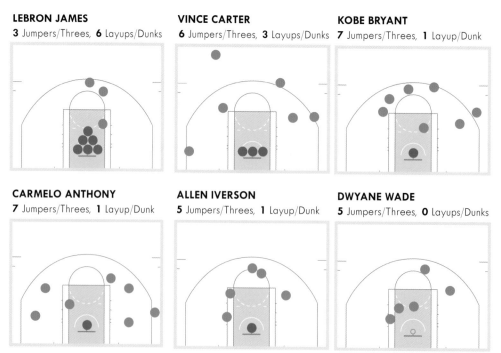

LEBRON JAMES
3 Jumpers/Threes, **6** Layups/Dunks

VINCE CARTER
6 Jumpers/Threes, **3** Layups/Dunks

KOBE BRYANT
7 Jumpers/Threes, **1** Layup/Dunk

CARMELO ANTHONY
7 Jumpers/Threes, **1** Layup/Dunk

ALLEN IVERSON
5 Jumpers/Threes, **1** Layup/Dunk

DWYANE WADE
5 Jumpers/Threes, **0** Layups/Dunks

Regular-season and playoff games from 2004 to 2007

Source: ESPN.com shot charts

STYLE GUIDE

1 LeBron takes the inbounds pass and holds the ball for several seconds as the clock winds down.

STYLE: **Custer's Last Stand**
Tense, guns at dawn

2 He recognizes the defense is funneling him to his right. Goes right anyway with an explosive first step.

STYLE: **Shark**
Fast, fearless, bloodthirsty

3 Gaining velocity, he lowers shoulder and leans into first defender.

STYLE: **Locomotive**
Steam, power, speed

4 Uses elbows and shoulders to break through two defenders in stride.

STYLE: **Running Back**
Size and strength in the service of forward motion

5 Manages to continue forward and upward even after absorbing contact.

STYLE: **Extra Gear**
High-speed object achieves abrupt, improbable acceleration

6 Shoves the third defender out of the way in midair and lays in the ball with his left hand.

STYLE: **Triple Layer Chocolate Cake**
Robust yet delicate

CHRIS PAUL

Trove of Special

In the most formative moment of his basketball career, Chris Paul didn't even have the ball in his hands: In a game during his college days at Wake Forest, a riled-up Paul punched North Carolina State swingman Julius Hodge square in the testes. An unremarkable violation—but one that would have wildly unforeseen consequences for Paul. In the immediate term, it sparked concerns about his character, his psychological fortitude, even the fundamental fitness of his game. Was he too small for the NBA? Did he commit too many turnovers? Amid the resulting chatter, Paul fell to fourth in the 2005 draft, behind Andrew Bogut, Marvin Williams, and Deron Williams, and was selected by the New Orleans Hornets.

It was a fateful choice. The Hornets were hanging by the thinnest of threads when Paul joined. The team was just coming off an 18–64 season, during which the former franchise leader, point guard Baron Davis, had forced a trade to Golden State. Worse, the league had realigned the conferences, thrusting New Orleans out of the relatively survivable East and into the highly competitive West. As the team fell into financial decrepitude, their notoriously

WHAT HE GIVES US:
An unmistakable Hall of Famer in the making.

WHAT HE STANDS FOR:
Definitive proof that point guard, and no longer center, is the most important position in the pro game.

WHY WE CARE:
Wouldn't you care if you stumbled upon a portal into the future of existence?

shifty owner, George Shinn, stood passively by (likely plotting a way out of the traditionally cruddy sports market of New Orleans). Hurricane Katrina would follow shortly, adding a whole new dimension of gloom. The displaced Hornets would spend the majority of that year playing in Oklahoma City, lacking a true home court for the duration of the season.

All the forces of nature and NBA fickleness were pushing against Paul, but CP3 pushed back harder. Orphaned in Oklahoma, with a dispersed fan base and no semblance of playoff aspirations, Paul had full license to become the next Steve Francis—a narcissistic bloat, forever concerned with personal stats over wins. Instead, he found inspiration in head coach Byron Scott, who, as a former Los Angeles Laker during their 1980s glory days, knew exactly what championship basketball consisted of. The rookie Paul developed the confidence of a 12-year veteran and embarked on a quiet vendetta against the entire league.

In the midst of all of the turmoil, he would lead his team in an unanticipated turnaround and put up startling numbers of his own in the process. And as he became the public face of the franchise, Paul went to work for New Orleans, undertaking numerous efforts to revive the city, including work with Habitat for Humanity and Feed the Children, all of which would earn him the David Robinson NBA Community Assist award.

Beneath this cloak of generosity and kindness, though, is a violent and ferocious competitor. His pinpoint handles, bull's-eye passing, and high field goal percentage are bolstered by a truly searing competitive spirit. This lamb-lion paradox informs Paul's signature move on the court, a slashing dribble into the lane culminating in a floating toss of the ball over a taller defender's head—equal parts sublimated aggression and genteel creativity.

This style has fed a heated but friendly rivalry with Deron Williams, the Jazz's Jerry Sloan–approved blue-collar "right-way" pick at number three—one slot higher than Paul. Through their first season in the league, Williams would not prove to be an easy matchup for Paul, with the Jazz besting the Hornets in three out of four games and Williams averaging 17 points per contest on 55 percent shooting. The Jazz would also finish the season with a .500 record, whereas Paul's Hornets would finish six games under. In the end, though, Sloan's rookie restrictions on D-Will's minutes kept him on the bench while Paul surpassed him. This rivalry between the two guards has continued to the present day, with Williams typically locking down Paul one-on-one, yet nonetheless remaining firmly planted as the *second*-best young PG in the league.

Although Williams has nearly matched Paul's skills and statistics in recent years, Paul's rookie-year triumph was an important one (and one for which D-Will maintains a chip on his shoulder). The popular narrative—ACC-ite Paul versus Big Ten–bred Williams—was really the tale of a battle of flash against grit, and Paul definitively proved that flash would triumph. Critics had disparaged Paul's supposed nut-punching cockiness and turnover-prone spontaneity; now, he proved that all the sniping just gave him even more fire as a ballplayer. To make matters worse for his "play the right way" detractors, CP3 has developed into a tremendous on-the-ball defender, a master of the art of the steal. Paul's game is now as complete as they come; at twenty-three years of age, he is one of the few players who exhibit no flaws. Thus exalted, Paul has provided redemption to his teammates. In 2007–08, the Hornets quickly found themselves near the top of the Western Conference standings—and stayed there, due in large part to what Paul made of everyone around him. Through a steady force-feeding of lobs, he has turned Tyson Chandler—whom the Bulls had all but given up on—into a top big man in the league. Paul's presence has taken the pressure off of Peja Stojakovic to be the Man, thus allowing ol' Predrag to do what he does best: make threes. And he has found a running mate in David West; a solid addition on any other team, West has become an All-Star playing alongside Paul, and a legitimate double-double threat every night.

As Paul's minute six-foot frame continues to bulldoze all who stand in his way, the league trembles and the body count rises. His charitable deeds, his bashful interviews with John Thompson, his golden-boy look, and his genuine respect for the game—all should strike fear in his opponents. Killing with kindness is not a mere idiom for Paul. He is a clean-cut, do-gooding diablo who harbors a penchant for retribution and cares only for the safety of his teammates. As Paul's status continues to rise, he's inspiring a very different set of questions: Best point guard in the league? Assist record? MVP? It will be a bloody joy watching him provide the answers, one by one.

NAME: Christopher Emmanuel Paul
BORN: December 30, 1984
HEIGHT: 6 ft 0 in (1.83 m)
WEIGHT: 175 lb (79 kg)
HOMETOWN: Winston-Salem, NC

SPIRIT ANIMAL: Mindoro stripe-faced fruit bat

PLAYER COMPARISON: Isiah Thomas if everyone didn't hate him; the yin to Deron Williams's yang.

PRESERVATION: Paul was friendly with the late Clarence "Big House" Gaines, a legendary basketball figure at the historically black Winston-Salem State University for 47 years. Big House coached players ranging from Earl Monroe to a young Stephen A. Smith, and most notably led WSSU to the 1967 NCAA championship, the first ever by an HBCU. Paul introduced part two of the documentary *Black Magic*, which paid tribute to the HBCU legacy.

LEGEND: While Paul was playing for West Forsyth High in 2002, his grandfather was beaten to death during a robbery, and Paul pledged to score 61 points in his honor—one for each year he had lived. He made good by dropping an astonishing 61 points, then intentionally missing the free throw that would have given him 62.

Fire on the Bayou

After Katrina ravaged the soul of New Orleans, the city's residents were left destitute, with little hope that their bright and bustling metropolis would ever regain its place among the world's great cities. The city needed a grand spokesfigure to tell the people that things would get better, to bring hope their way. This messiah would not be a misguided Ray Nagin, nor a brash Harry Connick Jr., nor a tentative Reggie Bush. Rather, it would be a cocksure young man who can play basketball like Allen Toussaint tickles the piano keys. The lyrics of NOLA soul and funk, which constitutes the major limbs and organs of that sacred city on the Gulf, tell the story of Chris Paul's embrace and revival of New Orleans.

LAKE PONTCHARTRAIN

From this day on, I'll dry your fears. (Eddie Bo, "From this day on.") I'm a go through your life (I just wanna turn me with a fine toothed comb. (Willie West, "Fair Child", "you don't know how to turn me to be your one and only man. (Deacon John, "make gumbo, a drunken man into the hatchet. I can't love you a creole can't, I'm getting there gumble. (Lee Dorsey.) Just the hatchet put up your nickels and dimes over was born, I'm makin it better say the Big Chief Magnolias some, I feel like a King some people fly high. (The Barons It's wine. (The Wild Magnolias) just kissed.") (The Meters If you don't wanta reborn, reborn, reborn, reborn, my baby better take helping hand you (Marilyn Barbarin reborn.) there's a will (Allen Toussaint care) & the Reborn) I'm gonna Don't they lay down.) On your homework friend. the old folks say. (Curley you go by pity me.") How to pick a winner your hand and sow my way is hard. (Curley tell me. and the size, the weight, the bigger won't somebody tell me. (Dial Joe the bigger they fall. the lower or the personality? "How to pick the harder they fall Roger & the Gypsies

In Other Words: Translating CP3

In 2007–08 Chris Paul completed one of the most statistically impressive seasons of any point guard in NBA history and became the first player in eighteen years to average 21 points and 11 assists. But when it comes to the beauty of statistics, sometimes numbers are not enough. To better reveal the scale and breadth of Paul's statistical accomplishment, here we show how Paul would have ranked among his contemporaries, had his achievements come not on the basketball court but in other rarefied fields of human endeavor. By outlining what distinguished people or things correspond to Paul's statistical accomplishments, we have turned quantitative code into a staggeringly humanist achievement.

CHRIS PAUL'S 2007–2008 SEASON STAT LINE

POINTS	REBOUNDS	ASSISTS	STEALS	FIELD GOAL %	FREE THROW %
21.1	**4.0**	**11.6**	**2.7**	**.488**	**.851**
19th in NBA	110th in NBA	1st in NBA	1st in NBA	38th in NBA	21st in NBA
Most basic and historically important form of output	Provides insurance and safety that conserves hope	The rarest but most valuable of essential commodities	As undervalued as beauty has been on our warring planet	Only in dreams can man be perfect and thus make every shot	Entitled, but able to make something of that opportunity
↓	↓	↓	↓	↓	↓
WORLD GDP 2006 Rankings	**SAFEST U.S. CITIES** 2007 Rankings	**PRECIOUS METALS** $/oz as of 3/29/08	**MISS UNIVERSE** 1993 Contest	**GREATEST PEOPLE** Who Never Lived	**RICHEST PEOPLE** Feb. 2007 Rankings
15. Australia	103. Peoria, AZ	**1. Rhodium**	**1. Miss Puerto Rico**	34. Dracula	15. Karl Albrecht
16. Netherlands	104. Cambridge, MA	2. Platinum	2. Miss Colombia	35. Citizen Kane	16. Roman Abramovich
17. Turkey	105. San Angelo, TX	3. Gold	3. Miss Venezuela	36. Faust	17. Stefan Persson
18. Belgium	106. Concord, CA	4. Palladium	4. Miss Australia	37. Figaro	18. Anil Ambani
19. Switzerland	107. Evansville, IN	5. Iridium	5. Miss India	**38. Godzilla**	19. Paul Allen
20. Sweden	108. Antioch, CA	6. Ruthenium	6. Miss USA	39. Mary Richards	20. Theo Albrecht
21. Taiwan	109. Hampton, VA	7. Osmium	7. Miss Brazil	40. Don Juan	**21. Azim Premji**
22. Indonesia	**110. Yonkers, NY**	8. Rhenium	8. Miss Czech Republic	41. Bambi	22. Lee Shau Kee
23. Saudi Arabia	111. Lincoln, NE	9. Silver	9. Miss Finland	42. William Tell	23. Jim Walton
24. Poland	112. Erie, PA	10. Electrum	10. Miss Spain	43. Barbie	24. Christy Walton

CHRIS PAUL'S 2007–2008 SEASON STAT LINE TRANSLATED

POINTS	REBOUNDS	ASSISTS	STEALS	FIELD GOAL %	FREE THROW %
Switzerland's GDP	Yonkers's safety record	Rhodium's price per oz.	Miss Puerto Rico's beauty	Godzilla's importance as a fictional character	Azim Premji's personal fortune

STYLE GUIDE

1

Paul dribbles up court and surveys the floor.

STYLE: **Bifocals**

Exacting vision at multiple depths

2

As his defender picks him up, Paul hesitates for a split second.

STYLE: **Freeze Frame**

Infinitesimally brief stoppage of time

3

Crosses over to to his left, throwing the defender off balance.

STYLE: **Paddle Ball**

Extremely quick change of direction within fixed space

4

Crosses over again, bursting through the tiny space he has created.

STYLE: **Scalpel**

Minute incisions, precise and sharp

5

As second defender slides over to help, Paul takes a hard dribble.

STYLE: **Sling**

Sidearm projectile, accuracy

6

Splits the two defenders by un-expectedly going over the top of them.

STYLE: **Rollercoaster**

Surprising changes in elevation

7

Lands hard as a third defender picks him up in the paint.

STYLE: **Trampoline**

Redirects impact, low to the ground

8

Leaps upward and throws in a scoop shot.

STYLE: **Cradle**

Safety, delicacy, precious cargo

AMARE STOUDEMIRE
Prodigal Sun

There are no second acts in American lives. We all get fifteen minutes of fame. It's better to burn out than to fade away. Only the good die young. These are the clichés Amare Stoudemire stewed in for all but two games of the 2005–06 season, as he recovered from a knee injury. His last real action had come in the 2005 Western Conference Finals, where he'd averaged nearly 40 points a game against that year's eventual champs, the Spurs.

Slashing scorers are known for their first steps, bursts of speed and strength that allow them to explode past a defender. Amare, at a statuesque 6'10", took that horizontal principle and applied it vertically, depth-charging rims like he'd never touched the ground. At once sleek and gory, futuristic and primordial, Amare had even the curmudgeonly Charles Barkley speaking in tongues.

And then, the injury—and, worse, the cure. In October, his knee didn't feel right, so doctors went in to look around and clean out debris. It was supposed to be a routine procedure. Instead, they detected a slight tear in the cartilage, a sure portent of eventual deterioration. That necessitated the dreaded microfracture procedure, in which a deliberate cracking of the bone leads to the growth of healthy, whole cartilage. In basketball, though, it was notorious for robbing explosive players

WHAT HE GIVES US:
The refinement of reckless, raw power.

WHAT HE STANDS FOR:
Proof of maturation and miracles.

WHY WE CARE:
We had no idea what we might have missed.

like Penny Hardaway and Chris Webber of their hops.

A pall of sadness fell over the league that day, as Amare's career threatened to be meteoric in more ways than one. It was somehow worse that the Phoenix Suns barely missed a beat without him, dissecting defenses and churning out points at a historic pace. In fact, with the smooth-passing Frenchman Boris Diaw taking Amare's place, they had become an even more efficient outfit. Point guard Steve Nash repeated as MVP, and Coach Mike D'Antoni proved that, despite losing key weapons like Amare and ATL-bound defector Joe Johnson, his vision could still be realized. In some ways, it was now even more utopian and pure.

Amare's bombastic presence was now only the faintest echo, as if he'd barely ever existed. But had we ever really known him? Did he even really know himself?

Flash back to Amare's rookie year, when he was a twenty-year-old just out of high school. In recounting the way a young player finds himself, the sports scribes speak of "statement games" and "coming-out parties" and all sorts of other pseudo-events. But there was something truly indelible about Amare Stoudemire's performance on December 30, 2002. Against All-Everything Kevin Garnett, the Suns rookie exploded for 38 points and 14 boards, leading his teammate (and one-time KG sidekick) Stephon Marbury to proclaim, "Once he learns the game, it's over with. He's right now by far the best player I've ever seen come out of high school. It's amazing how strong and dominant he is."

Marbury came off as the raving madman in the alley. But there was no denying that Amare was having the most productive preps-to-pro rookie year since Moses Malone. Kobe, Garnett—even they'd needed at least a year of acclimation. Not him. When Stoudemire immediately started grabbing boards and throwing down ear-splitting, spring-loaded dunks with abandon, he looked like an instant-success story: hood kid straightened out, safe in the game, a one-in-a-million beneficiary of sports uplift. A key part of a franchise's future, set for life and career. As the Hebrews say, *dayenu*: It would have been enough . . . if you supposed that was all Amare aspired to.

Amare came from a background that could be charitably described as turbulent: His father died when Amare was twelve; his mother was in and out of jail. Stoudemire attended six different high schools; he had taken up organized ball only at age fourteen, and between that and all that moving around, he got proper seasons only in his junior and senior years. Nevertheless, he was named Florida's Mr. Basketball for 2001–02. When he decided to enter the 2002 draft, his imposing physique and outlandish athleticism were known. However, no one had any idea how he'd fare in the pro context. There were whispers about an attitude problem, a lack of grounding, a general waywardness.

In fact, he couldn't have been more grounded. He hadn't just survived; he'd held together his family as best he could. With almost everyone around him dead or in jail, he'd resolved to be the steady core, pushing himself to make the league as circumstance conspired to drag him down. And he wasn't just going to succeed in the NBA, he was going to rule the roost one day.

That day came two years later, when Steve

Nash came to Phoenix. You could say that Nash made Stoudemire, but we'd seen Amare's prowess since that rookie season. He found Nash as much as Nash found him. The 2004–05 Suns were a high-powered offense for the ages, specializing in brash fast breaks and eye-popping alley-oops, a method that verged on complete anarchy. Nash's sleight of hand and pristine feel for the game made it all possible, and D'Antoni had the vision. But it was Amare, catapulting himself at the basket and putting real fangs on the sprint, that made the team so impressive. Maybe it was style over substance, with Amare way out at that less reputable end of the spectrum. Yet before that fateful operation, Amare Stoudemire was poised to spread giddy mayhem across the league for years to come, and the Suns were set to make this frenzy a valid path to victory.

But there was the injury.

No one knows for sure how, during his hiatus, Stoudemire himself saw his future—there were reports of depression, uncertainty, low morale, and denial. But in other realms of his being, there were outward signs of positive transformation, even growth. He began to display a marked eccentricity in his dress, and the *New York Times* revealed that he'd written a series of poems concerning "faith, truth and African-American women raising children on their own." Amare declined to make his poetry public until he was "ready to reveal it."

There were setbacks. Amare made one brief return to play in 2005, looking balky and bad. That summer, there was an abortive attempt to train with the Olympic team. The season started rough, until he convinced D'Antoni to insert him into the starting line-up. Some saw hubris in this request, others, a need to

NAME: Amare Carsares Stoudemire
BORN: November 16, 1982
HEIGHT: 6 ft 10 in (2.08 m)
WEIGHT: 249 lb (113 kg)
HOMETOWN: Cyprus Creek, FL

SPIRIT ANIMAL: Piranha

PLAYER COMPARISON: Karl Malone with ADHD; Shawn Kemp's redemption.

NOTABLE REMARK: "It felt like it was just me and the rim."

NOTABLE REMARK ABOUT HIM: "He is committed [to defense] in thought and spirit. Now we have to find out if he's committed in execution."—Former Suns assistant Marc Iavaroni.

PUBLIC RELATIONS: The 2001 *Real Sports* segment on Stoudemire's convoluted journey through amateur ball may have scared off some NBA folks, but it let him demonstrate poise and character well before entering the draft.

NOTABLE FASHION STATEMENT: At Kenny Smith's Katrina benefit game, showed up in a T-shirt with a photo of Tupac Shakur and Mike Tyson together.

INTERNATIONAL RELATIONS: In 2008, Amare joked he would move to China to break Yao Ming's stranglehold on the West's starting center slot.

be set free. Right away, Amare began having the most accomplished season of his young career.

He wasn't the Amare of old. His athleticism, which had been otherworldly before, was now merely extraordinary. But his game had diversified in ways that showed both maturity and imagination. Amare didn't dunk every time down the floor; he could now use his speed to maneuver in the lane, playing angles and taking smart lay-ins when it was the better play. Instead of constantly committing offensive fouls, he sought out contact that would take *him* to the line. His outside shooting and free throws improved tremendously.

In short, he'd become a more complete player; the dominating brute of 2004–05 had given way to a guy who could stand shoulder-to-shoulder with great power forwards of the past. Despite having long complained about playing out of position at center, Stoudemire first made the All-NBA Team at the five, over giants like Yao Ming and Dwight Howard. Then, in 2008, the Suns acquired an aging Shaquille O'Neal to give themselves some real big-man heft. They gave up Shawn Marion, but the presence of O'Neal and the extra minutes for Boris Diaw meant that Stoudemire could spend most of his time at his natural position of PF. His production skyrocketed, his play reached new levels of expertise, and, almost as an afterthought, his pre-surgery explosiveness was now very nearly restored. Again, a seemingly chaotic turn of events that set him up to ascend to even higher echelons of greatness.

Amare wasn't reborn or afforded a rare second chance. Step back and you'll see that he's gotten wiser and more imposing with each passing season. Please don't call his saga a comeback. For Amare Stoudemire, everything happens for a reason. Some in the media have called the injury a blessing in disguise. Those who knew better, though, could tell you otherwise. Amare had always been headed somewhere special. Those delays, those hitches in the road, have actually helped him get there faster.

Motion Is a Man's Best Friend

TYPE OF SHOT	2006–2007	2007–2008	CHANGE
Driving Dunks	16	33	+17
Driving Layups	30	34	+4
Running Jumpers	7	19	+12
Offensive Fouls	68	44	-24

Amare has gone from a one-dimensional dunker to a well-rounded offensive force. After missing almost all of 2005–06, Stoudemire returned for 2006–07 with increased mobility, range, and fluidity. He could now put the ball on the floor with confidence, shift his body for the optimal look, and avoid offensive fouls by playing under control. These trends continued in 2007–08, showing a player intent on honing his already dominant game.

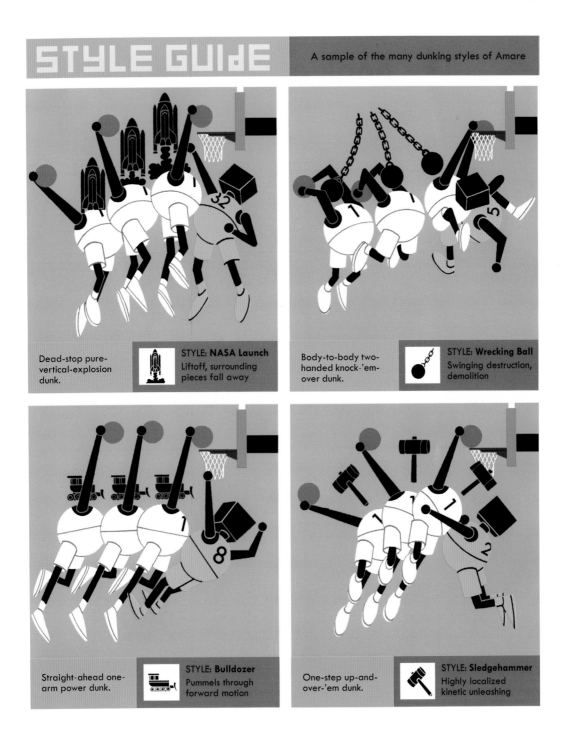

STYLE GUIDE

A sample of the many dunking styles of Amare

Dead-stop pure-vertical-explosion dunk.

STYLE: **NASA Launch**
Liftoff, surrounding pieces fall away

Body-to-body two-handed knock-'em-over dunk.

STYLE: **Wrecking Ball**
Swinging destruction, demolition

Straight-ahead one-arm power dunk.

STYLE: **Bulldozer**
Pummels through forward motion

One-step up-and-over-'em dunk.

STYLE: **Sledgehammer**
Highly localized kinetic unleashing

The Book of Stoudemire

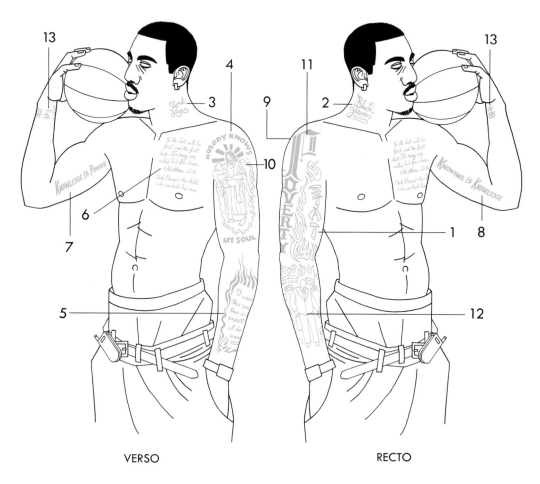

VERSO   RECTO

Tattoos have become an essential NBA accessory—yet another way in which the sport demands we acknowledge individuality. And no one's tats are more evocative, or mysterious, than those of Amare Stoudemire. Amare has said, "When I die, all you have to do is read my tattoos, and you will know a lot about me and what I lived for." This is easier said than done; indeed, this collection of words and images has sparked an entire community of discourse, one fanatically devoted to understanding the individual works and the web of meaning that links them. Taking the Talmud as their model, these scholars map out layer upon layer of meaning, all in hopes of getting a more complete picture of Amare himself.

7. KNOWLEDGE IS POWER: As Amare has spoken: "They always say what you don't know won't hurt you. I think what you don't know will kill you." And here is the wisdom of ages shown. For it is truly said that the way of riches is smoothly paved for the man of wisdom, and that for the foolish, there is death worse than pain. And do not Amare's college classes evince his love of knowledge? Yet some sages speak of another truth. As a young man, Stoudemire studied the words of Tupac Shakur: To speak wisdom in the palace, must not one first seize the scepter of power from the king?

8. KNOWING IS KNOWLEDGE: On his inner right bicep, Amare has written: Knowledge is power. And yet, on his inner left bicep, the edict has changed: Knowing is knowledge.

3. LORD KNOWS: Amare has proclaimed: This work "explains the 'Black Jesus'" known by scholars to be on the other side of his neck. And the wise man understands this to mean: The Lord knows that he, Amare, is the Black Jesus. But is this not also a cry of uncertainty, of man's awe before the divine? For no man can know the plans of G-d. Or, as some say, might not "Lord Knows" be the miserable wailing of Amare's enemies, who have been so broken and scattered to the four winds that nothing is left to them but to appeal to the mercy of the divine? Some scholars have suggested that "Lord Knows" is meant to be read first of the neck texts. If this is so, "Black Jesus" should be understood as the answer to a question, an identity revealed through divine guidance. Fusing them into "Lord knows Black Jesus" is infrequently suggested, due to the complete incoherence of the resulting text.

4. NOBODY KNOWS MY SOUL: A cry, a lamentation, and a mysterious reply to "Lord Knows"—and yet not a rejection. Instead, it is a reply to Amare's enemies, those among the NBA press corps who would sully his name in the marketplace. The wise man who reads this knows that words of truth come from within, not from the mouths of jackals.

1 S.T.A.T.: This is first among the marks of Stoudemire, and another name by which he is known. The elders say the letters signify "Standing Tall and Talented," and truly it is said: Does not Amare have powers beyond that of size? Stoudemire has proclaimed: "It also means I put up a lot of stats."

2 BLACK JESUS: What will become of the man who proclaims himself a prophet? Will he not find a home among the dogs? And yet here Stoudemire speaks only in the tongues of scholars: "Throughout history, it says Jesus was black." Thus knowledge of self and consciousness is made manifest. Was not "Black Jesus" also the name by which the great Earl Monroe was known? And did not Ghostface Killah also take the same name unto himself? Thus, Amare Stoudemire has placed himself among those who walk the earth like giants. The fool sees the boundless arrogance of a man; the scholar knows the righteousness of submission.

5. I WAS RAISED IN THIS SOCIETY AND THIS IS HOW YOU EXPECT ME TO BE. I DO WHAT I WANT TO DO: As it is written on Amare's forearm. The society of men has misused him and his brethren, and Amare has learned to keep his own hand strong unto himself. The fool sees rebellion; the wise man sees knowledge of self.

6. SO THE LAST WILL BE FIRST, AND THE FIRST LAST. FOR MANY ARE CALLED BUT FEW CHOSEN. MATTHEW 20:16. GOD BLESSED THE CHILD WHO CAN HOLD HIS OWN: And here Stoudemire interpolates two twines of Scripture with the words of Billie Holiday, declaring the words of the Black Jesus a Scripture unto themselves.

9. STILL I RISE: Located on his back, it accompanies a picture of Christ carrying a cross. "He's kind of standing up with it, trying to rise up with it," Stoudemire has stated.

10. JESUS CARRYING A MAN: Amare has proclaimed this a "footprint painting." "It's about a guy who can't really handle it no more, so Jesus carries him. When he wakes up he sees footprints but knows he wasn't walking so he knows Jesus was taking care of him."

11. POVERTY One of Amare's most prominent works, it confirms his dedication to the mitzvah of helping the poor.

12. BUSINESS MAN: Beneath "Poverty" is an image of a faceless man in a business suit in front of a city skyline. Though the meaning is unclear, Amare assures us that all his tattoos are "positive." "I never get anything negative," he has stated. "They're kind of motivational for me. I don't want any skeletons or skulls on my arm or anything like that."

13. THE REALIST: Written in Chinese characters, "The" is on his left wrist and "Realist" is on his right. Does he announce his realness, or his refusal to entertain idle hopes?

edge. Scholars have long argued the relationship between the two statements. Do they work as one, like the hands of neighbors as they turn the wheel to mill grain? Or do they oppose each other, like a pack of dirty, starving Hittites dividing the remains of a roasted goat carcass? Some have said: To know is powerful, and to know is to partake of the knowing of knowledge, and that knowing is power. Others have said: Yes, but not to know is to know not nothing of knowledge but rather to know the knowledge of no thing, which is in itself a knowing of the powerful knowledge that is known. Amare is an athlete with one hand, a basketball scholar with the other. He knows that he knows and knows not that he knows not; of knowledge, he is knowing; and what is known to him is known, save that which is not known. And that is powerful.

MOTN

MYTH OF THE NEXT

Since man first became conscious of the passage of time, he has struggled to achieve a glimpse of the future. He has cast bones and read entrails, sought visions and oracles. In modern times, he has consulted computer simulations, high-priced think tanks, and fortune cookies. This impulse is especially strong among the practitioners of basketball scouting, the inexact science by which teams decide which non-pro players to add to their rosters. The choices made in each summer's NBA draft involve millions of dollars in contract money. The right choice can revive a franchise; the wrong one can set it back four steps. With the prospects at hand being entirely unproven in the NBA game, there is no small measure of uncertainty, even danger, inherent in the process.

Some front offices rely on the hunches of grizzled intuitives, others on mountains of data. At times, out of weakness or frustration, these brave men and women turn toward a false idol: the Myth of the Next. Based, some say, on the Stoic notion of Eternal Return, the principle states that everything that has happened before in the NBA must happen again, and soon; in each year's crop of fresh meat, they see reflected the images of last season's All-Star rosters. Its effect is insidious, as what begins as an offhand comparison becomes hype, which is then all too easily transformed into regrettable action. Hopefully, these recent examples can serve as a cautionary tale for organizations everywhere.

MONDN

MYTH OF THE NEXT DIRK NOWITZKI

Somewhere in Europe, there's a very young, very skinny player who defies categorization. He must be drafted.

EXAMPLES:

Pau Gasol (2001): He zoomed up scouts' boards, going third overall. Has matured into an All-Star big man who combines ferocity with finesse, even if he really doesn't break any molds. PROPHECY FULFILLMENT: +3

Darko Milicic (2003): Picked over Melo and Wade, he was rumored to have a "mean streak" and real moves around the basket. Instead, he's a periodically competent shot blocker and undying punch line. PROPHECY FULFILL-MENT: -5

Nikoloz Tskitishvili (2002): A tall, scrawny Georgian teen with a pure shot and footwork refined in his national folk dance troupe. Sadly, he couldn't make a shot in games and fell out of the league. PROPHECY FULFILLMENT: -9

OTHERS: **Zarko Cabarkapa** (-8), **Maciej Lampe** (-32)

MONDW

MYTH OF THE NEXT DWYANE WADE

If an undersized combo guard can be a star in college, he can be an All-Star shooting guard in the NBA.

EXAMPLES:

Brandon Roy (2006): Not all that athletic in the tradi-tional sense, but a multipurpose backcourt All-Star who has helped rekindle the Blazers. Basically a duller, smarter Wade. PROPHECY FULFILLMENT: +8

Rodney Stuckey (2007): This inventive Pistons pick came on strong late in his rookie season as a potent scorer who could handle the ball when necessary. Has a nasty quotient that almost equals Wade's. PROPHECY FULFILLMENT: +4

Randy Foye (2006): Held back by injuries. Most notable for being traded for Roy on draft night and for situs inver-sus, a rare medical condition in which the organs' positions are reversed. PROPHECY FULFILLMENT: -2

MONJO

MYTH OF THE NEXT JERMAINE O'NEAL

MONKG

MYTH OF THE NEXT KEVIN GARNETT

Draft a high school big man, plant him on the bench for several years, and he'll grow into an All-Star.

EXAMPLES:

Andrew Bynum (2005): This lottery pick confused fans and pissed off Kobe. Then, 2007–08 rolled around, and Bynum suddenly looked like one of the league's top centers. PROPHECY FULFILLMENT: +10

Tyson Chandler and Eddy Curry (2001): The new version of the Spurs' Twin Towers, they were to be. Unfortunately, they developed bad habits, clashed with coaches, and spent their time in Chicago pondering their own incompleteness. Chandler went on to achieve maturity in NOLA. PROPHECY FULFILLMENT: +3

Kwame Brown (2001): Brown had the bad fortune to come to D.C. right when Jordan made his comeback. This made patience and slow development impossible, and Brown was stunted by His Airness. We're still waiting. PROPHECY FULFILLMENT: -5

OTHERS: **Amir Johnson (+6)**, **Robert Swift (-7)**

A tall, skinny guy with guard skills will turn into one of the league's best players.

EXAMPLES:

Lamar Odom (1999): Odom's career, detailed elsewhere in this volume, has been a study in self-effacing brilliance, even if he has never risen to KG's level of importance. PROPHECY FULFILLMENT: +2

Chris Bosh (2003), Kevin Durant (2007): Both college stars and highly touted prospects drew comparisons to KG, largely due to their skinny frames and outside shooting— but both have gone on to define their own legacies. PROPHECY FULFILLMENT: N/A

Darius Miles (2000): Superficially, high school draftee Miles looked like the evolutionary advancement over Garnett. More sinewy, faster, and with better ups, D. Miles became a Clippers favorite best known for his angry, elastic dunks before stagnating in Cleveland and Portland. PROPHECY FULFILLMENT: -7

OTHERS: **Andray Blatche (+1)**, **Jonathan Bender (-10)**

MONAS
MYTH OF THE NEXT ARVYDAS SABONIS

The next great big man will come from overseas and wallop the American competition.

EXAMPLES:

Yao Ming (2002): The best true center playing the game today, Yao is multiskilled in a way that would make Arvydas proud. Plus, he idolized Sabonis growing up, even using his name as a message-board handle. PROPHECY FULFILLMENT: +15

Andrew Bogut (2005): Australian, but, as he points out all the time, actually of Croatian descent in a way that draws him regionally closer to Sabonis. Rumored to pass well; went first overall. Didn't do much until 2007–08, when he decided to start blocking shots. PROPHECY FULFILLMENT: +3

Pavel Podkolzin (2004): Dogged by a gland problem that required surgery, rumored to have once dribbled with both hands and hit a three in a workout, he was the great white whale of 2003 draft boards. He's like Saba in that he's from Eastern Europe, but his NBA output remains negligible. PROPHECY FULFILLMENT: -12

MONGA
MYTH OF THE NEXT GILBERT ARENAS

Buried in the second round, there lurks a guard without a position who will one day set the world on fire.

EXAMPLES:

Monta Ellis (2005): Picked in the second round by Arenas's original team, the Warriors, Ellis emerged as an explosive element during the 2006–07 campaign. Would've likely been lost in the same way that Gilbert was, but changes in the collective bargaining agreement prompted by Gil's escape allowed the Dubs to keep him on board. PROPHECY FULFILLMENT: +12

Luther Head (2005): A first-rounder, thanks mostly to the widespread discussion of MONGA. Has become more a three-point specialist than a Monta-like demon, but nonetheless uplifted himself through the third-party power of scout rhetoric. PROPHECY FULFILLMENT: +2

Troy Bell (2003): Drafted way too soon, the first sign that Jerry West was mortal. These days, Bell pursues semipro boxing on YouTube. PROPHECY FULFILLMENT: -8

OTHERS: **C. J. Miles** (+1), **Louis Williams** (+1.5)

MONGP
MYTH OF THE NEXT GINOBILI-PARKER

MONTM
MYTH OF THE NEXT TRACY MCGRADY

Every foreigner that the San Antonio Spurs draft will turn out to be a star.

EXAMPLES:

Luis Scola (2002): This Argentinean, a vet of European ball, didn't come to the U.S. until his late twenties. The Spurs had secured his rights years before, but inexplicably traded him to divisional rival the Houston Rockets before the start of the 2007–08 season. Made a late push for Rookie of the Year, just not with the Spurs. PROPHECY FULFILLMENT: +5

Beno Udrih (2004): Like many international Spurs picks, he was taken late in the draft and showed up roughly ten years later. Coach Popovich hated him because he once turned the ball over, and he was kicked out the door only to be born anew in Sacramento—again, not with the Spurs, and with overtones of Spurs condemnation. PROPHECY FULFILLMENT: +3

Ian Mahinmi (2005): A total unknown who stayed far away from us all until he played well for France in the 2007 Worlds. In this case, this Myth served as an important form of motivation. PROPHECY FULFILLMENT: +1

Every formerly obscure athletic high school wing will eventually dominate the league.

EXAMPLES:

J. R. Smith (2004): Can jump out of the gym and hit a three from anywhere. After a promising rookie year with New Orleans, he was exiled to the bench, then traded to the Bulls, then immediately moved again to the Nuggets. Has grown into an important role player under the tutelage of Carmelo Anthony and then Allen Iverson. PROPHECY FULFILLMENT: +3

Dorell Wright (2004): Can jump out of the gym and hit a three four or five times a season. Miami's Pat Riley kept him off the court until injuries and large-scale failure gave him no choice. Broke the mold by excelling at rebounding and defense. PROPHECY FULFILLMENT: +2

Gerald Green (2005): Can jump out of the gym and hit a three from anywhere. Managed to produce a bit, first in Boston and then in Minnesota, before being dealt to the Rockets and promptly released. Winning the 2007 Dunk Contest didn't help his frivolous rep. PROPHECY FULFILLMENT: -6

MONDR

MYTH OF THE NEXT DENNIS RODMAN

A guy who can't score but cares a lot and hits the floor frequently can transform your team.

EXAMPLES:

Renaldo Balkman (2006): Isiah was widely mocked for taking Balkman over better-known prospects. However, once people got over making Rolando Blackman jokes, they noticed that Balkman was energetic, determined, and capable of changing a game through sheer hustle. PROPHECY FULFILLMENT: +8

Joakim Noah (2007): Noah was hardly a secret, since the Gators had just won their second NCAA title. Still, by the end of 2007–08, Noah's zany fire was helping re-define the Bulls for the umpteenth time in as many years. PROPHECY FULFILLMENT: +4

Jerome Beasley (2003): Hard-rebounding power for-ward who did his dirt in the midst of a Dakota blizzard. This second-rounder never really got a shot at establishing him-self; there's a reason these are called "myths." PROPHECY FULFILLMENT: -5

MONMJ

MYTH OF THE NEXT MAGIC JOHNSON

Forward-size guys with handles and the ability to see the floor can play point guard in the NBA.

EXAMPLES:

Penny Hardaway (1993): Magic himself signed off on the comparison. Although he lacked Magic's charisma, Penny looked well on his way to living up to the hype with his play before injuries cut short his career. PROPHECY FULFILLMENT: +7

Jalen Rose (1994): Hails from the same state as Magic and also achieved NCAA success at a young age, but Rose never got to play much point guard in the NBA. Reinvented himself as a high-scoring wing, averaging 20+ per game for the Pacers and Bulls. PROPHECY FULFILLMENT: -3

Toni Kukoc (1990): In the days before Euros were a com-mon fixture in the NBA, Kukoc was something of a legend—a 6'11" point guard known as the greatest European-league player of all time. When he finally joined the Bulls in 1993, he created the stereotype of European players as soft and only obliquely motivated. PROPHECY FULFILLMENT: -6

GLOSSARY

A

ABA—An alternative league that semiflourished in the 1970s, it featured high scoring, acrobatic play, funny hair, and outlandish garb; later took on cult significance in the 1990s. Although it began life as a pyramid scheme, it ended up hosting the first dunk contest and is widely credited with disseminating style, especially when exports like Dr. J arrived in the NBA.

Adande, J. A.—An ESPN and L.A. *Times* sports correspondent who specializes in NBA culture. Appears regularly on ESPN's *Around the Horn* as a foil to the Woody Paiges and Jay Mariottis of the world.

Allen, Woody—A rabid Knicks fan whose essay on trying to meet Earl Monroe is this book's most prized antecedent. In the filming of *Annie Hall*, he directed a scene in Madison Square Garden in which a team of famous philosophers (featuring Nietzsche) played against the 1970s Knicks (featuring Phil Jackson); the scene was later cut.

All-Star Weekend—A great source of racial division in the country. Seen by some as only a jumble of glorified exhibitions and riotous nightlife, it is fondly referred to by journalist Michael Wilbon as "the Black Super Bowl."

And1—Company often credited with mainstreaming raw, uncut street ball. Used pejoratively to describe excessive in-game flair.

Andersen, Chris—Also known as "the Birdman." An erstwhile Hornets player best known for trying the same dunk twenty times in the 2005 contest, and for catching a two-year ban for undisclosed hard-drug use.

Association, the—Shorthand for the National Basketball Association; not to be confused with the seminal soft rock act of the same name.

B

"Basketball is jazz"—Specious claim frequently made by academics who have never heard James Brown or Rakim.

Bias, Len—Picked second overall by the Celtics in 1986, this Maryland star had greatness written all over him and was expected to extend the life of Boston's dynasty. Instead, he died of a cocaine overdose just hours after the draft. The Celtics took years to recover.

Big Aristotle—One of Shaquille O'Neal's innumerable self-invented nicknames, intended as a tribute to the profundity of his post-game insight.

Bird rights—Complicated rule instituted to ensure that franchise players (a la Larry Bird) could tango around certain salary-cap restrictions when their contracts expired so that they could stay with their cash-hampered teams.

Birthday Cake, the—Dunk executed in the 2008 contest by Gerald Green, who threw down while blowing out a candle on a cupcake. What secured its immortality was 1) the priceless, Chaplinesque acting of teammate Rashad McCants, 2) the fact that it was a cupcake, not a cake, and 3) the fact that it was nobody's birthday.

Black Jesus 1—The most rapturous nickname of Earl Monroe during his Baltimore Bullets days, when his every move was like a miracle.

Black Jesus 2—Depending on whom you ask, Amare Stoudemire, Ghostface Killah, or Marvin Lewis.

Black Planet—David Shields's book chronicling his experience of the 1995 implosion of the Seattle SuperSonics, seen through the lens of race, class, and Jewish self-loathing.

Brawl, the—Early in the 2004 season, some Pistons shoved some Pacers at Auburn Hills. A number of bystanding fans got involved, got their asses kicked for it, and decided to start a riot to assert their right to assault professional ballplayers without retribution.

Brown, Hubie—Former coach turned network commentator, beloved for his fireside-chat tone, avuncular warmth, and boundless knowledge of the game.

Brown, Larry—Coiner of the phrase "Right Way," celebrated as a teacher of the game and the only coach to win a pro and NCAA title. Actually a disloyal grump always on the hunt for a new job; he allowed the Knicks to court him while his Pistons were in the midst of a playoff series. Got his comeuppance when his "dream job" with the Knicks turned into the NBA's answer to Iraq.

Bullet Fedora—For Game 3 of the historic 2007 Warriors/Mavs series—the only time a number-eight seed has upset a number-one seed in a seven-game contest—star Warriors point guard Baron Davis arrived at Oracle Arena rocking a fedora with several bullets on the side, lashed on with a silk scarf.

Butler, Caron—Tough-as-nails Wizards forward who promised himself to basketball while in the hole at juvy. Favorite player of indie rockers Stephen Malkmus and Janet Weiss.

BynumSpace—A reference to Andrew Bynum's hilarious MySpace profile, in which he presented a self-revealing quiz that included such gems as: "Q: Are you suicidal? A: Only in the mourning" and "Q: Have you ever went barefoot in the snow? A: NO . . . im black [sic]."

C

competitive style—A grand synthesis of style and substance, it presumes that players win games by just being themselves.

country—A term used to describe players hailing from the Deep South, this became especially relevant when players stopped going to college and thus hit the league as very tall, highly regionalized ingenues.

Cuban, Mark—Outspoken owner of the Dallas Mavericks, best known for his personal blog, constant bickering with refs during Mavs games, and seemingly bottomless coffers. In the early 2000s, he turned the Mavericks into a basketball model UN.

D

D-Block—The National Basketball Developmental League, established in 2001, essentially as a farm system for the NBA. Most players hate getting sent down to D-Block, except for Pistons youngster Amir Johnson, who requested an assignment because not playing hurt his soul.

Detroit Pistons—Team that in 2004 somehow defied convention by becoming the only non-Shaq/Duncan team of the Shaq/Duncan era to win a championship; said

to have done so by harnessing energy from the outpouring of love that Coach Larry Brown bestowed upon them.

Donaghy scandal—In the summer of 2007, referee Tim Donaghy admitted to betting on NBA games. This brought cries that the league had been fixed and would take years to recover its integrity; instead, people forgot about it by Opening Day.

dunk contest—Breeding ground for innovation and artistry that may or may not ever be realized in an actual game. Increasingly, participants may or may not even be appearing in actual NBA games. Has been deemed "back" on numerous occasions, most recently after Dwight Howard's costumed Superman "dunk" in 2008.

E

Eastern Conference—The worst basketball in the league, played in the first states of the Union.

Eddie—Classic 1996 film in which Knicks fan Whoopi Goldberg ends up coaching the hapless squad. Was funny then because the Knicks were good. Not to be confused with 1995's *Theodore Rex*, in which Whoopi teams up with a talking dinosaur to fight crime, or the totally unrelated bummer documentary *Stevie*.

Elevating the Game—Nelson George volume chronicling the development and cultural significance of the expressive, creative style in basketball. Tends extensively to the hidden history of HBCUs and the New York City courts.

Euro Invasion—The influx of European players into the NBA following the success of Drazen Petrovic.

F

FBP—"first black president": Term applied to players who appear to have a bright future in politics, or approach the media as if they did. Ray Allen is the all-time leader.

Fields, Ronnie—High-flying high school teammate of Kevin Garnett who once ruled the city of Chicago. A car accident, personal problems, and low test scores kept him from finding his way to the promised land, but the murals remain.

Flood, Curt—St. Louis Cardinals outfielder who sacrificed his career so that free agency could be granted as a civil right to all athletes.

Ford, Chad—An ESPN.com writer who works the predraft beat, he spent a lot of time chasing down leads in Europe and submitting fantastic bits of travel writing. Is widely blamed for the hype surrounding Darko Milicic.

freakish—Scouting adjective used to characterize the truly mind-boggling, as in "freakish athleticism." Never applied to matters of the mind or heart.

free agency—When, in theory, a player gets to listen to offers and pick who he wants to work for.

fundamentals—The basic building blocks of orderly basketball, which some believe are a sacrosanct end in themselves.

G

Gaedel, Eddie—American dwarf who was asked—as a publicity stunt conjured up by oddball GM Bill Veeck—to pinch-hit for the St. Louis Browns MLB team in 1951. The absurdist spirit of this moment is something that the NBA under Commissioner Stern has decidedly lacked.

Golden State Warriors—Band of whirling dervishes playing basketball games set to Oakland psychedelic funk music.

H

half-court offense—Anti-freewheeling and anti-fast-breaking offense, based on set plays and jump shooting. Some teams have consistently struggled with this style of offense (see Denver Nuggets).

Hawkins, Connie—NYC playground legend who attended Iowa, where he was falsely implicated in Jack Molinas's ring of corruption and banned from the NBA. Forced into exile, he joined the Globetrotters, played in the ABL, and became the ABA's first star. Was pardoned by the NBA in 1969 and subsequently enjoyed several productive seasons that nonetheless only suggested what might have been.

haymaker—Meme circulated among the media following the 2004 brawl at Auburn Hills: Any and all punches, no matter how feckless, were to be known as "haymakers."

Haywood, Spencer—Very fashionable 1970s

star who fought the league's de facto age limit in court and won. Married the supermodel Iman (before she married David Bowie).

He Got Game—Spike Lee joint about a heavily recruited high school prospect and his estranged dad. Stars Ray Allen, who doesn't come off at all like an athlete playing one.

I

Inside the NBA—Premier program of NBA analysis, where Charles Barkley, Kenny Smith, and straight man Ernie Johnson good-naturedly trash everyone in sight and sedulously avoid any real technical talk.

Iverson, Allen—The personification of every reason uninformed people give for why they prefer NCAA basketball to the NBA. Also credited with single-handedly destroying the league after Jordan's second retirement.

J

Jackson, Phil—The Zen master. Motivates players by treating them like people who don't like sports.

Jackson, Stephen—The NBA's most misunderstood, underrated badass, as well as its edgy Zelig. The real firestarter at the Auburn Hills Brawl, a key member of the Spurs' 2003 championship, inspiration for the 8th-seeded Warriors' uprooting of the 1st-seeded Dallas Mavericks in the 2007

playoffs. Has dealt with firearms issues, but got a tattoo on his chest of two praying hands holding a gun to keep him straight.

Jailblazers—The Portland Trailblazers teams of the late 1990s/early 2000s, centered around the boneheaded behavior of Rasheed Wallace, Damon Stoudamire, and Ruben Patterson. The Jailblazers era jumped the shark when Qyntel Woods was arrested for running a dogfighting ring.

Jewelz—Nom de rap of Allen Iverson, whose album generated controversy for fairly standard lyrics such as "Come to me wit faggot tendencies / You'll be sleepin where the maggots be." It was never released. One of the NBA's most awkward cross-cultural moments.

Johnson, Amir—Spirited Pistons youngster who was the last high school player picked before the age limit took effect. Some see him as karmic redemption for Darko, since Johnson—picked 56th overall in 2005—is only a few easy steps away from stardom.

Jordan, Michael—The greatest the league has ever seen, he's also its North Star. Hence the terms "pre-Jordan," "Jordan era," and "post-Jordan," all of which are remarkably misleading.

K

Kareem's jacket—Bizarre Native American–meets-David Crosby leather-fringe joint that Kareem Abdul-Jabbar wore at a 2006 playoff game. Still known around the Internet as simply "the Jacket."

Kemp, Shawn—Father of hundreds and former high-flying highlight-reel staple who transformed into a doughy wasteland of a man after he left the Seattle SuperSonics.

KRS-TIC—Nickname for Nenad Krstic, oft-injured lynchpin of any future success for the New Jersey Nets. Proof that vowels are overrated—or, alternately, an indication of hip-hop's strong influence on Serbian culture.

L

Larry O'Brien Trophy—The NBA championship trophy, which Joe Kleine, Glenn Robinson, and Scott Brooks have held claim to, among others.

length—A measure of how much taller disproportionately long arms make players seem.

M

microfracture surgery—Procedure that punctures bone to force new growth of cartilage. Was career-ending for Penny and Chris Webber, but less than a decade later, Amare came back from the same procedure to make All-NBA.

Milicic, Darko—A seven-foot Serbian teen drafted ahead of Carmelo Anthony, Dwyane Wade, and Chris Bosh. As a child during wartime, he saw his family sell their car to buy a cow so he that he'd have milk for strong bones.

Molinas, Jack—Talented baller of the olden days; also a criminal mastermind and compulsive gambler who turned to full-time fixing after the NBA banned him for throwing games. Proceeded to nearly destroy college hoops through a series of point-shaving scandals and served some time before being shot in the back of the head in 1975.

N

NBA art collections—The truly erudite men of this league spend their money thus. Bill Russell was the originator; Ray Allen is the current champ, with pieces by Joan Miró, Andy Warhol, and Marc Chagall.

NBA draft—Day on which people with humorous names wear funny baseball caps and ill-advised suits.

NBA racial semiotics—The fine art of decoding situations like the following: Darius Miles calling his older coach Maurice Cheeks the "n-word," or white guard Bob Sura taking offense at Kirk Snyder's use of a racial epithet in reference to another black player.

Nelson, Don—Fondly known as "Nellie," the mastermind behind Nellieball, an up-tempo, size-deficient style of play that everyone loves but no one takes seriously.

Nice Oakley—Nickname for Kevin Willis, who throughout his career displayed the same tough-style hard-core 1980s-caliber ball as Charles Oakley but wasn't as much of a hard-ass.

No Walton—A parenthetical note meant to clarify that a bit of spoken hyperbole is offered in earnest, not in the cynical, narcissistic manner of commentator Bill Walton. Derived from the expression "no homo."

Nowitzki, Dirk—Saxophone prodigy who was guided to a life of basketball by Holger Geschwinder and Charles Barkley.

O

organic style—When a guy looks like he's making everything up as he goes along.

P

playoff atmosphere—Said of any regular-season game where fans show up and both teams play hard.

positional revolution—An ongoing attempt to change the physical and functional archetypes of positions on the floor. At its most extreme, it does away with the notion of fixed positions.

practice (the AI usage)—From an infamous news conference where Iverson answered accusations that he sometimes missed practice. Quoth Iverson: "We're sitting here, and I'm supposed to be the franchise player, and we're in here talking about practice. I mean, listen, we're talking about practice, not a game, not a game, not a *game*. We're talking about *practice*. Not the game that I go out there and die for and play every game like it's my last. Not the *game*. We're talking about *practice*, man. I mean, how silly is that?"

preps-to-pro—The now-defunct practice by which talented high school kids had the right to jump straight to the basketball big leagues. Still permissible in baseball.

R

Ricky Davis's triple-double—With the clock running down on a 2003 Jazz/Cavs game, Cleveland's Davis was one board away from a triple-double. He shot on his own basket for the easy solution, and Utah coach Jerry Sloan tried to have him executed.

Rider, J. R.—Rider began his controversial career with the Timberwolves, where he won the Slam Dunk Contest his rookie year, performing the much-copied between-the-legs move that he named the "East Bay Funk" dunk. Things were all downhill from there, as Rider was arrested numerous times over the next ten years and played for four different teams. Notably, he can be seen on the bench during the episode of *Curb Your Enthusiasm* in which Shaq makes a cameo.

Right Way—Fantastical approach to the game in which every decision is either/or rational, no mistakes are ever made, defense is championed above all, and human error is attributable only to showboating.

Run-TMC—High-scoring late-1980s/early-1990s Golden State trio of Tim Hardaway, Mitch Richmond, and Chris Mullin. Collectively, a living textbook on how to be badass and lovable at the same time. Coached by Don Nelson.

S

Sacred Hoop—Dissolute, rapacious Palo

Alto hip-hop outfit often confused with Phil Jackson's book *Sacred Hoops*.

seven-footer—A man who has no choice but to earn millions in the NBA.

short shorts—A bygone form of lower-body basketball wear that didn't go much further than absolutely necessary and left little to the imagination. Jordan killed them, but John Stockton kept his shorts short well after baggy became the norm. Revived for one night by the Lakers, who ruined the stunt by wearing regular-size jerseys.

Skita Time—This organization's original name, and a cry of urgency for lottery bust Nikoloz Tskitishvili. Derived from Amiri Baraka's *It's Nation Time*.

SLAM—The magazine all the players read.

Smith, Stephen A.—A television personality known primarily for yelling nonstop and enjoying Cheez Doodles in public; vastly underrated as an interviewer.

soccer—A sport, reportedly very popular in other countries, whose cult of style puts the NBA's to shame.

Sprewell, Latrell—Dark Ages star best known for strangling obnoxious-as-hell coach P. J. Carlesimo in Golden State. Reborn as a Knicks favorite, and then again as Garnett's saving wingman. Disappeared amid demands for big money needed to "feed my family"; last noticed for losing a yacht to the bank.

streetball—The lawless, flashy game played at city playgrounds; used pejoratively to describe anything that involves too much fun.

summer league—A wild, unreasonable land where scrubs drop 50 and lottery picks are lost and doubted.

swag—Short for *swagger*. After hitting a game-winning shot in 2007, Gilbert Arenas famously proclaimed, "My swag was phenomenal." Nuggets forward Kenyon Martin makes it literal, actually swaggering so much it looks like he's about to pull his own shorts off at any moment.

T

tanking—Deliberate late-season losses by unsuccessful teams, undertaken to improve their chances of winning the lottery. Almost became socially acceptable in 2007.

Tesh, John—Composer of the immortal *NBA on NBC* theme, a sweeping ode to all that is epic and swift in this game.

"This is a game of rules . . . and conventions!"—Hilariously untrue maxim articulated by David Stern on the television show *Pardon the Interruption*.

throwback—A jersey from long ago, brought back as a fashion statement. The trend began nerdishly at Philly's Mitchell and Ness store and spread to rappers; eventually, the league started dressing teams in them. Also refers to players whose style evokes the days of yore.

thug—What white people call black people who wear any jewelry or drive a luxury car without the factory package. Often applied to athletes, especially NBA players.

trade deadline—Traditionally, the day that

Jimmy Jackson switched uniforms. A generally anticlimactic finish to a flurry of trade talk among fans and pundits.

Troubled Griffin—Inseparable media appellation for Eddie Griffin, the saddest, most cursed NBA player of all time, who battled addiction and ultimately met his fate drunk-driving head-on into a train. Likely, he is in a better place now.

tweener—A player too small to play power forward and too slow to play small forward. Will continue to be used as an appellation even after he has carved out a niche for himself doing one or the other.

U

UNLV—The rascally, scandal-plagued University of Nevada, Las Vegas, which ran like hell and produced the likes of Larry Johnson and Shawn Marion. School logo became popular trademark for the Chicago Vice Lords gang, as the university's letters backward stand for "Vice Lords Nation United."

upside—A young player's hypothetical potential to get much, much better, in ways that would probably astonish all parties involved.

V

Van Gundy, Jeff—Former coach of the Knicks best known for his high anxiety level, ever-present Diet Coke, and attempt to enter an on-court brawl by grabbing the leg of Heat center Alonzo Mourning in 1998. Became a tragic figure when he

couldn't get the Yao/T-Mac tandem out of the first round. Was reborn as the game's wryest and most upbeat media voice.

Vasquez, Fran—Spanish prospect who, after being drafted 11th by the Orlando Magic in the 2005 draft, spurned the Magic (following his girlfriend's wishes) and returned to Europe. It remains unclear how an NBA draftee is legally allowed to do this.

veteran tricks—Mysterious techniques for pushing opponents and pissing them off that players learn only after their rookie contract is up. Have extended many a career well past its sell-by date.

W

Wade, Dwyane—Explosive Miami guard who somehow still manages to be boring as hell.

Walker, Antoine—Despicable fat guy who takes a lot of bad three-pointers and likes to shimmy. Became a sympathetic figure after being robbed at gunpoint in his own Chicago house.

Western Conference—Where the best teams have lurked since Jordan's retirement. As a result, due to the folly of American time zones, half the country now thinks the NBA sucks.

Worldwide Wes—William Wesley, a shadowy figure who may or may not control the entire NBA through his network of connections and contacts. This information alone took several years of investigative reporting to obtain.

BIOS

BETHLEHEM SHOALS is a perpetual student who has lived in every time zone. Before founding FreeDarko, he was a reputable newspaper reporter, feared for his absolute monopoly on Newark's dry-goods beat. His interests include fishing, world religions, and conspiracy theories about conspiracy theorists.

BIG BABY BELAFONTE is an illustrator and designer. He was formerly the art director of *The Philadelphia Independent.* He is married and lives in New Delhi.

BROWN RECLUSE, ESQ., lives in a cave in an undisclosed location where the power of the Internet allows him to follow the NBA, buy too many records, and do legal research.

DR. LAWYER INDIANCHIEF hails from the land of Humphrey, Mondale, and Wellstone. These days he spends his time rapping with vultures, plotting his next psychological experiment, and eating the bone-in rib-eye with garlic and fresh-cracked pepper, charred, medium-rare, at Chicago's Gene & Georgetti.

SILVERBIRD5000 is the founder, editor, and sole proprietor of the only blog devoted exclusively to the English Revolution of 1640 (www.theenglishrevolution.blogspot.com - Get Familiar!). He is unmarried and lives in New Haven, CT.

WITH THANKS TO

Amelia Abreu
Gilbert Arenas
Francis Davis
David Einhorn and Marilyn Baum
Andrew Friedman
Charles Friedman and Patti Abbott
Angela Garbes
Susan Gray and Paul Waytz
Eli Horowitz
Lakshmi IndraSimhan
K. P. and Nirmala IndraSimhan
Satoshi and Carolyn Ito
Avi Korine
Terence Lau
Will Leitch
Joey Litman
Alec MacDonald
Niamh McGuigan
Dave McMenamin

Alejandro Miyar
Boru O'Brien O'Connell
Mike O'Connor
Chris Parris-Lamb
Rob Peterson
Megha Ralapati
Dan Shanoff
J. E. Skeets
Dan Steinberg
Nick Trautwein
Matthew Watson
David Waytz
Josh Waytz
Josh and Johanna Weinstein
Patricia Weiss
Will Welch
Lang Whitaker
Tom Ziller